GOD HATES YOU, HATE HIM BACK

Making Sense of The Bible

CJ Werleman

First Published In Great Britain 2009
by Dangerous Little Books
www.dangerouslittlebooks.com

GOD HATES YOU, HATE HIM BACK

Contents

Acknowledgements

This is the part where I get to thank my beloved wife and children for the suffering I put them through in the eighteen months it took to research and write this book. At the very least I can now be sure that she truly does love me because she never once interrupted whilst I explained to her any of the Biblical stories in my own words. Even thought she wanted to. So very much.

As passé as it may seem, my darling wife truly provided me the resolve to complete this project, and I love her so.

This is also where I'd like to thank a long lost friend, who tracked me down after twelve years. A dear friend, who truly played the part of silencing the voices of doubt inside my own mind. I firmly believe that if every human being had a supporting friend like Oz, then we as humanity would have achieved so much more.

To my big brother Bryan I thank you. I thank you for showing me that anything is possible. It was in your lounge on that Christmas Day that you helped me shape the idea for the book, whilst also encouraging me along the way.

To all my Bali expatriate friends: You suffered with my incessant Bible talk, whilst I was set on this one track journey. You laughed when appropriate, and you never once told me to shut up. I love you all. Living in Bali for the past seven years has been one of, if not, the greatest experience of my life, and I thank you for playing your part in those memories.

Finally I'd like to thank my publisher, Dangerous Little Books. You took a gamble on me, and the book and I thank you for the opportunity you have given me to articulate my message.

Introducing The Bible

"The characters and events depicted in the damn bible are fictitious. Any similarity to actual persons, living or dead, is purely coincidental."
Penn and Teller

The Bible is a collection of 66 different books, the writings of at least 40 different authors over a period of time that spans at least 1,500 years. The Bible, however, is not a singular catalogue of these books as the sixty-six books are each respectively assigned to either the Old or New Testament. To illustrate this, the Old Testament comprises of thirty-nine of the sixty six, Genesis to Malachi; whilst the New Testament includes the balance of twenty-seven books, the Gospel of Matthew through the Book of Revelation. Now it is important for non-Jewish audiences to understand that the New Testament is not 'new' in the sense that it is a modernised or an updated version of the Old Testament, as an alarming number of Christians that I have spoken with incorrectly believe. Jews, for example, don't call it the Old Testament, as to them there is no 'new'. The Old Testament is *the* Hebrew Bible, starting there and ending there. Whereas the New Testament is a Christian 'addendum', or add on, so that their belief may allow for the introduction of their messianic hero - Jesus.

The Old Testament, or Hebrew Bible, is the catalogue of Judaism belief. The Hebrew Bible ends where the New Testament begins. For these reasons the Jewish religion is relatively straight forward and uncomplicated. In contrast the basis for Christianity is highly problematic and confusing because they introduced a special new character, Somewhat like writing a new super-hero into a script after filming had already begun. Christopher Hitchens, author of *God is Not Great,* eloquently makes his punchy position on this:

> *"[New Testament] is a work of crude carpentry, hammered together long after its purported events and full of attempts to make things come out right."*

The new Christian addendum for reasons of brand positioning became the New Testament and thus the Jews, of which Jesus and his disciples were, laugh and scoff at the Christian story in the same manner that most of us laugh at the idea that seventy-two virgins await in heaven for those that fly aircraft into buildings. But, much to their chagrin, Christians cannot divorce themselves from the Old Testament, or Hebrew Bible, because Jesus' biography is hammered and nailed together (bad pun) from Old Testament prophecy and genealogy, i.e. no Old Testament – no Jesus!

Further convoluting the whole mono-theistic party punch is the fact that the Koran, the Islamic Bible, has its roots in the Old Testament too, but at the risk of upsetting the unshaven Muslim guy seated next to me on this Trans-Pacific flight, I will dispense with any Islamic observations because I have seen what these are capable of when they get 'pissed'!

As you process the stories of the Bible it is important to remember that the respective authors were not men of modern enlightenment. To put that statement into some kind of context, if we could somehow build a time-travel device and transport Moses from 2000 BC to 2009 AD his knowledge of the universe would embarrass that of even a 3rd grader. This suggests that religious believers today spend their years on earth in worship of enlightenment and understanding of the same knowledge that an eight year old could provide.

The books of the Bible were crafted together by ancient man to explain how his universe, his surroundings, came to be. These were books that provided comfort to man, as he feared the dark, death in battle, the sound of thunder, or illness and disease. Within all civilizations, within all societies, the human existence has demonstrated its proclivity to create gods for when we cannot find meaning or understanding. For example, we knew the sun was good because it made our crops grow. No sun, no crops, no food. Therefore we created the Sun God. Similarly gods for water, fertility, healing, etc.

The earliest books of the Bible, Genesis in particular, were written by ancient Hebrews in an effort to explain how their existence and the things in their environment came about. All civilizations have their roots in folklore, mythology and legend. The ancient Romans believed their existence was founded by the twins Romulus and Remes, both orphaned and raised by a wolf. The ancient Hebrews believed a sky-god placed a man named Adam created from dust and a woman created by Adam's rib on earth, to be the first family of their existence.

There is little doubt the Bible, due to its wordiness, size and often incomprehensible translations, is an intimidating book which explains in large why people don't read it. This assertion is corroborated by my own anecdotal experiences, in which I am utterly flabbergasted as to how little my Christian friends actually know of the Bible's claims, commands, assertions, dictums and history. Interestingly my personal findings seem to be in synch with the findings published in an editorial titled *The Greatest Story Never Read: Recovering Biblical Literacy in the Church.* The author's findings include a swathe of statistical data that literally would blow the socks off any Baptist preacher. The research showed that 93% of American households own at least one copy of the Bible, but this is what is known of the 'Good Book':

- More than 35% of college attending Christians could not put the following in order: Abraham, the Old Testament prophets, the death of Christ and Pentecost.
- One-third could also not identify Matthew as an apostle from a list of New Testament names.

The above findings corroborated by an editorial published in *Politics Daily* titled, *Why a 'Year of the Bible' Would Horrify its Sponsors* showed:

- More than 50% don't know that Genesis is the first book of the Bible.
- More than 50% can't name even one of the Gospels.
- More than 60% can't name at least 5 of the 10 commandments.
- More than 20% think Moses was one of Jesus' disciples.
- More than 50% of High School seniors think Sodom and Gomorrah are a married couple.

Put the above data in context of a recent Rasmussen poll in which 44% of Americans believe in the literal translation of the Bible, which means 140 million Americans believe that a talking snake encouraged a woman to eat an apple; that a 900 year old man built an Arc to replenish humanity; that the sun revolves around the earth; and Jonah lived inside a whale for three days. It is the majority of these 140 million that enabled, by their votes, arguably the worst President in American history to inflict his Crusades paradigm upon the world. So I suggest the next time you see a guy step out of a car with a Bush-Cheney 04 sticker please be sure to kick him in the shins and tell him I made you do it.

To offer your life in servitude to an unseen sky-god based on the writings included in a book you have never read just seemed to me the far limit of irrationality. This irrationality seemed to be all around me, from my dearest friend's conversion to evangelical Christianity right through to the President of the United States who said when asked if English should be made the national language, "If English was good enough for the Bible it is good enough for me". A President who had either never read the Bible himself, or at the least did not understand what it was that he was reading and who once said on live television that faith in Christ was part of his foreign policy. This book, The Bible, is the blueprint for living a Judaist or Christian life, but simply the believers are choosing not to read it.

Is it possible that believers choose not to read it because Isaac Asimov's famous quote, in regards to the Bible, is a truism?

> *"Properly read, the bible is the most potent force for atheism ever conceived." – Isaac Asimov*

Therefore it is my objective in writing this book; *God Hates You, Hate Him Back,* to demystify the Bible for the layman. And I don't use 'layman' as some kind of elitist derogatory term, I use it because I consider myself a layman. I prefer simple explanations to things that I do not understand rather than a 'know it all' lecturing me in how smart they are. Therefore with that in mind I hope this book demonstrates the absurdity of religion in a modern context without me preaching from a theological or philosophical soap-box. If this book enables you to win a dinner table argument against one of your 'happy-clapper' Christian fundamentalist friends then this book has achieved what I set out to do in writing it.

The God I refer to in the title is the God of The Bible, and it's important to make this distinction as we in the western world mistakenly assume that God is God. God as we know in The Bible is not everyone's god now, nor was he everyone's god 4,000 years ago. The God you know through the 'good book' was purely the god of the Hebrew tribes in ancient Middle Eastern times. The Egyptians had their own gods. The Greeks had their own gods. The Romans had theirs, as did the Assyrians and Babylonians. All of these hundreds, maybe thousands, of gods hold equal evidence for their claim of being the one true god. NONE! The God you are familiar with is only such because historical events approximately 1,500 years ago, and more recently, shaped it so.

The Bible

The Bible begins with a story of how the Hebrew God, whom we shall just refer to as 'God' from now forth, created the earth and all living things. It explains how God revealed himself to Abraham in 2100BC and how Abraham took his descendents to Egypt involuntarily due to famine, to become slaves of the Pharaoh. Subsequently, God made a covenant with Abraham and promised not to forget his people, the Israelites and in 1400BC he summoned Moses to lead them out of Egyptian captivity to go directly to the 'promised land'. However, their bickering, whining and continual questioning of God led to a 40 year wait in the Sinai desert.

Under the leadership of Joshua they established the nation of Israel, grouped into 12 tribes or clans. In approximately 1050BC the nation of Israel asked for a human king. In turn Saul was appointed by the prophet

Samuel, who turned out to be a complete flop and thus was followed by David and then Solomon who built the Temple in Jerusalem as the centre of Israelite worship.

Israel was then conquered and destroyed by Assyria in 722BC and then Babylon in 586BC. Its people were taken as captives to Babylon but after 40 or 50 years were allowed to return to rebuild Jerusalem and the Temple under the leadership of Ezra and Nehemiah. This, in effect, ends the Old Testament story at approximately 430BC.

Israel continually fell under the control of other powers and at the time of Roman control Jesus was born. He was recognized by a handful of eccentric Jews as the Messiah, or God in human form, and his teachings lasted only for a period of three years. Thus commencing the stories of The New Testament, that has its origins nearly one hundred years after the supposed death of Jesus Christ.

"The great unquestionable evil at the centre of our culture is monotheism. From a barbaric Bronze Age text known as the Old Testament, three anti-human religions have evolved – Judaism, Christianity and Islam. These are the sky-god religions. They are, literally, patriarchal – God is the Omnipotent Father – hence the loathing of women for 2,000 years in those countries afflicted by the sky-god and his earthly male delegates." – Gore Vidal

With the Old Testament laying the foundation for the respective Judaist, Muslim and Christian faiths, one can assert that the Bible as the written or inspired word of God is in the minds of more than 4 billion people alive today. But what does the 'inspired word of God' actually mean? This is not an easy question to answer because the texts of the Bible are unarguably written by human hands. As a matter of fact not one single word of the 'Good Book' was penned by the Lord Almighty. Allegedly and without any empirical supporting evidence, the more than 40 various authors who contributed to the texts claim that God spoke to them alone on a mountain top, or he spoke to someone else that that person personally knew. This always befuddled me as a child, the fact that God only spoke to Middle Eastern men one-to-one, with the risk of the message being lost in translation, rather than just sit us all down for a chat collectively. Thus believers must believe it is the 'inspired' word of God or the book has no meaning at all and if it has no meaning then you have no religion. Therefore their belief is based on the fact that the Bible says it is the word of God. Nothing more.

If you ever get into a religious discussion with a Christian, for example, a circular rationale usually ensues, something like this: "The Bible is true because it is the word of God and I know it is the word of God because the Bible says so. And if the Bible says so, then it must be true, because I know the Bible is true because it is the word of God and God wouldn't lie. I know that because the Bible says so." Are you dizzy yet?

At the risk of further extending the circular roundabout, the theological conundrum is that the onus is now on the believer to prove the existence of the Biblical God, because if he isn't real then the book isn't inspired! And because we know that there were no Xerox machines or Kinkos on the Arabian Peninsula four millennia ago, we can conclude that the words were passed down orally from generation to generation, from one copy to another copy, each producing a slightly different version of the same story. Therefore for the Bible to be truly inspired by a Heavenly creator it would require that all the hundreds and thousands of men that took part in the copying and translating to have been 'inspired' by God. I now need to get off this merry-go-round.

But if we grant the believers their faith and be gracious enough to offer our humour, then shouldn't we expect the Bible to be brim-filled with wisdom, wonder, enlightenment and beauty? Shouldn't this book, co-authored by the supreme-being, the creator of all, be the most marvellous thing ever written? To stand side by side with progressive scientific discovery and not starkly against it? Is this too much to ask? Because having read the Bible back to front, front to back, right to left, left to right, I think it is one of the most uninspiring books ever written. God's greatest preachings to mankind, his creation, counts for little more than who I can and can't shag; what I can and can't eat; when I can and can't work; how I should treat my slaves; under what terms I can annihilate my neighbours; and how to slaughter an animal as a token of my gratitude to him. Furthermore, this God has some bizarre and brutish methods for getting his point across including forcing his prophet Ezekiel to eat nothing but bread smeared with human shit for 430 consecutive days; vaporizing people into salt for innocuous errs; and of course seeing to the slaughter of entire civilizations because they may happen to be in the way of an Israelite land grab.

Really? Is this his best effort? My god, I can literally walk into any Border's bookstore blindfolded, march directly to the self-help section and find more wisdom in '*Awaken the Giant within*' or '*Chicken soup for the soul*' and these respective books are just full of pseudo pop-psychology at best and utter meaningless bullshit at worst!

To borrow Lewis Black's comedic wisdom once more:

"...even if the Bible is a dead-on accurate transcription of God's words, it's rather shocking that God only had two books in him, the Old and the New Testament. I've actually written two books and I am sure God would have written more than me. Two books? That was all he had to say to us? You think he would have put at least a pamphlet in response to the Holocaust. And if not, a pamphlet, a couple of well placed fire-balls, for crying out loud. This is the Supreme Being we're talking about, who whacks Sodom and Gomorrah and turns Lot's wife to salt and Hitler doesn't get so much as a twisted ankle? It seems a little suspicious to me."

It becomes obvious that the Bible is far from the writings of an omniscient, super-intellectual being, but rather the often incoherent rants of a few violent, self-serving, nomadic Middle Eastern yokels, that created these writings with not only the intention of explaining the inexplicable but also for the moral justifications of slavery, subjugation of women and domination of neighbouring societies to steal their land, rape their women and plunder their treasures.

Who better to put this all into some realm of reality than the great late comedian Mr. George Carlin?

"When it comes to bullshit, big-time, major league bullshit, you have to stand in awe of the all-time champion of false promises and exaggerated claims, religion. No contest. No contest. Religion. Religion easily has the greatest bullshit story ever told. Think about it. Religion has actually convinced people that there's an invisible man living in the sky who watches everything you do, every minute of every day. And the invisible man has a special list of ten things he does not want you to do. And if you do any of these ten things, he has a special place, full of fire and smoke and burning and torture and anguish, where he will send you to live and suffer and burn and choke and scream and cry forever and ever 'til the end of time! But He loves you."

If the God of the Bible is all-powerful and therefore omnipotent, then his wickedness is second to none. To be omnipotent means that not only did he create evil but he does nothing to prevent it. When small children were being thrown alive into burning furnaces during the Second World War God did nothing to prevent their agonizing deaths, therefore permitting evil to take its course. By the time you have completed reading this page another few hundred children will die of thirst or starvation. Or as Epicurus the Greek Philosopher had the common sense to write way back in 300 B.C:

Is God willing to prevent evil, but not able?
Then he is not omnipotent.

Is he able, but not willing?
Then he is malevolent.
Is he both able and willing?
Then whence cometh evil?
Is he neither able nor willing?
Then why call him God?

God and evil in the one sentence surely challenges the Public Relations spin of God being a loving, just, peace-endorsing heavenly father. But with 'spoiler alert' disclaimer up front, this examination will ultimately lead you to one of the following two conclusions, that either:

- God is just a creation of man's imagination or,
- God is an evil bastard.

Be assured that my caricature of the celestial cloud merchant is not just something that I have grasped on my own, as much smarter men than I contend similar. Take Richard Dawkins', biologist and author of *God Delusion*, depiction of God from chapter two of his book:

"The God of the Old Testament is arguably the most unpleasant character in all fiction. Jealous and proud of it; a petty, unjust, unforgiving control freak; a vindictive blood thirsty ethnic cleanser; a misogynistic, homophobic, racist, infanticidal, genocidal, megalomaniacal, capriciously malevolent bully."

And don't be fooled into thinking that anti-God rhetoric is confined solely to 21st century scientists. To the eternal surprise of American Christians, Thomas Jefferson, one of the founding fathers of America shared his biographical portrayal of God with Dawkins more than 200 years earlier when he wrote:

"The Christian God is a being of terrific character – cruel, vindictive, capricious and unjust."

If your knowledge of the Bible is confined to the religious preacher soundbites then I am sure the aforementioned quotations from Messrs. Dawkins and Jefferson come as a bit of a shock. But I dare anyone to come up with a better personality profile of the God of Abraham having read the Bible from Genesis right through to Revelations. This God created by the Hebrews is far removed from the propaganda spun by priests, pastors and popes, who use these pithy soundbites of 'love thy neighbour' and 'do unto others', or 'turn the other cheek' as means of packaging Christianity for sale. The Biblical reality is that this particular God will smote you for working on the wrong day; wearing the wrong clothes; sex with the wrong person; thought crimes such as wanting a new car, a new boat, or a holiday; complaining about a lack of food; complaining about the quality of the food; eating the wrong food; occupying land allotted for his 'chosen' people; talking back to your parents; questioning authority; looking back to see his destruction of a city; breaking the rules for owning or buying slaves; and ultimately hates you for not being an Israelite, to name but a few. He truly punctuates the air with far more reasons to hate the human condition than love it.

Henceforth for every 'love thy enemy' there are dozens of God's commands endorsing the rape and killing of thy neighbour. The sprinkles of self-evident moral ideals are well and truly outnumbered by some truly wicked ideas, barbaric rituals and genocidal endorsements. The God of hate is revealed within the Bible and therefore my intent is to demonstrate that assertion throughout my summary of the 'Bad Book'.

So the claim that God is a tyrannical monster has been made – let's find the proof of such a contrarian assertion within the passages of the Bible. But before we do I just want to tackle the issue of religion and morality. The argument of morality is the tip of the sword that Christians use in defence of their beliefs.

So what about morality? A question often posed to atheists and agnostics. Where do we get our morality from if not the Bible? This is a daft question that many free thinkers take utter umbrage to. Especially so when one considers that morality is older than religion itself. As human beings with a higher consciousness to our fellow mammals in the animal kingdom we have an innate sense that what is good for our society is also good for us. Gene survival in social animals depends on the principle of looking after one's peers. The 'I'll scratch your back if you scratch mine' ideal is law of nature. Which is a nice segue for introducing our cousins the chimpanzees.

Consider that chimpanzees are socially evolved enough to take care of their young and elderly; perform roles in social teams; and are able to compete for social promotion for what zoologists label the principle of social service. They are able to do all of this without a sky-god to watch over them, without the benefit of a book written 4000 years ago by other chimpanzees. With this in mind why do Christians, Muslims and Jews continue the self-loathing and self-doubting assertion that the Bible forms the framework for human morality? Laughable isn't it? Like the chimps, we have a mutual investment and moral empathy in ensuring that perpetrators of deeds that cause harm to us are ultimately isolated from us, whether by imprisonment or ostracization. The reality-show 'Survivor' makes a dim-witted case in point for this dynamic. Watch any elimination episode and it is primarily those individuals that offer no altruistic value to the tribe, whether physically or politically, who are sent home for an early shower.

To defend the Bible as an argument for morality places one on a very slippery slope. By what standards or framework do we cherry-pick the Bible? What do we leave in and what do we omit? And who decides? Do we stone our daughters to death for working part-time at Burger King on the Sabbath? Or do we remove the law that demands we take our sons to the edge of the city limits and execute them for calling their fathers, "A cranky old bastard", in a heated teen-angst moment? And if we are picking and choosing the laws worthy of following, then aren't we playing God ourselves? Furthermore, if we accept that it is barbaric in the 21st century to sell our daughters into slavery, then it is evident that morals, like everything else in the human experience *evolve*. Resulting in the conclusion that moral evolution is at the behest of man and not by God.

Further, if belief in God were inextricably tied to morality then it would be fair to assume that statistical, analytical or anecdotal data would demonstrate that societies with a higher degree of religiosity would be safer places to live, as those citizens abided by the moral code prescribed by the respective religion. What we find, however, is the opposite. This data is best described by Sam Harris in his '*Letter to a Christian Nation*':

> *"While political party affiliation in the United States is not a perfect indicator of religiosity, it is no secret that the 'red (Republican) states' are primarily red due to the overwhelming political influence of conservative Christians. If there were a strong correlation between Christian conservatism and societal health, we might expect to see some sign of it in red-state America. We don't. Of the twenty-five cities with the lowest rates of violent crime, 62 percent are in 'blue' (Democrat) states and 38 percent are in 'red' (Republican) states. Of the twenty-five most dangerous cities, 76 percent are in red states and 24 percent are in blue states. In fact, three of the five most dangerous cities in the U.S. are in the most pious state of Texas. The twelve states with the highest rate of burglary are red. Twenty-four of the twenty-nine states with the highest rates of theft are red. Of the twenty-two states with highest rates of murder, seventeen are red."*

Harris' social data is consistent with a paper published in July 2009 on the online journal *Evolutionary Psychology* by Gregory Paul. Paul finds that countries with the lowest rates of social dysfunction – based on more than 20 indicators, including rates for poverty, unemployment, crime and sexually transmitted disease – have become the most secular or anti-religious. Whereas those nations listed as the most socially dysfunctional including the US, are listed as the most religious. Hasn't history taught us well enough that when you oppress or prohibit a certain behaviour the 'blowback' is double?

So with the continual decline of religion and with a collective awakening around the world that if there is a God then surely there can't be just one path to him, the question becomes what part will religion play in the future? I will let you ponder that as you read this book, but in the interim you may want to consider Harris' brilliant hypothesis, included in 'End of Faith':

> *"What if all our knowledge about the world were suddenly to disappear? Imagine that six billion of us wake up tomorrow morning in a state of utter ignorance and confusion. Our books and computers are still here, but we can't make heads or tails of their contents. We have even forgotten how to drive our cars and brush our teeth. What knowledge would we want to reclaim first? Well, there's that business about getting food and building shelter that we would to get reacquainted with. We would want to relearn how to use and repair many of our machines. Learning to understand spoken and written language would also be a top priority, given that these skills are necessary for acquiring most others. When in this process of reclaiming our humanity will it be important to know that Jesus was born of a virgin? Or that he was resurrected? And how would we relearn these truths, if they are indeed true? By reading the Bible? Our tour of the shelves will deliver similar pearls from antiquity – like the 'fact' that Isis, the goddess of fertility, sports an impressive pair of cow horns. Reading further, we will learn that Thor carries a hammer and that Marduk's sacred animals are horses, dogs and a dragon with a forked tongue......and when we will want to relearn that premarital sex is a sin? Or that adultresses should be stoned to death?"*

Harris further contends that if the above all-humanity memory loss were to occur, then our relearning of all things of relevance would place the Bible and Qur'an on the shelf next to Ovid's 'Metamorphoses' and the 'Egyptian Book of the Dead'.

Alright enough with the Theology 101 lesson, let's have some fun in exploring the ancient Biblical world of murder, barbarism, bestiality, rape and plunder.

PS: God doesn't know you are reading this book, so don't be scared.

The Books of The Pentateuch

Chapter One - The Book of Genesis

"Do you think that, if you were granted omnipotence and omniscience and millions of years in which to perfect your world, you could produce nothing better than the Ku Klux Klan or the Fascists?"
Bertand Russell (London, 1927)

Genesis is the first book of the Bible of Judaism and of Christianity and the first of five books of the Pentateuch or Torah. It recounts Judeo-Christian beliefs regarding the world, from creation to the descent of the children of Israel into Egypt, and contains some of the best-known stories of the Old Testament, including Adam and Eve, Cain and Abel, Noah's Ark, the Tower of Babel and the biblical Patriarchs.

For Jews the theological importance of Genesis centres on the covenants linking God to his Chosen People and the people to the Promised Land. Christianity has reinterpreted Genesis as the prefiguration of Christian beliefs, notably the Christian view of Christ as the new Adam and the New Testament as the culmination of the covenants.

The Creation

The very first sentence of Genesis and therefore the Bible states:

"In the beginning God created the heavens and the earth." (Genesis 1:1 NIV)

That's it! Doesn't tell us how he made it; what building materials were used; if any of the work was outsourced to India; or from where he sourced the materials. The Bible's explanation of the creation of the universe is paramount to the smart-ass kid in the classroom telling you, "It just is and you wouldn't understand it even if I told you anyway!"

The next time someone says there is still a debate between evolution versus the Biblical creation, know that on one hand we have a library full of two thousand years of scientific research cataloguing the origins of our species; natural selection; and the wondrous beauty of evolutionary development and on the other hand, that being the Bible, the good book has compressed all that natural world wonderment into a single pithy sentence. Magic! Scientists are the first to admit that there are some still some missing links in understanding the finer details as to the creation of the universe, but any 'gap' that we currently have today is not logically resolved by the Bible's explanation of 'wham here it is'!

The remainder of the opening sentence of Genesis continues:

> *"Now the earth was formless and empty, darkness was over the surface of the deep and the Spirit of God was hovering over the waters." (Genesis 1:2 NIV)*

So the question becomes what was God doing with himself all that time? Sitting idle in the formless empty darkness? How long was he sitting on his ass doing sweet bugger all? Did he create us out of sheer boredom? In between inventing the dinosaurs 35 million years ago and then man 7,000 years ago – what was he doing during this extraordinary lengthy hiatus? Evidently he was indeed content with floating around in the dark until all of a sudden he says to himself, "Fuck it, I want to create a planet, a heaven, some people and sit back and watch them destroy each other in my honour because Monday Night Football is still 6,000 years away."

This Genesis explanation for the origins of our universe is based on less rationality than the Hindu belief that the universe is a cosmic egg that cycles between expansion and total collapse. Sure, evolution may not have all the answers and there are a few gaps in the evolutionary timeline that science is still figuring out the answers to, but to argue that an invisible man floating around in the cosmos just decided on a whim one day to wave his hands and *bang* everything familiar to our natural physical environment appeared out of literal thin air – is too far a stretch even for the most deluded individuals whom are sadly confined to a life in a padded cell, and should be.

From a scientific point of view, and I am armed only with a 5th grade scientific mind (the kids on 'Are You Smarter Than a 5th Grader' routinely kick my ass), the errors, follies and fables of the Bible begin with that very first sentence of Genesis, *"In the beginning God created the heavens and the earth"*. This is completely untrue and unequivocally at odds with what we know of our universe today. The truth is that in the beginning a natural event created the universe as we know it and the earth did not form until billions of years later, thus an immediate booboo on behalf of the desert nomads who wrote this. For example, the Bible says that light and darkness are created after the water but before the sun. Discovery and

Discovery Channel, have proven that the sun came first, then the planet and its rotation, which gives us light and darkness and day and night, and then the water, and this all happened over millions of years.

Put into a more humorous way, there is an interesting observation included in a pocket-sized book of quotations titled *The Atheist's Bible.* A quote that is not attributed to anyone, but for a citation of an anonymous author, it reads:

> *"Geology shows that fossils are of different ages. Paleontology shows a fossil sequence, the list of species representing changes through time. Taxonomy shows biological relationships among species. Evolution is the explanation that threads it all together. Creationism is the practice of squeezing your eyes shut and wailing 'DOES NOT!'"*

I find it excessively humorous that God made light out of nothing, on the second day, which means he made the heavens and the earth in the dark! Now if creating everything we know out of nothing wasn't a challenge enough, he did it in complete darkness. Pretty clever isn't it? I can't even write my own name in the dark, let alone create a fucking great big shark.

God Messes Up The Order

Irrefutably the total balls up of the Genesis order of events is the smoking gun for demonstrating that God is the figure of 2000 BC man's imagination, but in keeping with the spirit of things let's pretend he did create all of this. Then we must ask, "How?"

God created light and darkness on day one and the sun and the planets didn't come until day four. So where did the light come from? No sun, no light. Oops!

On day three he creates all the earth's vegetation, the plants and the trees, but as we now know God didn't create the sun until the following day, so how can there be plant life without photosynthesis? Oops!

Now we run into our very first contradiction and we are only on page one of the Bible mind you, as God says that on day five he created the birds and animals from nothing more than the water from the oceans, but then in the very next chapter as he is doing a summary of these heady seven days, it is written:

> *"Now the Lord God had formed out of the ground all the beasts of the land and all the birds of the air." (Genesis 2:19 NIV)*

God stays on message for less time than President Obama without a teleprompter. I've met goldfish with longer short-term memories.

God Creates Man

Moving onto the sixth day of his celestial architectural program he decides to create a human being:

> *"So God created man in his own image, in the image of God he created him." (Genesis 1:27 NIV)*

Think about this for a moment. Made in his own image? If we are truly made in his own image then why aren't we invisible? But clearly I can see you and you can see me, so I think this is another fallacy straight off the bat. And if we do look like him, which of us looks like him? Is he Asian? Is he black? Is he an NRA card-carrying member of the Texas branch of the Young Republicans? Or is he somewhat Tokyo metro-sexual in appearance? Does he stand naked in front of the mirror and wish he gave himself an extra inch or two, not that I do that, I'm just saying, ok! And what if he were anything like Bill O'Reilly? Because if he is anything like the white angry men at FOX News then I will violate all of the 10 Commandments right now, grab a gun, shoot myself, assuring myself a place in the sulphur fires of Hell.

Ok let's imagine that God is more like Morgan Freeman's portrayal in *God Almighty* and imagine for a moment that, *bam*! man is made out of thin air in God's own image. Right? Wrong! Well wrong according to the next contradiction, which follows in the chapter two summary alongside the birds foul up. Get it?

> *"The Lord God formed the man from the dust on the ground and breathed into his nostrils the breath of life and the man became a living being." (Genesis 2:7 NIV)*

So which one is it? Air or dust? Admittedly I am easily confused but now I am fully flummoxed. We have only travelled a page or two into the Bible and already God is contradicting himself. The opening should be the easy part! Once God has to remember names and locations after receiving all those prayer-mails and knee-mails, it's bound to get more difficult.At the start of the second chapter where it is said, God made man before all the plants and trees, we are in confusion again. This in complete contradiction to the first chapter's claim that wildlife was made on day three and man on day six. Here is the incriminating passage:

> *"When the Lord God made the earth and the heavens – and no shrub of the field had yet appeared on the earth and no plant of the field had yet sprung up – The Lord God formed man from the dust of the ground." (Genesis 2:4-7 NIV)*

It is now at this point that we can see that religion truly was man's first attempt to explain the natural world. An explanation constrained by the absence of crucial information to explain, what was 4,000 years ago, inexplicable:

"Let man rule over the fish and the sea and the birds of the air, over the livestock, over all of earth and over all creatures that move along the ground."

This evidently demonstrates that man falsely believed that he had dominion over all living things. An excusable false assumption one might make without what we know today about bacteria, microbes and germs, which undoubtedly hold dominion over us. Consider that in thousands of years of medical science, man has only had one success in defeating just one virus, small pox, which is certainly a humbling if not terrifying fact. Even more daunting with the rapid spread of new pandemics of bird flu and swine flu, illuminating the fragile hold we have as a species on this planet. Furthermore, isn't it deliciously curious that creationists doubt evolution's claims but accept without question that viruses, such as H1N1, display adaptive traits including mutation? To further underscore this point, ask yourself what is providing you comfort at night in relation to combating these viruses: science or religion? Yes interesting isn't it? Religion has never proven any scientific discovery wrong, but the same can't be said the other way around can it?

A further mistruth is the Genesis claim that all animals and man were made on the same day, the sixth. We now know this simply to be utterly false through evidence and understanding of palaeontology, carbon dating and radiation dating. 97% of the world's leading scientists concur that dinosaurs became extinct at least 65 million years before man inhabited the earth. And before you run off into the living room to clutch the 'Good Book' as a means of solace, carbon dating is real, just ask my friend Lewis Black:

"And while we're on the subject, I'd like to point out – for the benefit of the religious naysayers out there – carbon dating is real. It can help us tell how old something is. It can place things in time. THIS SHIT ISN'T MADE UP! You can carbon-date an object and it gives you a sense of how it is because of the carbon in it. No one is making these numbers up. It's not mumbo jumbo. THE EARTH IS OLDER THAN SIX THOUSAND YEARS, SO TOUGHSKI SHITSKI!"

Lewis adds further to his take, as a Jew, on the Genesis claim for the creation of the earth, in his typical acidic style:

"Jews know that earth was not created in seven days, because as Jews we know what we are good at. And what we are really good at is – bullshit! This is a wonderful story told to the Jewish people in the desert to distract

them from the fact that they did not have air-conditioning. I would love to have the faith to believe it took place in seven days BUT I have thoughts and that can really fuck up the faith thing."

The human arrogance of Genesis is further evident in the fact that it assumes that we, humans on planet earth, are the only occupants of the universe. There are 70,000 million million million stars within our universe (7 followed by 22 zeroes) and our sun is just one of those. Without getting all sci-fi on you, to live with the presumption that we are 'it' and that ours is the only civilisation among galaxies 4 billion years older than ours, is not only childish naivety but wilful arrogance.

A former US President had no difficulty in closing his eyes to all scientific evidence when he said:

"On the issue of evolution, the verdict is still out on how God created the Earth." – George W. Bush

I am optimistic that by the time we get to the next book of the Old Testament you will conclude that it is glaringly obvious we created God in our own image complete with human qualities such as anger, jealousy, vengeance and remorse rather than the other way around.

Introducing Adam and Eve

Oh the boyhood sexual fantasies this story provoked in my pre-pubescent childhood, with thoughts of frolicking naked in a garden of paradise with a super hot chick. Not a care in the world except for the precautionary methods in ensuring I didn't suffer sunburn to the roof of my pecker. Other than this penile concern, the last remaining stress would be to adhere to God's only command, that being, simply to avoid the temptation of eating from just one apple tree. But returning for a moment to the creation of man, Adam, I find it utterly, fucking incredulous that believers will be ignorantly quick in their dim-witted assertion that evolution is only a theory and thus cannot be believed with any certitude. However, the Judeo-Christian 'theory' that man was formed from the breath of God into the nostrils of Adam is accepted with arrogant certitude is too hilarious to justify serious debate. The comedy of this belief is that Christians feel aggrieved whenever scientists say that humans evolved from other life forms, but have no problem with the Bible's claim that we were created from dirt. So ludicrous that it amuses my little mind to recall comedian Bill Hicks' observation of happy-clapper Christians, when he said, "Why is it that those who believe in creation, appear, themselves, not to be fully evolved?"

Another question I have is, if God really did create Adam out of thin air or dust and thus not born from a mother, did Adam have a belly button? All jokes aside, I think of Adam as the luckiest man ever made for one reason only, he didn't have a mother-in-law.

So there is Adam the sole human being on earth, surrounded by vegetation, flowing rivers and an abundance of wildlife. Eden was truly paradise on earth! But God notices that Adam with his testosterone-fuelled penile urges is attempting to mate with the animals. God thinks to himself, 'This shit don't look right, I need to get him something with less hair and nicer boobies.' Herewith was the inspiration for God to create woman. Check it for yourself...

"Adam rejected the animals." (Genesis 2:18)

Now in case you were wondering the creation of woman doesn't get any less ridiculous. God recognising that he needs to provide a playmate for Adam so that he does not end up fathering a Taurus, comes up with the design blueprint for woman:

"So the Lord God caused the man to fall into a deep sleep; and while he was sleeping, he took one of the man's ribs and closed up the place with flesh. Then the Lord God made a woman from the rib he had taken out of the man and he brought her to the man." (Genesis 2:21-22 NIV)

Whilst Adam was sleeping, God snuck down to the garden, tip-toed up to him careful not to break any twigs, then slices Adam open with a pen-knife, snaps off one his ribs and whammo a woman. How delightfully simplistic is the origin of our species. Amen.

God Is Resting... Still

The last verse of chapter one is worth a chuckle too. Imagine God with his arms folded, leaning back in his rocking chair overlooking all that he had created in just six days with a broad smile of satisfactory accomplishment:

"God saw all that he had made and it was very good." (Genesis 1: 31 NIV)

The very next day he rested. And the day after that he rested. And that day and the next. Fuck, he was still resting yesterday and as of this morning. When is he ever going back to work? Surely he can't be satisfied with the earth he has created considering that four-fifths of it is uninhabitable and most parts are either too hot or too cold to sustain life and the polar bears are drowning. This guy works less than a Melbourne wharfie on strike. C'mon you lazy sod do us all a favour and get back to work for Christ sake! There are 26,000 children dying of thirst and starvation every single day whilst you continue to sit around and pat yourself on the back for a job half-done.

For these reasons my god is Thor, because he has a hammer. And if he is handy with the tools, he is more likely to get shit done.

The Talking Snake

> *"Then the Lord God took the man and put him in the Garden of Eden to work it and take care of it. And the Lord God commanded the man, 'You are free to eat from any tree in the garden; but you must not eat from the tree of the knowledge of good and evil, for when you eat it you will surely die.'" (Genesis 2:15-17 NIV)*

Are you kidding me? What a wicked sense of humour God has! His very first dialogue with his created humans is a rule. How about, "Welcome to Eden guys. Enjoy yourselves. Have wild outdoor sex to your heart's content. Make yourself comfortable and later I will be back to you with one or two rules of the house." But no he introduces himself with a mind-fuck technique, that being the power of negative suggestion, "Don't eat from *that* tree!" If God had said nothing of the tree I am sure Adam and Eve would have never come within several orchard fields of it, but because he said 'that' tree, it is human instinct to enquire. If you repeatedly tell a child to stay away from the cookie jar, what do you think he will do the next time you turn your back away from the kitchen? Cookies will be gone Mummy! Thus God either commanded this edict for his own humorous benefit, or he is an extremely poor psychologist.

I mean, why go to the effort of creating man from dust, woman from man's rib and all the planets and then play a trick of entrapment that completely fucks everything up for every man or woman ever since? Talk about a joke that backfired!

Thus a serpent, with demonstratively superior psychoanalytical skills made its way to Eve in the garden, tempting her with the words, "Did God really say, 'you must not eat from any tree in the garden'?" Where did this talking snake come from? Yes you guessed it, God. He made the snake and he put the snake there. The snake is Satan and Satan is the root of evil, therefore *God created evil*! Did that just blow your mind? I am smoking a cigarette as I ponder this personal logical discovery!

Ok, before we examine this interchange between talking snake and Eve, let me make this clear from my own perspective. If I am walking through the bush and accidentally stumble across a snake, I run for dear life in the opposite direction. The mere sight of a snake makes me shit my pants, so imagine what a talking one would do to me?

However, Eve is seemingly much braver than I and continues to engage in carefree casual dialogue with the serpent and answers:

> *"We may eat fruit from the trees in the garden, but God did say, 'You must not eat fruit from the tree that is in the middle of the garden and you must not touch it or you will surely die.'"* (Genesis 3:2-3 NIV)

To which the mouthy snake responds,

> *"You will not surely die, for God knows that when you eat of it your eyes will be opened and you will be like God, knowing good and evil."* (Genesis 3:4 NIV)

We all know that the talking snake succeeded in 'selling' the apple appetizer to Eve, who in turned sold the idea to Adam. How she sold the idea we will never know but I assume she offered the apple in one hand whilst stroking her naked ass with the other, "If you don't take a piece of this, then you don't get a piece of that!" Like any red-blooded male the sexualized version of the car salesman's alternative close sealed an event that Bible believers refer to as the moment of the 'original sin' and shamelessly the justification of man (gender) to treat women as sub-equals had begun. A theme we will continually revisit throughout this book.

This part of the Bible also provides our first glimpse into the malevolent, brutish, vindictive, uncompromising and unforgiving character traits of God. As God says to Eve:

> *"I will greatly increase your pains in childbearing; with pain you will give birth to children. Your desire will be for your husband and he will rule over you."* (Genesis 3:16 NIV)

What a wonderfully chauvinistic command, "He will rule over you". I have repeatedly tried unsuccessfully to point to this passage whenever my wife has forbidden me to join my mates on a night out trolling strip clubs. I still haven't given up.

Ok, that is Adam and Eve punished. Of note is the fact that God promised Adam that he would "surely die" upon eating the apple, but God has proved already that he is not a man of his word, as Adam went on to live for another 900 years.

And what of the snake you ask? The instigator of fucking things up for all of us? Well, here is the punitive measure God dishes out to the snake. Are you ready for this?

> *"You shall crawl along your belly for the rest of your life."* (Genesis 3:14 NIV)

Are you serious? Well, call me stupid, but that hardly seems much of a punishment for a snake, that had no legs in the first place! And I'm sure the snake made a big sounding sigh of relief before slithering off to wherever it came from. Which poses an interesting question doesn't it? The snake must have come from God and was put there by God in the first place, whether intentionally as a ploy to tempt Eve or not, but if so why punish the snake if God did create him and use him for that purpose? Oh well it seems Adam blamed Eve, Eve blamed the Serpent and the Serpent didn't have a leg to stand on!

Adam & Eve – The Aftermath

Adam and Eve now mere mortals like you and I were also shouldered with the punishment of knowing they would now no longer live for eternity. God says to Adam, that because of his error, human beings will live only to a maximum age of 120 years.

Adam and Eve married and kept their clothes on at all times because they were now ashamed of their nakedness, due to the awakening as a result of eating the forbidden fruit, which meant that outdoor sex in broad daylight was no longer kosher but lights-off coitus would be the sex du jour. Shortly after formalizing their union as man and wife, Eve gave birth to two sons named Cain and Abel.

Cain, Abel and Noah

On the surface this appears to be a story of an insecure son and a God who played favourites.

> *"Abel kept flocks and Cain worked the soil. In the course of time Cain brought some of the fruits of the soil as an offering to the Lord. But Abel brought fat portions from some of the firstborn his flock. The Lord looked with favour on Abel and his offering, but on Cain and his offering he did not look with favour. So Cain was very angry and his face was downcast." (Genesis 4:2-5 NIV)*

It seems highly suspicious to a moron like me that God would play the favourites game with the very first family he ever created and for reasons given that hardly warrant so. That reason being that Abel offered more worthy animal sacrifices in worship of the Lord. But Cain grew vegetables and it would hardly make any sense to offer your first carrot as a sacrifice to the Lord, would it?

This passage provides us with our first insight into God's insecurity complex, in that he plays favourites to those that worship or praise him better. And more importantly doesn't it seem somewhat 'human' to show partiality towards one over another?

Over time Cain gets the shits, his jealousy consumes him and in a remote field he murders his brother, Abel. But since God is subjected to the human emotion of jealousy too he opts not to punish Cain in any great manner and leaves the judicial process to his parents who decide to banish Cain to an undisclosed location.

But what of Adam and Eve? God helped Eve, at 130 years of age, to become pregnant with another son to replace Abel, his name Seth. Adam died in his prime at a whopping 930 years of age. The death of Eve is not mentioned, but needless to say both lived more than 800 years past what God had said was man's expiry date. Which poses the question, when do we obey God with certainty or when do we second guess his bluffs? He is one mean poker player.

We learn that Cain survives his banishment and lives a prosperous life. He finds a girl, marries her and together with his new wife produces a son named Enoch. Enoch had two children and more grandchildren, until approximately 600 or more years later one of Adam and Cain's descendents gave birth to Noah.

Now just in case you missed the flaw in the above story, like I did on the first go around. Where the hell did Cain's wife come from? As it is written quite clearly that God created first Adam and then later Eve. The two hook up and produce two sons of their own. The start of the human race! Abel is killed and Cain is banished but marries some broad. Who created her? I guess the author of Genesis doesn't include any mention of her lineage or creation because to do so would either discredit his original Genesis story, or make it one of incestuous beginnings.

At the grand old age of 500 years (and In case you didn't notice, I just made that coughing sound that intentionally, feebly conceals the sound of 'bullshit') Noah became the father of Shem, Ham and Japheth.

The Flood

God didn't stay happy with his creation for very long and in his heavenly loneliness he became irate that all of mankind seemed to be having too much of a good time enjoying guilt-free sex, drinking wine and smoking whatever they could get their hands on:

> *"The Lord saw how great man's wickedness on the earth had become and that every inclination of the thoughts of his heart was only evil all the time.*

The Lord was grieved that he had made man on the earth and his heart was filled with pain." (Genesis 6:5 NIV)

And judging by the proceeding words of God, this pain must have been a little more uncomfortable than a slight burning sensation of reflux:

"I will wipe mankind, whom I have created, from the face of the earth – men and animals and creatures that move along the ground and birds of the air – for I am grieved that I have made them." (Genesis 6:7 NIV)

So he wants to start all over again? This is the intelligent designer we are talking about and he wants to get rid of the entire human race on day one of the honeymoon.

Now, notwithstanding the obvious human blunder of applying human emotions to a celestial spirit we are now witnesses to the fact that God is a genocidal maniac.

Is this not mass-murder on the grandest level? Does it not beget the obvious question: Why do believers worship a mass murderer? And surely if God, the all-knowing creator, created man, would not he have foreseen this so called evil coming? This is nothing short of a senseless atrocity of the highest order, to destroy millions of people because he was displeased at the moral performance of 'some' of those that he created in his own image. And if we are the mirror of God does this mean that he too has a natural, instinctual urge to participate in drunken orgies? And if not, why did he fail to program us without these so called wicked desires? And more significantly, God hadn't prescribed any rules or commandments at this stage, so why were we being punished for breaking the rules when there weren't any yet to follow? And to punish by death for violating invisible rules seems a little harsh doesn't it? This is certainly can not be the act of a God of love, peace and mercy.

If this event were true then this is a violent, unforgiving, celestial dictator that requires unquestioning obedience, to not only follow his rules, but guess what he is thinking too.

Fortunately, the rationalists amongst us can be thankful that not only is God a character of wicked fiction but we can also take comfort that our ancestral forefathers did not meet a watery grave, as there is no evidence that Mt Everest was ever covered in flood water, nor do indigenous civilizations such as the Australian Aboriginals have a pause in their history that would denote such a catastrophe. Thus another bogus fable and a fable with similar tenets told in almost every religion since the dawn of time.

Furthermore, the credibility that all species of animal, insects (of which there are more than 1 million species of beetles alone) and man alive today are a result of the miraculous efforts of a 900 year old man, Noah, corralling two of every living thing onto his 450 foot long boat, and then successfully encouraging all these species to mate with one another after spending 150 days trapped on a wooden boat, is too stupid to imagine. The comical improbability of this story can be pictured with the mind's eye - a man that is nearly a millennia in age, wearing nothing but a flimsy sheep wool robe and a pair of ancient thongs probably held together by no more than a couple pieces of leather hide, prancing around the world trying to collect two of every species. Imagine his difficulty in getting a male and female Sumatran tiger. He had to clip clop his way all the way down to Indonesia, set traps in the Sumatran jungle then catch two of these powerful cats that could kill you with a playful swipe of their paws. Not only catch them but also imagine Noah carrying them all the way back to the Middle East, only to discover that both tigers had a set of testicles.

Or picture Noah there standing proudly before the completed Arc with most of the animals on board including the dinosaurs, asking his sons, "Alright lads let's make sure we have we got all the animals on God's list?" His sons reply, "No Dad there's a small problem, none of us have heard of a kangaroo, nor have we heard of a place called Australia." Noah then replied, "Must be one of God's typos. Ok what is next on the list?" "A Koala." "Shit!"

As a teenager I recall looking at a picture of an Aardvark and thinking that if ever there was animal that named itself then it must have been this mammal. There's Noah standing in front of the Arc, the rain pouring down. He's holding a clipboard and asking that all animals assemble in alphabetical order. Noah looks down at this strange looking creature and asks, "What is it that you are?" "I am an Aardvark," came the reply. "Ok well go stand behind the antelope?" To which Noah is hastily informed by the four legged critter that his species is spelt with two a's. As in a double stroke of animal genius.

American columnist Judith Hayes also pondered these kind of comical questions in relation to this childish story that frighteningly more than 60% of Americans believe to be literal truth when she wrote:

> *"The biblical account of Noah's Ark and the Flood is perhaps the most implausible story for fundamentalists to defend. Where, for example, while loading his ark did Noah find penguins and polar bears in Palestine?"*

Not only do we know that it would have been impossible to house all the millions and billions of living species on this boat, but we also know there is no DNA evidence to show that all animals on earth came from single breeding pairs just a few thousand years ago.

Final thoughts on this, where would Noah have kept the woodpeckers and the termites? With all these millions of animals, reptiles and insects on board this boat for months how big was the poo-room?

God's Covenant with Noah

As the flood waters receded Noah set forth to ensure all the animals were busy mating. He also encouraged his sons to mate with their wives so that mankind could begin to multiply once more. God made the following promise to Noah:

> *"Then God said to Noah and to his sons with him: 'I now establish my covenant with you and your descendents after you and with every living creature that is with you....Never again will all life be cut off by the waters of a flood; never again will there be a flood to destroy the earth.'" (Genesis 9:8-11 NIV)*

This promise was sealed with a rainbow:

> *"Whenever the rainbow appears in the clouds, I will see it and remember the everlasting covenant between God and all living creatures of every kind on the earth." (Genesis 9:16 NIV)*

Once more the Biblical explanation of the rainbow as God's covenant with Noah demonstrates that the Bible was indeed written by 2000BC man without crucial information we know to be true today, to explain things that were inexplicable to man 7,000 years ago. We now know, thanks to Isaac Newton in 1665, that the scientific explanation for a rainbow is a result of the passing of light from air into water, or water into air, where the different colours are refracted. Thus, the colours are separated into a spectrum, or rainbow.

A further question worth pondering in relation to this chapter of Genesis and its claim that all mankind are in effect descendents of Noah and his sons, is how does this explain from where Asians and Blacks descend? And if you argue that they too came from Noah and their features adjusted to their respective climatic locales, then aren't you now arguing the case for evolution?

Once more this chapter raises more questions than the zero answers it provides.

The Tower of Babel

As the authoring committee were piecing together the story for the genesis of civilization they quickly realized they would have to deal with the fact of explaining how it was that different cultures spoke different languages. You had the Egyptians speaking Egyptian, the Greeks speaking Greek, for example, all the while God was speaking only in fluent Hebrew. So they pondered an explanation for this whilst sitting around the campfire in the middle of the Canaan Desert. The Bible reconciles this in a manner that is arguably the most ridiculous of all.

The Bible has it written that the entire world, post-flood, spoke a single language. The world's inhabitants gathered together on a flood plain in the land of Shinar, presumably somewhere in what we know to be Israel today. All citizens of the world united to build a new city, with what would be an iconic tower, being so magnificent that its pinnacle would seem to touch the heavens. Working together in solidarity and with a common purpose, the 'world' built this impressive tower made of brick and mortar, and indeed, according to Bible lore, it reached into Heaven.

Was God happy with this engineering feat of human endeavour? Was he happy that man had united after the virtual elimination of man as a result of God's flood? The answer is no he wasn't. In fact God was pissed that man would do such a thing without it being specifically a monument in his honour. God travelled down to Babel, and this is what he said:

> *"'Behold, the people is one and they have all one language; and this they begin to do; and now nothing will be restrained from them, which they have imagined to do. Go to, let us go down and there confound their language, that they may not understand one another's speech.' So the Lord scattered them abroad from thence upon the face of all the earth: and they left off to build the city. Therefore is the name of it called Babel; because the Lord did there confound the language of all the earth: and from thence did the Lord scatter them abroad upon the face of all the earth." (Genesis 11:1-9 NIV)*

The inference being that the Tower of Babel was not built for the worship and praise of God, but was dedicated to the glory of man, with the motive of making a 'name' for the builders. God, seeing what the people were trying to achieve by working together, was not only pissed but evidently concerned that if man could create such an impressive structure without his input then man could achieve any number of things via human solidarity. I wonder what man could pull together by collaboration? Science or medicine maybe? Rational thinking? Anyway, in his fear and fury he confounded their languages and scattered the people of Babel throughout all four corners of the earth.

This being the Genesis explanation of the diversity of languages we know today. What nincompoop really believes this to be true? I can't go on, but I must!

Wouldn't you think it a little insightful if God kept all of mankind to a single language so that the Bible could've been written in a single language rather than have to be translated from Hebrew to Aramaic to Greek to English? I guess the principle of 'lost in translation' never occurred to the 'Great One'.

Introducing Abraham

The name Abraham translates in Hebrew to 'father of nations' and as is revealed in the writings of Genesis he is a critical figure as the founding patriarch of the Israelites. According to the Bible Abraham was brought from Mesopotamia, or Iraq-Iran as it is known today, to the land of Canaan. God had said to Abraham, in a dream, to leave his country, his people and his household to go to the land that God would reveal to him, in return he would be blessed with all of mankind.

Abraham was led into Egypt due to a severe famine, but upon entering Egypt he was concerned that the Egyptian Pharaoh would kill him and take his wife, who was said to have been stunningly beautiful. Thus he deceived the Pharaoh into believing that his wife, Sarah, was his sister. The scheme backfires somewhat as the Pharaoh takes Sarah and includes her in his harem and bonks her, along with tens of other willing sex slaves, at anytime of his choosing. But before you think to yourself, "Hey it's good to be the Pharaoh", Sarah was seventy-five years of age at this point. I mean c'mon how hot could she really have been?

What's further interesting about this story is that Abraham lied and deceived a Pharaoh with God's endorsement. What kind of moral teaching is this? I think all believers should find it somewhat unsettling that the human father of the Judaeo-Christian faith was a fraudster. The Church of Later Day Saints, the Mormon faith, was likewise founded by a convicted fraudster in Joseph Smith. But at least the Mormons got magic underwear in following him.

Somehow the Pharaoh learns that Sarah is Abraham's wife and he reunites the couple before banishing them from Egypt. Upon returning to Canaan, Abraham enters into a covenant with God. This covenant was based on a deal that in exchange for recognizing God as supreme universal deity and authority; he would be blessed with innumerable progeny. The Lord appearing to Abraham in a vision, told him,

"Do not be afraid, Abraham. I am your shield, your very great reward." (Genesis 15:1 NIV)

Abraham complains to God that his wife can bear no children and expresses his concern that should he die his inheritance will be left to one of his slaves. Yes the Patriarch of Israel, the chosen one of God is seemingly oblivious to the moral bankruptcy of slavery, but more on this later.

In return that Abraham offer unquestionable servitude of the Lord, the Lord says to Abraham:

"Look up at the heavens and count the stars – if indeed you can count them. So shall your offspring be." (Genesis 15:4-5 NIV)

But before Abraham could enjoy the fruits of this new baby-making pact with God, he is awoken later that same night with another vision from God, but this time with an eerie warning:

"Know for certain that your descendants will be strangers in a country not their own and they will be enslaved and ill-treated four hundred years." (Genesis 15:13 NIV)

A little later in the story, we discover that God is a shifty old shyster and reneges on his earlier covenant with Abraham, by moving the goal posts. God had told Abraham that he and his descendants would be given land and made into a great nation with kings out of Abraham's line. However, God informs his prophet that he must now seal this new deal by mutilating his genitals, at the age of 99 years mind you, along with the genitals of every other male in his household including the male slaves. Can you imagine being poor old Abraham's water carrier and he approaches you with a rusty old blunt knife and bellows to you, "Hey boy come here whilst I hack the tip of your dick off with this here knife". Who would've stayed around long enough for that to happen? And what sort of sick, fucking perverted, twisted god would demand such a barbaric act of senseless, immeasurable cruelty? And if God detested the foreskin so much, why create man with it in the first place?

God says to Abraham:

"Every male among you shall be circumcised. You are to undergo circumcision and it will be a sign of the covenant between me and you." (Genesis 17:10 NIV)

Thus if you are male and reading this book, chances are you too have no foreskin, which according to some scientific claims contains 75% of the erogenous nerves of the penis. You can point to this passage in the Bible to explain the reason why your uncircumcised friends are experiencing 300% more pleasure during sex. I have to say that I personally bear no grudge against God for this covenant, being circumcised myself, because if I were to enjoy sex anymore than I currently do then I would never get anything accomplished. It would be a case of 'goodbye outside world!'

As far as this being a brutish ritual there is no refute to this claim. To raise a new born infant into your hands, the look of innocence and trust on his face, before mutilating its genitals because of some ancient mythology is beyond the pale in this century. For this reason we opted against having our son circumcised when he was born, because it made no sense to inflict needless pain on him so as to perpetuate this ancient idiotic rite. Whilst I don't remember the day of my circumcision, I am sure it must have been painful because I didn't walk or talk for an entire year after. (An old Jewish joke.)

Sodom and Gomorrah Destroyed

Let's just start by saying that the citizens of Sodom and Gomorrah were having a 'gay' ole time. A suitable metaphor would describe the original twin cities as the ancient version of Las Vegas, but instead of $20 lap dancers these guys had to settle for an ass reaming in back of Jeremiah's barn! Like Vegas I'm sure the road through the desert leading into the cities lead to a welcome sign on the outskirts of town which read, 'Where the sinners are winners, and what happens in Sodom stays in Sodom'.

What is interesting in the passages leading up to God's destruction of these 'bum-fun' towns is firstly that Abraham tried to talk God down from wiping Sodom & Gomorrah off the face of the planet. He argues that the Lord should reserve his genocidal wrath as it's likely that not all Sodomites are bum-bandits or evil doers. The second thing that stands out in these passages is that the Bible asserts that it is morally preferable to offer your virgin daughter to be gang raped by a crowd of salivating perverts, than to surrender two male strangers you barely know to be molested by the same perpetrators. This is no joke by the way. I wish there was a joke in the tragedy of gang rape, but there plainly isn't. Rather than spew forth my inner anger and contempt for this immoral imbalance, I will quote the passage:

> *"Before they (Lot and his family) had gone to bed, all the men from every part of the city of Sodom – both young and old – surrounded the house. They called out to Lot, 'Where are the men who came to you tonight? Bring them out to us so that we can have sex with them'. Lot went outside to meet them and shut the door behind him and said, 'No, my friends. Don't do this wicked thing. Look, I have two daughters who have never slept with a man. Let me bring them out to you and you can do what you*

like to them. But don't do anything to these men, for they have come under the protection of my roof'." (Genesis 19:3-8 NIV)

I dare any follower of Judaism, Islam or Christianity to defend this moral position which is accepted as an act of decency or nobility in the book of God. This is abhorrent by any stretch and I hope demonstrates that religion is made by self-serving, morally corruptible men and not the work of a morally superior power.

But we can pause for a moment's sigh of relief as there is absolutely zilch evidence, archeologically or otherwise, that the twin-cities were anything but a piece of literary fabrication and therefore a story for our own amusement. Thus, there never existed any town of Sodom or Gomorrah in the sands of the Middle East or elsewhere. And more thankfully, these innocent daughters were not gang raped by a pack of lecherous bastards.

However we only have to move a few paragraphs from this point of the Bible before we stumble across further bizarre sexual standards or norms that do not solicit any moral judgment or condemnation. In Genesis 19 it describes Lot living alone with his two daughters in a cave outside of a town called Zoar.

"One day the older daughter said to the younger, 'Our father is old and there is no man around here to lie with us, as is the custom all over the earth. Let's get our father to drink wine and then lie with him to preserve our family line through our father.' That night they got their father to drink wine and the older daughter went in and lay with him. He was not aware of it when she lay down or when she got up."

On the following night, they got their father drunk again and this time the younger daughter slept with Lot and within a matter of weeks both daughters became pregnant and bore sons to him. There is no sub-text that follows this story. No footnote to say God was displeased with Lot or his daughters. Hell, God was smiting people all over the place for far less than this. Heck, he turned Lot's wife into salt for merely sneaking a peak at the destruction of Sodom, after God told her not to look back. Tough love!

I guess God, the jealous, petty god, was too consumed with his own jealousy and insecurities to be concerned over matters of gang rape and incestuous sexual relations. Too busy testing Abraham's faith, with his command that Abraham should sacrifice his own son, Isaac, on a nearby mountain. This guy, God, has a wicked sense of humor, huh? Abraham, always obliging though, does as God wishes and just before he slashes the throat of his only son an angel appears telling Abraham words to the effect, "Hey it was just a joke. You just got punked!"

What kind of god would ask you, as proof of your love for him, to look into the innocent and trusting eyes of your child before slashing his or her jugular vein, watching your very own bleed slowly to death before your very eyes? This can only be the test of a deeply wicked and insecure sadist.

Jacob, Esau... and the Invisible Man

At the age of one hundred and eighty years Abraham passed away, but on his deathbed he anointed his eldest son Isaac to lead the family. Isaac inherited all that was Abraham's and in his new role as patriarch he wasted no time in impregnating one of his favourite wives, Rebekah. Mind you it took God's IVF program to deliver the sperm to her ovaries as Rebekah had been 'barren' for many years in unsuccessfully trying for children. Rebekah and Isaac slaughtered an animal as a token of thanks for allowing them to finally become parents. The glowing mum-to-be realized mid-way through her pregnancy that she was bearing twins. Whilst a 'two-for-the-price-of-one' deal was reason to further praise God, Rebekah became confused and concerned because the two fetuses were punching the shit out of each other insider her womb, in what is positively the first in utero boxing showdown. Too bad Sodom and Gomorrah had already been destroyed, because the bookmakers from that city could've thrown down some handy odds. Rebekah became increasingly worrisome that the battle inside her womb continued, with unrelenting punches, kicks and some UFC 'ground n pound' taking place. She cried out to God for an explanation to this pre-natal sibling bickering and God answered:

> *"Two nations are in your womb and two peoples from within you will be separated; one people will be stronger than the other and the other will serve the younger." (Genesis 25:23 NIV)*

The due date for delivering the rival twins came and the first to emerge was a hairy, red-headed boy, a 'ginga' as we would say in Australia, they named Esau. The second child to pop was named Jacob and he emerged from Rebekah's womb clutching onto the heel of his five-minute older brother.

The boys became men, of which Esau became a skilled hunter and Jacob a lay-about, preferring to just spend his days hanging around the family tents whilst his elder brother chased wild game throughout the land. The story takes a devious turn at this point, as the scripture tells of Esau returning from a hunt. He is exhausted and near starving and returns home to find his brother cooking a stew. Esau pleads with his brother, Jacob, for some food as he is famished, but his brother initially refuses him. Esau pleads with his brother again. To which Jacob hatches a heinous bribe. Jacob tells Esau that he may have some stew on one condition:

"First sell me your birthright." (Genesis 25:31 NIV)

To give up one's birthright to a sibling is the equivalent of forfeiting all inheritance and family power, but Esau agrees to Jacob's wicked proposal, replying:

"What good is my birthright if I am about to die of starvation?" (Genesis 25:32 NIV)

Years later Isaac is now on his deathbed and in his final days he is anxious to bless his eldest son, whom he still believes is Esau, with the family trust. On his deathbed he summons Esau to his side and asks that he go out and catch some tasty meat for what would probably be his father's last supper, a meal whereby he will announce his blessing to Esau. Esau agrees and sets forth into the wilderness with his spear.

Rebekah overhears the conversation between her husband and her eldest son and she runs to Jacob to tell him what had just transpired. Jacob was Rebekah's favourite son and she wanted to ensure the inheritance did not pass to Esau. Rebekah convinced Jacob to promptly slaughter two goats in the backyard and then to dress like Esau. Jacob protested to his mother that Isaac would recognize him as him and not as his brother and accordingly this plan would be doomed before it began. Rebekah convinces Jacob that her husband's eyesight is all but gone and if he covered himself in a fur rug Isaac would mistake the fur for the much physically hairier Esau.

Jacob did what was asked by his mother and walked into his father's bedroom. Isaac called out, "Who is there?" Jacob replied, "It is me father, Esau!" Isaac called to who he thought was Esau and demanded that he come closer so he could feel his skin, to be sure of his identity. Jacob leant in and Isaac felt the fur rug covering Jacob's smooth skin. Isaac had been duped! Isaac swallowed the devilish bait and unknowingly blessed the wrong son, Jacob:

"May God give you of heaven's dew and of earth's richness – an abundance of grain and new wine. May nations serve you and peoples bow down to you. Be lord over your brothers and may the sons of your mother bow down to you. May those who curse you be cursed and those who bless you be blessed." (Genesis 27:28-29 NIV)

Esau returned home from his hunting trip to discover the shocking treachery that had taken place whilst he was out obeying his dying father's wishes. Esau rushed into to speak with Isaac, crying, "Father what have you done?" Isaac, now confused, asked, "Who is that?" When Isaac realized he had been deceived into wrongly blessing his younger son, Jacob, he began to sob and tremble. But Isaac knew it was also too late to undo a blessing, i.e. you can't take it back once given.

Esau cried at his father's bedside:

> *"Jacob has deceived me two times. He took my birthright and now he's taken my blessing." (Genesis 27: 37 NIV)*

Esau pleads with his dying father to bless him too, which seems fair enough, but the blessing that comes forth is not the blessing that Esau either expects nor deserves. Isaac with an unjust callous voice says:

> *"Your dwelling will be away from the earth's richness, away from the dew of heaven above. You will live by the sword and you will serve your brother." (Genesis 27:39-40 NIV)*

Jacob, knowing his brother would be pissed and out for revenge flees into the countryside. After travelling for a full day he camps under a tree, using a rock as a pillow. As he drifts off to sleep, God descends from heaven and appears directly before him and says:

> *"I am the Lord, your God, the God of your father Abraham and the God of Isaac. I will give you and your descendents the land on which you are lying. Your descendents will be like the dust of the earth and you will spread out to the west and to the east, to the north and to the south. All peoples on earth will be blessed through you and your offspring. I am with you and will watch over you wherever you go and I will bring you back to this land. I will not leave you until I have done what I have promised you." (Genesis 28:13-15 NIV)*

What? Were you expecting God to punish Jacob for his deceit too? Not only does God choose not to punish this shyster, he rewards him with being the new 'chosen one'. I guess God likes people that behave like himself, huh?

This incredible injustice is a lesson that teaches that villainy is good and the ends do justify any means. God has set a terrible precedence in this example of judicial oversight. And it gets worse! A few years later Jacob becomes frightened that Esau has organized a few hundred men to attack him and his family. Jacob, ever cunning, formulates an elaborate plan for escape. The night before the attack, Jacob prays to God which reads less as a prayer and more as a reminder to God that he honour his promise to help Jacob lead his descendents as a great nation. As Jacob prepares to set off, an invisible man wrestles Jacob to the ground. I always thought the 'Invisible Man' was a product of Marvel comics, but clearly not. Jacob is thrown to the ground and bashed against rocks by this transparent attacker. This fight lasts a full twenty-four hours, before the invisible man eventually tired and pleaded:

"Let me go, for it is daybreak." (Genesis 32:24 NIV)

But Jacob wasn't prepared for the fight to end until he had been named victor:

"I will not let you go unless you bless me." (Genesis 32:26 NIV)

At this moment the invisible man revealed himself as God. And God said that because of Jacob's strength he was fit to found a nation:

"Your name will no longer be Jacob, but Israel." (Genesis 32:28)

The fraudulent man named Jacob had now been ordained a nation by God. The nation of Israel begins.

A number of years later, however, a new Pharaoh took the throne and slowly instituted laws that made the Jewish nation slaves and over the course of the next 80 odd years, the Israelites were forced into labour and unjustly mistreated.

Before I end this chapter on Genesis, I would like to say to those amongst us who believe the earth to be only 7,000 years old, DINOFUCKINGSAURS! If dinosaurs roamed the planet at the same time as early man, don't you think that somewhere in this Bible there would be a reference to some kind of lizard that stood 10 stories tall? Because I would expect something of the following to be included in the scripture:

"And then Jacob led the Israelites into Egypt due to severe famine that had ravaged their lands in Canaan, as they marched through the desert and upon seeing the fertile lands of Egypt, there was a fucking, great, big Brontosaurus Rex blocking their path."

Genesis Body Count: 30,040,001

Wikipedia estimates the world's population at the time of the supposed flood, three millennia BCE, to be approximately 30,000,000.

The destruction of the mythical twin-cities of Sodom & Gomorrah is estimated, by some Biblical scholars who believe the fable, to include approximately 1,000 inhabitants.

Lot's wife = 1

A seven year worldwide famine = 40,000

Cumulative Body Count: 30,040,001

Chapter Two - The Book of Exodus

"When did I realize I was God? Well, I was praying and I suddenly realized I was talking to myself."
Peter O'Toole

Exodus is the second book of the Jewish Torah and of the Christian Old Testament. It tells how Moses leads the Israelites out of Egypt and through the wilderness to the Mountain of God, Mount Sinai. There God, through Moses, gives the Israelites their laws and enters into a covenant with them, by which he will give them the land of Canaan in return for their faithfulness. The book ends with the construction of the Tabernacle.

According to tradition, Exodus and the other four books of the Torah were written by Moses in the latter half of the 2nd millennium BC. But the character Moses is certainly one of fiction. Thus, even though the following events were factually true, they were recorded nearly 3,000 years after the fact.

Exodus is not a historical document in the true scheme of things. It has never been proven archaeologically and more significantly the story has never been concurred by Egyptian history which has one of the longest recorded documented histories of any civilization, nor has it been validated by any other external historical records. The story is simply a myth. Egypt being one of the primary storage centres of ancient history has no recording of a character named Moses, nor is there any evidence that suggests the Israelites ever lived or worked as slaves under Pharaoh rule. We also know that the events that took place as claimed by Exodus occurred centuries before they were written about and with legend of hearsay and good ole 'Chinese whispers' we can feel safe in our educated assertion that the story of Exodus is utter fabrication.

What is further perplexing and problematic for religious scholars is the question, "Where did the nation of Egypt come from?" In the generations before or after Noah the Bible makes no mention of such a place, with Pharaoh Kings. And if there was an Egypt prior to the flood then why weren't they all killed? This nation and their people literally pop up out of nowhere, with no chronology.

The Slavery of The Israelites in Egypt

The story claims that after such time that Joseph and his brothers had died, the Israelite population in Egypt had grown significant, so that the land was filled with them. Then a new Pharaoh came to power and fearing that the Jews had become too numerous in his land and concerned that one day their rising numbers would have the strength to take control of Egypt, the Pharaoh empowered slave masters over the Israelites forcing them into slave labour. The greater the Israelites numbered the greater the Egyptians came to despise them and subsequently worked them tirelessly and ruthlessly, with all kinds of hard labour.

Oppressing the Israelites did not have any affect in reducing their numbers and with ruthless tyranny the Pharaoh ordered that all new born male Hebrew babies be killed at birth.

Enter Moses

This early passage refers to the well known birth of Moses, to Levitie parents. Obviously under the new Pharaoh law that decreed the death of all Israelite new born males, his mother hid baby Moses in a papyrus basket along the banks of the Nile. The floating baby capsule made its way with the flowing currents of the river, until it reached a group of women bathing and frolicking downstream. The women bathers were shocked to discover a baby inside the papyrus basket and recognised the boy baby to be of Israelite descent. However, as it turned out one of the women bathers happened to the sister of the Pharaoh and having no children of her own she decided that she would raise the baby as her own and therefore as an Egyptian. She named him Moses, which in Hebrew means to 'draw out', because she drew him out of the water. Why an Egyptian would bestow a Hebrew name to her adopted son at a time when Hebrew babies were being murdered makes absolutely no sense.

Moses grew into a young man in line to the throne of Pharaoh, as the Pharaoh's sister maintained Moses' Israelite identity a secret to all. But Moses suffering some sort of identity crisis in his thirties felt naturally drawn and partial to the Israelites for reasons he could not yet comprehend. Then one day whilst working in the fields as an Egyptian project manager for the construction of some monuments in the Pharaoh's honour he witnessed an Egyptian slave master viciously beating an Israelite slave for falling behind in his daily work quota. Upon seeing that there were no witnesses, Moses murdered the Egyptian master of the whip and hid his body in the sand. Concerned that his vengeful defense of a fellow Israelite had become known, he fled Egypt for a town called Midian.

Moses wandered aimlessly throughout the desert, with little or no food or water to preserve his survival. Nearing death a Midianite shepherd discovered the emaciated Moses and brought him to his family to be rehabilitated. His shepherd saviour not only nourished him to health, but also offered his eldest daughter, Zipprorah, up for marriage to Moses. Moses and Zipprorah wasted no time in 'getting busy' in their designated tent and shortly thereafter gave birth to a son they named Gershom.

Meanwhile back in Egypt the conditions for the Israelite slaves worsened:

> *"The Israelites groaned in their slavery and cried out and their cry for help because of their slavery went up to God. God heard their groaning and he remembered his covenant with Abraham, with Isaac and with Jacob. So God looked on the Israelites and was concerned about them." (Exodus 2:23-25 NIV)*

Moses and The Burning Bush

In terms of comedic value and degree of rational believability, you can lump the story of Moses and the burning bush right amongst the talking snake in the Garden of Eden; Jonah surviving three days inside the stomach of a whale; and Noah and the Ark. Another fable that is well outside the boundaries of physical reality.

According to Exodus, the story has it that Moses, whilst leaving Midian and in continued exile from Egypt was leading his flock to Horeb, the mountain of God. There an angel of the Lord appeared to him from within the flames of a burning bush. Upon seeing this remarkable occurrence, Moses says to himself:

> *"I will go over and see this strange sight – why the bush does not burn up." (Exodus 3:2-3 NIV)*

God, seeing that Moses had walked curiously towards the bush alight in flames, called Moses from within the bush. "Moses! Moses!" summoned the voice of God. Moses looks around doesn't see anyone speaking to him. Again the voice called, "Moses, Moses." "Holy Shit!" Moses presumably said aloud, "The Bush is not only on fire but has a voice." The Bush then called out:

> *"Do not come any closer. Take off your sandals, for the place where you are standing is holy ground. I am the God of your father, the God of your Abraham, the God of Isaac and the God of Jacob." (Exodus 3:7-8 NIV)*

God then proceeds to have a lengthy dialogue with Moses using the flames as his vocal cords, telling him that he has seen the misery his people the Israelites are enduring in Egypt, and that he has a plan to liberate them. If Moses plays his part in God's strategy he will endow the Israelites with a land of milk and honey, actual words.

Moses argues with God that he is not worthy of such an undertaking and expresses his concerns that the Israelites would never listen or follow him, and the Egyptian Pharaoh would laugh him out of Egypt for daring to ask the release of the Israelites. Remember, Moses is talking to a bush on fire. In turn God promises to Moses that he will perform miracles and send signs that God was behind him and the people would follow him.

God demonstrates his support by throwing down a long wooden stick, a staff, as his first sign. Moses looks at this stick on the ground and remarks, "My God this is but just a stick!" God replies to Moses with words to the effect, "C'mon pal I am God, this is but no ordinary stick. This be a special magic stick." Moses obeys and picks the stick up from the ground. But just as his hand went to clutch the staff, it turns into a slithering snake to Moses' obvious amazement. I mean who wouldn't be impressed? That is one awesome party trick!

"This," said the Lord, "Is so that they may believe that the Lord, the God of their fathers – the God of Abraham, Isaac and the God of Jacob – has appeared to you."

There is subsequent to and fro banter between Moses and God, mostly God offering his reassurance to Moses that he, the Lord, will perform the necessary miracles, actions and assistance when the time is apt.

> *"I am the Lord and I will bring you out from under the yoke of the Egyptians. I will free you from being slaves to them and I will redeem you with an outstretched arm with mighty acts of judgement. I will take you as my own people and I will be your God, who brought you from under the yoke of the Egyptians. And will bring you to the land I swore with uplifted hand to give to Abraham, to Isaac and to Jacob." (Exodus 6:6-8 NIV)*

Clearly a problematic issue presents itself in these passages, as the writings clearly now claim that God has chosen the Israelites as his people. Which seems at odds with the Genesis claim that God created all of man, but now seems eager to play 'favorites'. Wouldn't an all knowing creator surely see that favoring a 'chosen people' would surely lead to war, conflict and divisiveness down the track? Wouldn't a god of peace, justice and love promote unity rather than division? This seems to be a major lack of foresight on God's behalf, even I would've seen this and I can't even create an elementary school level diorama of a plasticine volcano.

With God at his back Moses arrives in Egypt to instruct the Pharaoh to free the Jewish nation. The Pharaoh is dismayed that not only is his former non-blood related brother alive after surviving in the desert all these years, but is now making far reaching demands to free the Israelite slaves. Naturally the Pharaoh dismisses Moses' God sponsored request, to which Moses demonstrates the 'stick into snake trick' to prove that he is the messenger of God's divine will. The Pharaoh clearly unimpressed with this sorcery, summons one of his own magicians and the Egyptian father of David Copperfield was able to mirror Moses' punchline.

Temporarily defeated Moses turns to God for a plan B strategy. God instructs Moses to lead the Pharaoh to the banks of the Nile and once there Moses is to strike the water with his staff and God will turn the water of the Nile into a river of blood, with all the fish destroyed and the water undrinkable for the Egyptians. A few days later Moses does exactly as God orders in the presence of the Pharaoh. Surprisingly once more, the Pharaoh is seemingly unmoved and replies that his magicians can perform the same trick too.

There sure was no shortage of magicians in Biblical times, which meant someone was running a pretty darn good magic trick school in the Nile region and pumping out a streamline of graduates.

God being God wasn't going to sit back and be outstaged by one or two of David Blain's forefathers and the 'big guy in the sky' sent down a series of plagues to be sure that the Egyptian Pharaoh would eventually see that God via Moses would not be budged from their ultimatum to release the Israelites.

The plague of frogs covered the land with the stench of rotting frog carcasses until the Egyptian houses were smothered in the amphibians. However, the Pharaoh would not be moved.

God steps his game up again and sends down a plague of gnats to little persuasive effect, which preceded a plague of flies; a plague on livestock; a plague of boils; a plague of Locusts; and a plague of darkness. All the while the Pharaoh stood steadfast to his refusal to emancipate the Israelites. This guy was one tough cookie!

God, as you can imagine, is now pissed off and I'm sure uttered the words of fictional character Tony Montana from *Scarface*: "You wanna go to war, I take you to war!"

With all his power and now obvious rage it begets the question why didn't God just smite the Pharaoh and his people so that the Jews could escape the clutches of their slave masters? As you will see in later books of the Old Testament, God repeatedly demonstrates zero restraint in exterminating entire cities and civilizations.

The Holocaust of The Passover

We know God is now pissed at the continual defiance of the Pharaoh and so we come to the origin of the Jewish holiday of the Passover. A name of relative innocuous inference, but one which in reality celebrates baby killing on a grand scale.

With the failure of all the plagues inflicted on Egypt, God bumps up the ante and says to Moses, in a manner that only Stephen King could fortell:

"About midnight I will go throughout Egypt. Every firstborn son in Egypt will die, from the first born son of the Pharaoh who sits on the throne, to the firstborn son the slave girl, who is at her hand mill and all the firstborn cattle as well. There will be a loud wailing throughout Egypt – worse than there ever been or ever will be again. But among the Israelites not a dog will bark at any man or animal. Then you will know that the Lord makes a distinction between Egypt and Israel." (Exodus 11:4-8 NIV)

What follows next is equally diabolical and senseless, with God instructing Moses that all Israelites are to slaughter a one year old lamb perfect of defect, then with the blood of this infant mammal each household is to grotesquely paint the doorway to his or her house on the fourteenth day of the New Year.

"On the same night I will pass through Egypt and strike down every firstborn – both men and animals – and I will bring judgement on all the gods of Egypt. I am the Lord. The blood will be a sign for you on the houses where you are; and when I see the blood, I will pass over you. No destructive plague will touch you when I strike Egypt. This is a day you are to commemorate; for the generations to come you shall celebrate it as a festival to the Lord – a lasting ordinance." (Exodus 12:12-15 NIV)

Looking past the obvious unjustifiable barbarism of death and destruction of innocents, it seems incredible that the omniscient, omnipresent God who supposedly can hear our prayers and audit our sins and convict us of thought crimes, would require the homes of his 'chosen people' to be stained in blood as a signpost to prevent the Jews from inadvertent death as a result of a mythical form of death by friendly fire.

Good to his word, God did exactly as he promised and murdered all first born sons and animals of Egypt at midnight. Not a single Egyptian household was spared of death, including the Pharaoh's son.

Finally, with the Pharaoh's heart broken, he eventually caved and begrudgingly permitted Moses to lead the Israelites out of Egypt as Moses had requested.

I am sure Henry Kissinger has his own view on the means justifying the ends in warfare, but surely this Biblical event, even if it were true, must disturb even the most religiously apathetic.

The Parting of The Sea

With Moses successfully leading the Israelites out of Egypt and slavery, one would not expect the Pharaoh with the lifeless body of his firstborn son clutched in his arms to just sit back and watch the Israelites flee without hindrance. He sent his army to pursue and destroy the self-proclaimed 'chosen people'. Before long the Egyptians had cornered the Israelites against the Red Sea with no route for escape. Naturally the Israelites were terrified of their pending doom and despite all the aforementioned miraculous divine interventions that God had performed to ensure their Exodus from Egypt in the previous days, the Jews still doubted their saviour and complained and whined bitterly to Moses:

> *"Was it because there were no graves in Egypt that you brought us here to die? What have you done to us bringing us out of Egypt? Didn't we say to you in Egypt, 'Leave us alone; Let us serve the Egyptians?' It would have been better for us to serve the Egyptians than to die in the desert!" (Exodus 14:11-12 NIV)*

But God hadn't finished working his wonders and as the Pharaoh's armies closed in on the Israelites, the Lord whipped up a storm cloud of sand that encircled the rear of the fleeing Jews to protect them from vengeful plunder.

> *"Throughout the night the cloud brought darkness to the one side and light to the other; so neither went near each other all night long." (Exodus 14:20 NIV)*

God then instructs Moses that come the following morning, he should hold out his staff and stretch out his hand over the sea and then God would do his part to divide the water so that the Israelites can walk through the sea on dry ground.

> *"Then Moses stretched out his hand over the sea and all that night the Lord drive the sea back with a strong east wind and turned it into dry land. The waters were divided and the Israelites went through on dry ground, with a wall of water on their right and on their left." (Exodus 14:21 NIV)*

The oceans parted with Moses holding up a stick! A scene no less comical than that portrayed in Cecil B. De Miles *Ten Commandments*, with walls of water held at bay on either side of the ocean bed. Of course this event never took place and only a child would believe such suspension of natural law to be possible. But what Biblical scholars do agree on is that an event like this may have taken place with the Israelites fleeing a pursuing army, but due to mistranslation from Hebrew to Aramaic to Greek the original wording was meant to have said, "The Israelites crossed a sea of reeds", rather than the Red Sea. Thus a teeny bit of incorrect syntax created the parting of the waters mythology, rather than what may have occurred in that a bunch of Jews crossed a swamp.

The Egyptian armies follow the Israelites into the parted sea. So, why did God give Pharaoh half-a-chance by releasing the protective cloud he had earlier sent down to defend his people? Nevertheless the Egyptian chariots made it approximately half way across before God wills the wheels of their chariots to come off thus making survival impossible when the waters returned to drown the entire Egyptian Army.

Significantly, once again an event of dramatic proportions whereby there is not a single recorded word in Egyptian history that even hints or implies that any of the above ever occurred. Whilst this is yet another fable, it does make for a fantastic film plot.

The Amalekites Defeated

After the implausible God driven escape from the Egyptians, Moses led the Israelites on a directionless meandering path through barren middle-eastern wasteland for the next forty years. Yes forty long years, of moving from camp to camp in search of some real estate that would foster livestock and crops. Where was God in this entire period of Jewish 'walkabout'? God doesn't even utter a whisper. Was he taking a deserved forty year nap whilst his chosen people suffered all kinds of hardships, such as thirst? The plagues, the baby killing and the parting of the Red Sea must be exhausting work, but surely a long weekend to recover would suffice? Forty years seems a tad extreme even to the most ardent teamster.

Eventually the Israelites began to complain and quarrel with Moses, demanding that he find them water to drink. Moses tells them that they should not put God to the test and that he will be there for them when they really need him. But this third-party explanation did not satisfy the whining Israelites and they grumbled,

> *"Why did you bring us out of Egypt to make us and our children and livestock die of thirst?" (Exodus 17:3 NIV)*

These Israelites sure were a thankless bunch and it is astonishing that they still whined to Moses and to God even after God had performed miracles to lead them out of Egypt; then parted an ocean so that they would be spared a gruesome death at the hands of the Egyptian swords. Not only were they thankless but they were now ready to turn on Moses, their prophet from God, with threats of stoning him:

"Then Moses cried out to the Lord, 'What am I to with these people? They are almost ready to stone me.'" (Exodus 17:4 NIV)

God answers Moses' gripe and instructs him to lead some of the tribe elders to a rock at a town called Horeb. Once there God gives Moses a little 'heads up' and says that upon striking the rock with his magic staff (which had previously turned into a snake and parted a sea) water would come out of it.

The quantity of water from the rock was inadequate to replenish an entire tribe, but was another demonstration that God was on their side and looking out for them.

Awhile later, the Amalekites came and attacked the Israelites at a town called Rephidim. Moses ordered Joshua to lead the men, whilst he, Aaron and Hur went to the top of a hill that overlooked the battlefield. What comes next is truly a laugh!

"As long as Moses held up his hands, the Israelites were winning, but whenever he lowered his hands, the Amalekites were winning. When Moses' hands grew tired, they took a stone and put it under him and he sat on it. Aaron and Hur held his hands up – one on one side, one on the other – so that his hands remained steady till sunset. So Joshua overcame the Amalekite army with the sword." (Exodus 17:10-13 NIV)

This would make an hilarious Saturday Night Live comedy parody, picturing a tired old sports coach having his hands held up above him so that his team could win a football game. "Hey Moses, for Christ's sake we are losing the game, keep your fucking arms in the air or the Patriots are going to take the division!"

The final paragraph of this passage is one that many conservative Jews have tragically interpreted as God's will to destroy the Palestinians, believing that they are the descendents of the Amalekites.

"For hands were lifted up to the throne of the Lord. The Lord will be at war with the Amalekites from generation to generation." (Exodus 17:16 NIV)

Mount Sinai and The Ten Commandments

Let us ignore the obvious flaw in the title of this story, that being there is no Mount Sinai nor has there ever been such a location. So notwithstanding this immediate irreconcilable component of the fable of the Ten Commandments, let us at least examine what this story predicates.

According to the Old Testament, the Israelites had camped themselves at the bottom of this mythical mountain for some time, before God called to Moses from the mountain top:

"This is what you are to say to the house of Jacob and what you are to tell the people of Israel: You yourselves have seen what I did to Egypt and how I carried you on eagle's wings and brought you to myself. Now if you obey me fully and keep my covenant, then out of all nations you will be treasured possession. Although the whole earth is mine, you will be for me a kingdom of priests and a holy nation." (Exodus 19:3-6 NIV)

Playing favourites again? Surely God would have the foresight to envision what pain and suffering words like this would foreshadow for thousands of years to come. Revisiting Sam Harris for a moment,

"A glance at history, or the pages of any newspaper, reveals that ideas which divide one group of human beings from another, only to unite them in slaughter, generally have their roots in religion."

Why would God want to divide mankind rather than unite? After all did he not make all of us in his own image as claimed earlier in Genesis? Just further proof that the origin of the Bible is man-constructed and not the word, or inspired word, of a super-intellectual being. And as well-known American political activist Anne Lamott stated:

"You can safely assume that you've created God in your own image when it turns out that God hates all the same people you do."

Moses tells the people that God will soon lay out some instructions to him and that they should prepare themselves by washing their clothes and abstaining from sex. On the morning of the third day, after Moses had spoken:

"...there was thunder and lightening, with a thick cloud over the mountain and a very loud trumpet blast. Everyone in the camp trembled. Then Moses led the people out of the camp to meet with God and they stood at the foot of the mountain. Mount Sinai was covered with smoke, because the Lord descended fire upon it. The smoke billowed up from it like smoke from a furnace, the whole mountain trembled violently and the sound of the trumpet grew louder and louder. Then Moses spoke and the voice of God answered him." (Exodus 19:16-19 NIV)

God then commands Moses to leave the people at the bottom of the mountain, whilst he alone his to ascend to meet God. My cynical mind can't help but smell a rat here! Why is it that throughout all religious history God never speaks to anymore than one or two people at a time? Why can't he ever speak to all of us, like equals, so that we can all be sure that he is real and not be vulnerable to the manipulations and fraud of others? The needless suffering caused by religious conflict would cease immediately if only God addressed all of us one time and clearly enough so that we can replay it on youtube.com

With Aaron by Moses' side God issued his ten commandments, which are to form the moral code for man's ethical conduct on earth:

1. *You shall have no other Gods before me.*
2. *You shall not make for yourself an idol in the form of anything in heaven above or on the earth below. You shall not bow down to them or worship them; for I, the Lord your God am a jealous God, punishing the children for the sin of the fathers to the third and fourth generation of those that hate me, but showing love to a thousand generations of those who love me and keep my commandments.*
3. *You shall not misuse the name of the Lord your God.*
4. *Remember the Sabbath day by keeping it holy. Six days you shall labour and do all your work, but the seventh day is a Sabbath to the Lord your God.*
5. *Honour your father and your mother, so that they may live long in the land the Lord your God is giving you.*
6. *You shall not commit murder.*
7. *You shall not commit adultery.*
8. *You shall not steal.*
9. *You shall not give false testimony against your neighbor.*
10. *You shall not covet your neighbour's house. You shall not covet your neighbour's wife, or his manservant or maidservant, his ox or donkey, or anything that belongs to him.*

Surely he could have, would have produced something a little more profound and inspirational than the ten he proclaimed. Any person with even a teaspoon of intellectual honesty will have difficulty at defending the claim that the Ten Commandments can only be that of dim-witted man rather than an entity of the highest intellectual enlightenment. Notwithstanding the fact that civilizations such as China, India and Egypt had written legal codes, containing prohibitions against murder, theft, adultery and fraud, thousands of years before the Israelites fled into the desert.

The first four commandments are simply a reminder of who's boss and depict a God that suffers the human emotion of petty jealousy, namely of other Gods. This is interesting in itself as it reveals an argument that even God acknowledges, the presence of peers, which is at odds and inconsistent with the entirety of the Bible. I find it particularly clever that Christopher Hitchens has nicknamed the first four commandments as that of "maniacal throat-clearing". A dictum that plainly forewarns that you better worship me alone or watch out! Interesting is the second commandment which God promises to condemn up to four generations of a sinner's descendents, which throws out the claim that all children are born without sin and further suggests that no matter how righteous your Judeo-Christian life should be, this will mater for naught if your great-great-grandfather believed in a Sun God and you are thus surely doomed.

The fifth goes without saying. A majority of mammals respect or show a sense of endearment towards their mother, father or both. However, God does not stipulate any reciprocal respect or honour of thy children in return. Parents are commanded, in later chapters, to stone their children to death should they blaspheme (Deuteronomy). This, at the very least, contravenes the 6th commandment.

The sixth through ninth 'shall nots' are self-evident for any functioning society to progress on a day to day basis and the tenth commandment is a promise that you will be condemned for committing a thought crime, for envying your neighbour's property. Any supporter of capitalism would admit that if it were not for envy progress, advancement and commercial gain would never be possible, thus this is a stupid command. Does this mean that advertising agencies or marketing managers are agents of Satan? These commandments more than anything else provide substantive proof that these laws did not originate from a profound being of enlightenment but rather from misogynistic, barbaric, Bronze-age man, as women are lumped alongside a donkey on a man's personal balance sheet as property. Thus as man's property he is free to sell them for a profit.

It must be said that the Ten Commandments provided God, if he were true, a real opportunity to proclaim his wisdom, understanding and insight that would ensure human solidarity for ad infinitum. But he squandered it with proclamations of petty jealousy and omitting of a number of truly wicked acts that have stained our human existence. There is no mention of rape, child abuse, racism and slavery to name but a few examples. There is certainly no condemnation of genocide because that comes later when God inspires the whole wiping out of cities and civilizations.

Interestingly, an often neglected fact is that the Ten Commandments are just the start of what are actually 613 commandments from God to Moses, as written in Exodus, Leviticus and Deuteronomy. Others include:

"Anyone who has sexual relations with an animal must be put to death." (Exodus 22: 19 NIV)

This suggests that the Israelites were actually having sex with their goats or God wouldn't have any reason to create this law.

> *"Anyone who kidnaps another and either sells him or still has him when he is caught must be put to death." (Exodus 21:16 NIV)*

Does this mean all is forgiven if you gave the kidnapee away free of charge?

God then goes into granular detail when it comes to property law, with dozens of specific laws for some very specific agricultural concerns:

> *"If a man borrows an animal from his neighbour and it is injured or dies while the owner is not present, he must make restitution. But if the owner is with the animal, the borrower will not have to pay. If the animal was hired, the money paid for the hire covers the loss." (Exodus 22:14-15 NIV)*

Selling Your Daughter as a Slave

God even allows the morally unthinkable, of permitting a man to sell his own daughter into slavery, whether for sexual or labor purposes. God says quite clearly:

> *"If a man sells his daughter as a servant, she is not to free as manservants do. If she does not please her master who has selected her for himself, he must let her be redeemed." (Exodus 21:7-8 NIV)*

Not even in Tasmania in the 1800s was it permissible to do such a thing! And if Tasmania is more holy than heaven, then god help us all.

The Covenant Confirmed

At the conclusion of God's dictation of the commandments to Moses, there is the usual required ceremonial bloodbath with the slaughter of calves, lambs and bulls in honour of God's glory. Then Moses is summoned to the mountain once more:

> *"Come up to me on the mountain and stay here and I will give you the tablets of stone, with the law and the commands I have written for their instruction." (Exodus 24:12 NIV)*

Moses did as asked and sat upon the mountain for forty days and forty nights, whilst God covered the mountain in cloud.

The Tabernacle

God surely kept Moses busy, if he wasn't demanding him to scribe the Ten Commandments into stone atop a mountain, then he was demanding that he build for him a Tabernacle. Not sure what a Tabernacle is? Think of it simply as a 'portable worshipping tent' and thus it is often referred to as the 'Tent of Meeting' in the Bible. God instructions to Moses were:

> *"They shall build me a sanctuary and I will dwell among them. You must make the Tabernacle and all its furnishings following the plan that I am showing you." (Exodus 25:8-10 NIV)*

The Tabernacle comprised of a tent draped with colorful curtains of finely twisted linen and yarn. It consisted of a rectangular, perimeter fence of fabric, poles and staked cords. This rectangle was always erected when the Israelites would set up a new camp. In the center of this enclosure was a rectangular sanctuary draped with goats' hair curtains, with the roof made from rams' skins. Inside, it was divided into two areas, the Holy Place and the Most Holy Place. These two compartments were separated by a curtain or veil. Entering the first space, one would see 3 pieces of sacred furniture: a seven-branched oil lamp stand on the left (south), a table for twelve loaves of show bread on the right (north) and straight ahead before the dividing curtain (west) was an altar for incense-burning. Beyond this curtain was the cube-shaped inner room known as the *Holy of Holies*. This sacred space contained a single article called the Ark of the Covenant, which would house the tablets of the Ten Commandments.

> *"The Lord would often come down and visit Moses and speak to him face to face inside the Tabernacle, as a man speaks to a friend." (Exodus 33:11 NIV)*

The concluding instructions for the Tabernacle's construction are stated at the end of the Book of Exodus. Immediately following the words about the Tabernacle, God reminds Moses about the importance of the Jewish Sabbath:

> *"God told Moses to speak to the Israelites and say to them: You must still keep my Sabbaths. It is a sign between me and you for all generations, to make you realize that I, God, am making you holy. Keep the Sabbath as something sacred to you. Anyone doing work shall be cut off spiritually from his people and therefore, anyone violating it shall be put to death." (Exodus: 31: 12-17 NIV).*

But unlike God we have to go back to work the day after the Sabbath whilst God continues to rest and rest and rest...

God Will Strike Terror

At the conclusion of these laws God promises that he will deal with Israel's enemies. Not because they have sinned against God in any particular way, but because they have land that the Israelites desire:

> *"My angel will go ahead of you and bring you into the land of Amorites, Hittites, Perizzites, Canaanites, Hivites and Jebusites and I will wipe them out." (Exodus 23:23 NIV)*

If that didn't give the Israelites the stomach for waging war on their neighbours then God's next promise certainly should have:

> *"I will send terror ahead of you and throw into confusion every nation you encounter. I will make all your enemies turn their backs and run." (Exodus 23:27 NIV)*

Exodus Body Count: 1,031,700

The 7th plague hail. Wikipedia estimates the population of Egypt to be anywhere up to 5 million at the time of Exodus. If we allow for a 0.05% death rate = 25,000.

God murders every Egyptian firstborn child during the Passover. If one in 5 of the population were firstborn = 1,000,000.

God drowns the Egyptian army as they pursued the fleeing Israelites during the parting of the Red Sea = 5,000 as a crude estimate.

God helps Moses and Joshua kill the Amalekites = 1,500.

God incinerated an unknown number of Israelites that complained during their wanderings in the Desert = 200 as crude estimate.

Cumulative Body Count: 31,032,701

Chapter Three: The Book of Leviticus

"If absolute power corrupts absolutely, where does that leave God?"
George Deacon

Leviticus is the third book of the Torah (Pentateuch).

Leviticus is where God really ratchets up the babbling rhetoric, with the first seven chapters or so a complete mish-mash of dribble in relation to animal sacrifice. Thus this book has little meaning in today's terms as Jews and Christians have ceased, in the most part, to slaughter animals in God's name. Which is a lovely anecdote as to the irrelevancy of most of what is written in the scriptures in today's modern world.

This book is a celebration of the mundane, and really highlights that the Bible is more an ancient agriculturalists' how to guide rather than a book of profound revelation to enlighten the human experience. Here's an example of how bogged down in the laborious Leviticus truly is. God commands that the Israelites must offer him not just animal sacrifice in worshipping him, but also grain offerings. His instruction for this includes:

> *Take a vase of oil pour it onto fine flour that has had a stick of incense burnt on it. Then take this to Aaron's sons, the priests. It is then to be cooked in an oven without being mixed with oil. Once cooked it is to be smeared in oil. If the grain offering is prepared on a griddle it is to be mixed with fine flour and oil, but without yeast. Because all offerings made to the Lord must be without yeast or honey.*

Did you write all this down?

But if you are in search of literature to make yourself feel guilty as a result of your sexual fantasies then this is the book for you. A diatribe with whom you can and can't sleep with and under what circumstances is prescribed herewith. Thus this is the book that declares homosexuality as an abomination. But if guys have been shagging guys since the dawn of time, bearing in mind that we were created in God's image, wouldn't this suggest that the practice of gay sex be consistent with the laws of nature, as evidently it is? And therefore is it not probable that God too wears ass-less chaps and a policeman's cap?

What makes this book special is that it is the best argument in demonstrating religious hypocrisy. With all the laws, some contradictory, others plainly immoral an atheist can really exploit this book of law to counter fundamentalist zealots. For example a Christian will reference Leviticus 18:22 as proof that God hates homosexuals:

"Do not lie with a man as one lies with a woman; that is detestable."

If I were gay I would counter this assertion with, "Yeah but Leviticus says that I may also sell my daughter into sexual slavery and that I am to put my son to death if he curses me." Twenty-first century Christians have, by the majority, determined that these moral laws are outdated and repugnant. The paradox, however, is they believe God is still righty-right on the gay issue. Hmm! Thus the coining of the phrase 'cafeteria Christian' - choose which laws suit you from the buffet selection of commandments.

All jokes aside the one positive we can draw from Leviticus is that at least it is conscious of inequality, so much so that one may be forgiven for accusing this book as being the origins of Marxism: Each time it describes a sacrifice, it specifies what a rich man must do, before providing a more affordable alternative for the poor:

"If he cannot afford a lamb, he is to bring two doves or two young pigeons to the Lord." (Leviticus 5:7 NIV)

A read of this book makes it glaringly obvious that it is written by a different author than that of the preceding books of Genesis and Exodus who at least told their fictionalized version of events in an imaginative way full of literary vigour. Conversely, Leviticus is a horrible book to read due to its monotonous repetition in reciting the precise method for killing each kind of animal; the preparing of each kind of offering; and the rules for preparing food.

The boring tedium of the first half dozen chapters is suddenly broken, however, with a return of the all too familiar vengeance of God. Moses had ordained Aaron and his sons as priests, but only two chapters later, the sons of Aaron (Nadab and Abihu) made the unforgiving error of burning the wrong incense as an offering. Bloody evil-doers!

"...and they offered unauthorized fire before the Lord, contrary to his command. So fire came out from the presence of the Lord and consumed them and they died before the Lord." (Leviticus 10:1-2 NIV)

Two priests incinerated on the spot for burning the wrong smelling sticks! Wow the ruthlessness of this guy, but boy oh boy what a clean hit. With their smouldering corpses lying in the dust, the Lord then gives Moses instructions to 'take the bodies out the back', in true 'Godfather' style.

As we move forward Leviticus prescribes in incredibly painstaking minute details the dietary laws that God had commanded Moses. Animals that don't chew their cud, or don't have hooves are forbidden as food. Sea creatures without fins and scales are out. Eagles, vultures, ravens, owls, hawks, osprey and bats are out. All insects that walk on all fours are out. All kinds of lizards are out. Basically any creature that moves along the ground is to be detested.

> *"I am the Lord your God; consecrate yourselves and be Holy, because I am Holy. Do not make yourselves unclean by any creature that moves about on the ground. I am the Lord who brought you out of Egypt to be your God; therefore be Holy because I am Holy." (Leviticus 11:44-45 NIV)*

What an insecure little fella the Lord is, always having to remind everyone of his accomplishments, "Hey, psst, it was me that brought you out of Egypt and don't you forget it," and the repetitive language of God coincidentally mirrors that of the Leviticus author! Helllllloooo!

We also learn from God that women are wretched and dirty for at least one week after having given birth to a son; but are so for two weeks if delivering a daughter. There's a fine message to all the young ladies out there, further illustrating God's distaste for women.

> *"A woman who becomes pregnant and gives birth to a son will be ceremonially unclean for seven days. If she gives birth to a daughter, for two weeks the woman will be unclean." (Leviticus 12:2-5 NIV)*

Sex Laws

The second part of Leviticus ventures into the laws of holiness, such as those pertaining to sexual conduct and stipulations made upon bestiality, homosexuality and incest. Of the latter, it flaws me that God had to take the time to stipulate every relative that cannot have sex with me, as it seems obvious just to say, "Hey, don't fuck anyone that is family, you perverts!" But he lists a whole litany of blood and non-blood relatives off limits in Leviticus 18; The Lord said:

> *"Do not dishonor your father by having sexual relations with your mother."*
> *"Do not have sexual relations with your father's wife."*
> *"Do not have sexual relations with your sister."*
> *"Do not have sexual relations with your son's daughter."*
> *"Do not have sexual relations with your father's sister."*
> *"Do not have sexual relations with your mother's sister."*
> *"Do not have sexual relations with your aunt."*
> *(Isn't this a repeat of the above two?)*
> *"Do not have sexual relations with your daughter-in-law."*
> *"Do not have sexual relations with your brother's wife."*
> *"Do not have sexual relations with the mother and her daughter."*

"Do not have sexual relations with your brother's wife."
"Do not have sexual relations with your wife's sister, whilst your sister is alive."
(I can't help but giggle it this one.)
"Do not approach a woman to have sexual relations with her during her monthly period."
"Do not have sexual relations with your neighbour's wife."
"Do not lie with a man, as you do with a woman. This is detestable."

Bestiality

A standout command is one that concerns bestiality, whilst also hinting that it is women and their relationships with horses that we should worry about, which is an image I have tried to delete from my memory that stemmed from an email sent to me from a friend:

> *"Do not have sexual relations with an animal and defile yourself with it. A woman must not present herself to an animal to have sexual relations with it; that is perversion." (Leviticus 18:23 NIV)*

Which suggests that some of the Israelites were shagging the sheep or there'd be no reason to offer this law. Further I can't figure out if this permits men to have their ways with animals or not? Thankfully clarification comes a few chapters later:

> *"If a man, or woman has sexual relations with an animal, the man, or woman must be put to death and you must kill the animal." (Leviticus 21:15-16 NIV)*

Hardly seems fair on the poor old sheep does it? Not like an overpowered animal has much say in the matter.

I am but a mere mortal and I had difficulty in putting together Human Resource rules for managing my previous business, but even I can see a few glaring omissions that God had overlooked in compiling his list of sexual dos & don'ts. Including:

- Do not have sex or inappropriately touch a child under the age of 18. This rule applies to Catholic clergy too.
- Do not rape. If a woman says, "No," no means no.
- Do not forcibly attempt to replicate what you watched on a pornographic movie with your wife and/or girlfriend.
- Do not suggest a threesome with your wife's best friend to her best friend without your wife knowing.

The thing that stands out from the God's sexual laws is that a majority are clearly written from a man's perspective. For example it forbids a man to have sex with your brother's wife, but does not state that a woman cannot sleep with his sister's husband; forbids sex with your aunt, but not with your uncle. I guess a moral oversight not of God, but of the Hebrew men who wrote this stuff. You see under Hebrew laws a woman was property of a man and thus adultery in the Bible applies only to a married woman. Married women were not to sleep around but polygamy for men was encouraged. As we will read later, all the great men of Biblical times such as King David and Solomon had hundreds of wives. It was good to be a man and it was good to write the rules being a man.

Punishment for Sin

The moral malice and wickedness of Leviticus is telegraphed with the first stated punishment for sin:

> *"If anyone curses his father or mother, he must be put to death. He has cursed his father, or his mother and his blood will be on his own head." (Leviticus 20:9 NIV)*

How many of us are required to now go out and take our rebellious teenage sons or daughters out into the backyard and butcher them? Had God already forgotten his commandment that 'thou shall not kill' which was dictated only a few passages ago in Exodus? Seems the various authors of the Bible never got together to synchronize their respective stories. Even a bunch of keystone cops could pull this apart under cross examination.

Death warrants are spelt out for a host of indiscretions including blasphemy. Leviticus 24 tells of a story of a fight between the son of an Israelite mother and an Egyptian father. The son of the Israelite mother, in the heat of the fight, assumedly cried, "Jumping Jehovah you are big fucker!" Subsequently the blasphemer was taken into custody and led to Moses, who would in turn get on the 1800-Godhotline to await the sentence. The Lord then said to Moses:

> *"Take the blasphemer outside the camp. All those that heard him are to lay their hands on his head and the entire assembly is to stone him." (Leviticus 24: 13-14 NIV)*

The moral of this passage is don't bother turning to God for any compassion or mercy. It is also in this chapter that we get the first half of the 'eye for an eye' versus the 'turn the other cheek' conundrum:

> *"If anyone injures his neighbor, whatever he has done to him: fracture for fracture, eye for eye, tooth for tooth. As he has injured, so is he to be injured." (Leviticus 24:19-20 NIV)*

Seems like an unjust justice system. What if you caught your neighbour going one step further than merely coveting your wife's ass and as rightful revenge you punched him in the face, forcing one of his teeth out. According to the law, your wife's pro-bono gigolo can now knock out one of your teeth. Now both of you are absent a tooth, but he has still shagged your wife.

Various Other Laws

Amazingly God delves into some laws of seemingly obvious minutiae including one that just boggles the mind:

> *"Do not seek revenge or bear a grudge against one of your people, but love your neighbour as yourself, for I am the Lord." (Leviticus 19:18 NIV)*

Did the God with a current body count of greater than 30 million and growing, just say, "Do not seek revenge"? Ok let's back up a moment. It was only in the preceding book, Exodus, that God issued vengeful pay-back against the Amalekites. God said to Moses:

> *"Make sure Joshua hears that I will completely blot out the memory of the Amalek from under heaven... The Lord will be at war against the Amalekites from generation to generation." (Exodus 17:14-16 NIV)*

For God it really is a case of do what I say not as I do! Which overtly implies that we should behave more like humans, ourselves, rather than God.

How To Buy Your Slaves

How the almighty overlooked this irrefutable moral abomination would remain a mystery if God were true:

> *"Your male and female slaves are to come to you from nations around you; from them you may buy slaves...You can will them to your children as inherited property and can make them slaves for life." (Leviticus 25:44-46 NIV)*

If God had said that slavery was wrong and it's moral bankruptcy, placed at least below that of cursing your father, then the argument that God is real, or at least just, would have a little more credibility. Rather, God lists the commercial terms and conditions of buying and owning slaves, including the command that Israelites are not to be kept as slaves, as all Jews are his chosen people. Uhuh!

In my personal debates with Christians regarding God's endorsement of slavery, my religious friends will argue that these were the times these Israelites lived in and slavery was socially acceptable back then, therefore no problem that God applied his rules to it. My counter-argument is a reminder to my zealot buddies that this is God's only book and wouldn't they be on far firmer argumentative ground if God demonstrated a little bit of enlightened foresight to tell his people that what they were doing was morally reprehensible, just as shagging the goats is? I mean why go to the lengths of protecting the rights of animals from bestiality assaults but dismiss the human rights of those in bondage?

It's important also to appreciate the ugly dynamics of slavery by understanding where slaves came from, or how they came to be. Slaves were defeated enemy. Men, women and children. When, for example, the Hebrews conquered the Amalekites, children were torn from their mothers and sold to the highest bidding Hebrew family. There is hardly an uglier scar on man's past than slavery, and God sanctions our ugliest.

Reward for Obedience, Punishment for Disobedience

Reward for obedience:

> *"If you follow my decrees and are careful to obey my commands, I will send you rain in its season and the ground will yield its crops and trees of the field their fruit. I will grant peace in the land and you will lie down and no-one will make you afraid. You will pursue your enemies and they will fall by the sword before you. Five of you will chase a hundred and a hundred will chase ten thousand and your enemies will fall by the sword before you. I will look on you with favour and make you fruitful and increase your numbers. I am the Lord your God, who brought out of Egypt so that you would no longer be slaves to the Egyptians." (Leviticus 26:3-13 NIV)*

The reward for obedience is some fruit and the ability to fight better. Modest rewards for having to live one's life in serfdom to a capricious celestial dictator. Contrast the above with the following decree for Punishment for disobedience:

> *"But if you will not listen to me and carry out my commands, then I will do this to you: I will bring upon you sudden terror, wasting diseases and fever that will destroy your sight and drain away your life. You will plant seed in vain, because your enemies will eat it. I will set my face against you so that you will be defeated by your enemies; those that hate you will rule over you....I will multiply your afflictions seven times over, as your sins deserve. I will send wild animals against you and they will rob you of your children, destroy your cattle and make you so few in number that your roads will be deserted.....You will eat the flesh of your sons and the flesh of your daughters." (Leviticus 26:14-29 NIV)*

We can spend your and my valuable time considering the implications of God's warning that he will convert us to cannibalism but it really is too absurd to warrant serious discussion. What is significant is that the above passage from Leviticus, as spoken by God, are just the headline comments, as the actual passage contains approximately twenty paragraphs of venomous vile spewed from the Great one's mouth.

Leviticus Body Count: 0
Cumulative Body Count: 31,032,701

Chapter Four: The Book of Numbers

"When I was a kid I used to pray every night for a new bicycle. Then I realised that the Lord doesn't work that way so I stole one and asked Him to forgive me."
Emo Philips

The fourth book of the Torah begins with God's command to Moses to count the number of men amongst all Israelite tribes that are fit and able for military service, from 20 years of age and up. But I prefer to think of this as the Book of Moaning, for reasons that will become obvious.

It had been nearly forty years since the Exodus from Egypt and the Israelites had moved from camp to camp suffering at the hands of famine and war. Thus this book begins with the counting of the Israelite tribe, before they set out on their journey from Sinai to Moab, then later across the River Jordan.

The result of this census is that 603,500 Israelites are found fit and strong enough to serve in the military. Let the war begin.

God then prescribes how the tribes are to position themselves in formation around the Tabernacle, with the Levites given the honour of exclusive service of the Tabernacle, whilst also displaying no reduction for his appetite for death and destruction.

"The Lord said to Moses, 'Bring the tribe of Levi and present them to Aaron the priest to assist him. They are to perform duties for him and for the whole community at the Tent of Meeting by doing the work of the Tabernacle... Appoint Aaron and his sons to serve as priests; anyone else who approaches the sanctuary must be put to death.'" (Numbers 3:5-10 NIV)

The Test for an Unfaithful Wife

God informs Moses that he has constructed a test for wives that are suspected by their husbands of being unfaithful. Firstly, who but only a man could come up with this? And secondly, there is no test for an unfaithful husband. Not the first time and certainly won't be last time that the prejudice against women in the three Abrahamic religions astonishes me. That so many women commit their lives to a doctrine of female discrimination appals me. I am sure if women believers around the world actually read the tenets of the three monotheistic religions then it would have equal appeal to them as does Nascar racing!

God informs Moses that in circumstances where there are no witnesses, he has devised a holy forensic testing procedure to prove if a woman has or has not cheated on her husband. The suspicious husband is to drag his wife before the local priest. The priest will then stand her before God, before pouring a combination of holy water and dust from the Tabernacle floor through her hair. God's curse has now been placed upon her, and should she be impure then her abdomen will swell causing her excrutiating pain for days on end until death is her only relief. If she is innocent of the charge then she will live a normal and healthy life, not withstanding that a horse and cart whilst crossing the main street of Moab hit her accidentally.

This test of marital faithfulness is no more advanced than Haitian tribes practicing Voodoo magic. An ancient ritual that is so preposterously ridiculous and flawed, that it serves only to demonstrate its irrelevancy to modern societal values. I'd like to know how many Christians or Jews still prescribe this test to their wives that return home at three in the morning all liquored-up after a hen's night with her girlfriends. And what would we think of someone who still did this? Nutty!

The Israelites Leave Sinai

Moses awoke one morning after another visit from God in his dreams and says to his father-in-law Hobad, that they must set out in search for the land that God has procured on behalf of his people. Departing the mountain of the Lord they set out for three days, carrying the Ark of the Covenant with them, whilst God provided them shelter from the sun by positioning a cloud over them as a mobile UV beach tent.

Shortly after venturing out in search of God's 'promised land', the Israelites, being as slow learning as they seemingly were judging by past indiscretions of whining that were punished remorselessly by God, began to complain about the food, in the same manner high-school students do in a high school cafeteria.

"The rabble with them began to crave other food and again the Israelites started wailing and said, 'If only we had meat to eat! We remember the fish we ate in Egypt at no cost – also the cucumbers, melons, leaks, onions and garlic. But now we have lost our appetite; we never see anything but this manna.' The manna was like a coriander seed and looked like a resin." (Numbers 11:4-7 NIV)

Moses eventually becomes pissed off at all this whining about manna bread this and manna bread that and thus he escalates their continued gripes to God. So what does God do? Does he smite them? Send down another fireball that incinerated Aaron's sons for burning the wrong incense? No he takes the Bill Cosby lesson on fatherhood, the one in which his dad, upon catching a young Cosby smoking a cigar, locks him in the cupboard until such time that he had successfully smoked every single cigar in the box, so that he will never want to look sideways at a cigar again.

"Now the Lord will give you meat and you will eat it. You will not eat it for one day, or two days, or five, ten or twenty days, but for a whole month – until it comes out of your nostrils and you loathe it – because you have rejected the Lord, who is among you and have wailed before him, saying, 'Why did we ever leave Egypt?'"(Numbers11:18-21 NIV)

Hardly seems much of a punishment! I have friends that have eaten nothing but steak for twenty years and I've never seen a T-Bone pop out of their nostril. Stand table side at an all-you-can-eat Outback Steakhouse buffet promotion and you will witness dozens of 300lb men consuming enough steak to fall out their nostrils but it doesn't. It seems such a juvenile punishment too, one that hardly seems godly to me.

The dissension amongst the Israelite camps continues through the book of Numbers, as Miriam and Aaron begin to question Moses' authority and legitimacy.

"Why does the Lord speak only through Moses and not through us?" (Numbers 12:1 NIV)

Moses leads Miriam and Aaron to the Tent of Meeting and then a pillar of cloud descends from the sky carrying God. God says:

"Listen to my words. When a prophet of the Lord is among you, I reveal myself to him in visions, I speak to him in dreams. But this is not true of Moses; he is faithful in all my house. With him I speak face to face, clearly

and not in riddles; he sees the form of the Lord. Why then were you not afraid to speak against my servant Moses?" (Numbers 12:6-8 NIV)

This passage requires a few questions to be asked. Firstly, we now know God has a face. Well how about a little narrative that describes what he looks like? I would think that would be of some interest to the readers and faithful. Did he wear glasses? Was he sporting a white beard? Was he a she? Was he showing signs of aging? But nothing.

Significantly God claims not to speak in riddles when speaking to Moses. Well now, that throws out the religious apologist's defense of any of the immoral, inconsistent, incoherent and brutal laws of the Old Testament, with their rebuttal that much of God's instructions are 'metaphors'. I always found this refute such a hard to stomach cop-out. "Oh yes, umm ahh, God does say kill your disrespectful child, but that is just a metaphor for banning him from the television for a week."

At the conclusion of God's speech delivered to the two skeptics, he inflicted leprosy on Miriam:

"When the cloud lifted from the above the Tent, there stood Miriam – leprous like snow." (Numbers 12:10 NIV)

Anyway the quest to find the 'promised land' continues as they set up camp in the Desert of Paran. Once camped there, God advises Moses to send some men on an exploration mission of the land of Canaan. After forty days of having a gander of the area which encompassed the Desert of Zin, Rehob, Lebo and down to the Valley of Eshcol, the exploratory team returned back to Moses and Aaron to report their findings and they gave Moses this account:

"We went into the land to which you sent us and it does flow of milk and honey! Here is its fruit. But the people who live there are powerful and the cities are fortified and very large. We can't attack these people; they are stronger than we are…All the people we saw there are of great size… We seemed like grasshoppers in our own eyes and we looked the same to them." (Numbers 13:27-33 NIV)

The Israelite community upon learning of this Intel report began to scream and many of them wept openly. The people began to grumble again. Weren't they still suffering from nostrils full of meat as a result of their most recent displeasure with God and Moses? The Israelites shouted:

"'If only we had died in Egypt! Or in this desert! Why is the Lord bringing us to this land only to let us fall by the sword? Our wives and children will be taken as plunder. Wouldn't it be better for us to go back to

Egypt?' And then they said to each other, 'We should choose a leader and go back to Egypt.'" (Numbers 14:3-4 NIV)

Now might have been the appropriate time that Aaron stepped in and said. "Listen here you whinging fuckers, my wife not only has a rump steak coming out her left nostril, but she also has leprosy for questioning the Lord." Surely that would've suppressed the fledgling uprising!

Moses and Aaron take the gripes of the Israelites to the Lord. Which is strange in itself, as God is supposed to be omnipresent, thus he should be able to hear their complaints without Moses and Aaron relaying the message. Regardless I am just relaying to you what it says in the Bible and God learns of their displeasure. Upon hearing this God gets fucking pissy. He is not a happy Creator:

"How long will this wicked community grumble against me?" (Numbers 14: 27 NIV)

Wait a minute God! These are your chosen people. Nobody held a gun to your head and demanded that you 'choose' them. Seems in hindsight that the Egyptians would've been far less maintenance than this lot. But you made your bed now God. You did this all by yourself and now you are calling them a 'wicked community'. Well make up your mind for Christ's sake, which one is it? Chosen or wicked?

"I have heard the complaints of these grumbling Israelites. So tell them, 'As surely as I live, declares the Lord, I will do to you the very things I heard you say: In this desert your bodies will fall – everyone of you twenty years old or more who was counted in the census and who has grumbled against me. Not one of you will enter the land I swore with uplifted hand to make your home…Your children will be shepherds here for forty years, suffering unfaithfulness, until the last of your bodies lies in the desert.'" (Numbers 14:27-34 NIV)

Following this maniacal edict, God then sends down a plague to kill all the men that were responsible for creating the exploratory intelligence report of the new land.

God then goes on a killing spree and because he is so fed up with the complaining Israelites, he takes the drastic step of switching sides and therefore empowers the enemies of Israel, such as the Caanites and the Amalekites, to defeat his own chosen people in battle. God tells Moses to kill one of his tribe, by stoning, for gathering wood on the Sabbath. God opens up the earth to swallow Korah, his family, his tribe of 250 men and women and his possessions, for daring to question Moses' leadership.

"The ground underneath them split apart and the earth opened its mouth and swallowed them... They went down alive into the grave, with everything they owned." (Numbers 16:31-34 NIV)

More grumbling and quarrelling amongst the Israelites, with a shortage of water. The community makes the same grumbles they had made before, such as. "Why didn't we stay in Egypt? It sucks balls here!" Moses takes the tribal leaders to a huge rock, taps on the rock twice with his staff, the rock splits open and water pours out.

The Israelites thirst is now quenched, at least for the time being anyway. But it didn't take long for the 'water from rock' trick to lose its luster and the people began to whinge again, with the same old gripe heard a hundred times already, "Why did you lead us out of Egypt? Yadda, yadda, yadda". God hears their bickering and sends down some venomous snakes, which bit many and they died. If this has a matter-of-fact tone, it is because this is how it is told in the Bible. I guess the sight of God killing his own people for complaining was becoming old hat!

Talking Donkey

We've already had the talking snake (Genesis), but now a chatty ass. The story tells of an Israelite shepherd named Balaam. His donkey sees an angel on a narrow path, but Balaam does not see it, the donkey moves to get out of the way of it, but in taking evasive action the donkey accidentally crushed Balaam's foot against a rock wall. Balaam proceeds to beat the shit out of the donkey. The donkey looks up at Balaam and says:

"What have I done to you to make you beat me these three times?" (Numbers 22:28 NIV)

A conversation then follows between man and ass that is too stupefying to warrant mention even in this book.

The Red Cow

In terms of God trying to fuck with our small minds this passage surely ranks somewhere in his top 5. How so? Because he gives us a command that is impossible to follow, when he says to Moses to prepare an animal sacrifice in his honour:

"Tell the people of Israel to bring you a red heifer without defect. In which there is no blemish." (Numbers 19:2 NIV)

Whilst this may seem like any of the many number of animal sacrifices that God demands in worship of his name and for placating of his insecurities, there is but a wee little problem with this demand. *God hasn't invented a red cow!*

In fact 2000 evolutionary years later we still don't have a red cow. Although this hasn't stopped a group of fundamentalist nutbags from, ironically, trying to scientifically breed a red cow in Israel, to prove God's word on this clause true. Apparently one mob got close to breeding one but were eventually disappointed that she grew white hairs. Another bag full of money flushed down the drain in attempting to give Biblical mythology some scientific credence.

The Second Census

After God was done, for the time being anyway, with inflicting his umpteenth plague on his own people, he instructs Moses to take another census of the whole Israelite community so that he may number all those above the age of 20 years that are fit and able to serve in the army of Israel.

Yet another example that seems to belittle God's omnipresent eyes in the sky capabilities, because if he can hear us all murmur prayer to him then it would be fair to assume that at least he knows how many of us down here, right? Well wrong!

At the conclusion of the counting of the clans, the total number of men of Israel was 601,730.

Moses then reports the number back to God and God gives instructions on how the 'promised land' (when found) is to be divided amongst the clans. God now assuming the role of celestial real estate broker says:

> *"The land is to be allotted to them as an inheritance and to a smaller group a smaller one; each is to receive its inheritance according to the number of those listed. Be sure that the land is distributed by lot. What each group inherits will be according to the names for its ancestral tribe. Each inheritance is to be distributed by lot among the larger and smaller groups."*

Vengeance on the Midianites

God the lord of war and supreme endorser of ethnic cleansing commands Moses to take vengeance on the Midianites because they lured the Israelites into sexual promiscuity and the worshipping of other Gods. I am not sure what part of the Ten Commandments the Israelites didn't get when God spelt out his jealous pride? I guess the lure of a good ole toga themed orgy made it much easier to praise the Baal of Poer rather than the sex hating celibate God!

Moses marshals 12,000 men (1,000 from each Israelite tribe) ready for battle and the trumpets of war are sounded. The war rages and as was commanded of Moses by God, the Israelites kill every man and take hostage all the women and children; herds; flocks; and goods as plunder. They then raised all the Midianite villages to the ground.

The military Generals return to Moses to report their victorious triumph in battle, but are soon shocked to learn that Moses, obviously taking his remorseless cues from his boss, is displeased with the army's efforts.

> *"Have you allowed all the women to live? Moses asked them. They were the ones who followed Balaam's advice and were the means of turning the Israelites away from the Lord in what happened at Peor, so that a plague struck the Lord's people. Now kill all the boys. And kill every woman who has slept with a man, but save for yourself every girl who has never slept with a man." (Numbers 31:15-18 NIV)*

Now in case you were skimming through this book, or your powers of concentration have waned during the past five minutes, I want to make sure that you didn't miss the meaning of Moses' orders in the above passage. In essence Moses demanded that his military slaughter all the captured Midianite boys. Even the Geneva Convention forbids the killing of defenceless innocents, which makes the articles of that far more moralistic than the Bible. Then after all the boys aged 0-18 are hacked to death with spears and swords in front of their mums and sisters, the soldiers are then to turn their attention to butchering all women that slept with the Israelite men. This is their punishment for passing on a sexually transmitted disease (although evidently Moses believes an STD to be a plague sent from God). The surviving girls and women are spared, but spared only to become sexual slaves of the Israelites. Holy fucking shit is right!

This passage of the Old Testament basically teaches us the following moral lesson: If you are a man and fuck a woman by mutual consent, it is her fault for luring you towards her wicked breasts and vagina. Should you contract an STD, then that is too her fault for passing you a viral infection and she should be mercilessly punished by death for such dissent. Is it any wonder that the occurrence of religious inspired gang-rape/murder be on the rise?

[Article as featured on Australian news Commentary on August 4, 2006:]

Lebanese Muslim gang leader sentenced to 38 years jail for racially motivated pack-rapes of Australian girls.

Bilal Skaf, the leader of a Lebanese gang which perpetrated racially motivated pack-rapes on Australian teenage girls in Sydney in 2000, was last week sentenced to a further term of imprisonment. Added to the 28 years he is serving for other pack-rapes, his maximum term is 38 years.

To show their disdain for Australian culture and Australian females, gangs of Lebanese Muslims carried out violent, racist pack-rapes on young Australian girls around Sydney in 2000. Over 50 young girls were pack-raped during this rampage.

Bilal Skaf, the leader of one gang organised the pack rape of a sixteen-year-old girl known as Miss D near a soccer field in the Sydney suburb of Gosling on the night of August 12, 2000. Fourteen Lebanese youths pack raped Miss D that night.

Anna Marshall

I don't need to underscore the point, as I believe this article does it perfectly so.

Numbers Body Count: 15,300

God incinerated an unknown number of Israelites that complained during their wanderings in the Desert *again* = 100 as crude estimate.

God sent a great plague inflicted upon the Israelites for complaining about the food during their wanderings = 5000 as crude estimate out of 600,000 Israelites that left Egypt.

Slaughter of the Aradites = minimum estimate of 5,000.

God sent down a plague of snakes to bite the Israelites for complaining about a lack of food and beverage during their desert wanderings = 50 as crude estimate.

God helps Moses kill all of the Bashanites = 5000.

God opens up the ground to swallow Korah and his family for questioning Moses' authority = 250.

Cumulative Body Count: 31,048,001

Chapter Five - The Book of Deuteronomy

"I dislike blasphemy on purely rational grounds. If there is no God, blasphemy is stupid and unnecessary; if there is, then it's damned dangerous."
Flan O'Brien

The final book of the Torah and fifth book of the Old Testament is a set of three sermons delivered by Moses. The first sermon is a review of the previous forty years of walkabout in the desert and is also the continuation of the kind of maniacal madness we witnessed of Moses in the end passages of the book of Numbers. The second sermon is an elaboration of the laws and the way in which the Israelites must conduct themselves in the Promised Land. Whilst the third sermon articulates the blessings to the obedient and curses on the rebellious.

The start of Deuteronomy shows that God is evidently pissed off that the Israelites have been acting cowardly in their refusal to go forth and claim the Promised Land that God had allotted them. Moses launches into a tirade lambasting his people in a tone that can only be assumed to be of mockery:

> *"You grumbled in your tents and said, 'The Lord hates us; so he brought us out of Egypt to deliver is into the hands of the Amorites to destroy us. Their people are stronger and taller than we are; the cities are larger, with walls up to the sky.'" (Deuteronomy 1:27-28 NIV)*

What a bunch of namby-pamby, wimpy, whiney sods! The Israelites have God and Moses on their side, so what are they worried about? Up to now their Lord had performed a shopping list of miracles and a bunch of vengeful acts that surely must have proved his powers. But evidently not good enough for this hard to impress lot. And Moses let them know all about it too, launching into a long diatribe reminding them of what God had done for his miserable bunch, from the exodus of Egypt through their endless wanderings in the desert to this point. With a gentle tap on the shoulder, Moses told them that if they didn't pull their socks up then more heaven-sent wrath was headed their way. Moses clearly had more patience than me, because I surely would've told them all to fuck off, stop following me and headed to the coastal plains with a few of the more attractive females to massage my shoulders to soothe me from the desert heat.

The first four chapters are a summary of forty years of wandering; a review of God's covenants and laws; and a motivational pep talk to remind the Israelites that they were the people of God:

"Ask now about the former days, long before your time, from the day God created man on the earth; ask from one end of the heavens to the other. Has anything so great as this ever happened, or has anything like it ever been heard of? Has any other people heard the voice of God speaking out of fire, as you have and lived? Has any god ever tried to take for himself one nation out of another nation, by testings, by miraculous signs and wonders, by war, by a military hand and an outstretched arm, or by great and awesome deeds, like all the things the Lord your God did for you in Egypt before your very eyes. You were shown these things so that you might know that the Lord is God; besides him there is no other." (Deuteronomy 4:12-38 NIV)

Reading the Old Testament it is not difficult to see why and I'm not taking sides here, the Jewish people will not give an inch in negotiating a lasting peace deal with the Palestinians. Why would you if you really believed God to be on your side? You're the chosen people right? When I read this kind of rhetoric I can't help but draw similarities with this elitism propaganda and the lunatic rants of Adolf Hitler. I unreservedly apologize to my Jewish friends for making what seems a vulgar simile, but I'm just trying to make the point that whenever a leader convinces his people that they are 'chosen' and no nation will stand in their way with a divine wind at their back, then history has proven to us time and time again that inevitably bad things follow.

Moses further reminds the Israelites of the Ten Commandments and the punishments that follow for disobedience. We are not afforded the luxury to forget that God is a jealous god and woe the retribution for those that dare worship another. Thus some repetition of the preceding books of the Torah, until we get to chapter seven whereby Moses really ratchets up his murderous rhetoric to solicit the Israelite thirst for battle and blood, for conquer and conquest:

"When the Lord your God brings you into the land you are entering to possess and drives out before you many nations – the Hittites, Girgashites, Amorites, Canaanites, Perizzites, Hevities and Jebusites, seven nations larger and stronger than you – and when the Lord your God has delivered them to you and you have defeated them, then you must destroy them totally. Make no treaty with them and show no mercy. Do not intermarry with them. Do not give your daughters to their sons or take their daughters for your sons, for they will turn your sons away from following

me to serve other gods and the Lord's anger will burn against you and you will quickly destroy you." (Deuteronomy 7:1-4 NIV)

"Make no treaty with them and show them no mercy." Whoa! But Moses is just warming up here, takes a step back, wipes his forehead, enjoys a couple of deep breaths before launching further into this venomous spray:

"This is what you are to do to them: Break down their altars, smash their sacred stones, cut down their Asherah poles and burn their idols in the fire. For you are a people holy to the Lord your God. The Lord your God has chosen you out of all peoples on the face of the earth to be his people, his treasure possession." (Deuteronomy 7:5-6 NIV)

Hmm, where have we heard such vitriol that stinks of intolerance and racial superiority? The tragic irony is that this language of intolerance resembles that of Hitler addressing (below) the German people in the Nuremberg rallies in the late-1920s:

"The only thing we may be proud of is this: We have this value, we have our blood-building value, the best proof of which is the great men of world history over the millennia. We have this value of race and personality. We have a third value: a sense of battle. It is there, it is only buried under a pile of foreign doctrines. A large and strong party is attempting to prove the opposite, until suddenly an ordinary military band begins to play. Then the sleeper awakes from his dreams and begins to feel himself a member of a people that is on the march and he marches along. That is how it is today. We only need to show our people the better way. They see: we are marching already!

"There had to be a way to build this unity at home and this was clear to them. Why was it possible at the front? Because of the enemy! Because one knew the danger that one faced. If I am to build unity among the people, I must first find a new front, a common enemy so that everyone knows: We must be united, because this enemy is the enemy of us all. If we are not united, the entire German people will sink into the abyss.

"We National Socialists therefore make the holy promise never to rest in raising the honour of this flag, making it our symbol of self-discipline, obedience and order. Let it be to us a symbol of eternal struggle. We see in this flag the victorious sign of freedom and the purity of our blood. We want this flag to be a symbol of salvation, a sign that faith in these great possessions is alive in our people. May in the coming years a party rally occur at which five times as many people march, even if their sacrifice is still greater than ever before!" (Excerpts from Adolf Hitler's Nuremburg Speech in 1927)

Experience has shown us that when you instil a belief into a people that they are racially and intellectually superior, with God on their side, then you create divisions. And with divisions the propensity for violence is increased, as it is easier to inflict bigotry, segregation and atrocities on any individual who you mistakenly deem to be inferior to you. Thus further highlighting the moral failings of the Bible and fundamental religious dogmas.

In chapter thirteen there is an expansion of the Ten Commandments, which is commonly referred to as the fundamentals of the Deuteronomic Code, which include extensive laws, admonitions and injunctions to the Israelites regarding how they ought to conduct themselves in Canaan, the land promised by the God of Israel.

Religious Freedom

If there is any passage of the Bible that proves that Christianity is every bit as dangerous a doctrine as the Islamic Koran it is this. This is an edict from God to murder those that believe in other religions. This is religious intolerance at its ugliest and most brutal.

> *"If your very own brother, or your son or daughter, or the wife you love, or your closest friend secretly entices you, saying, 'Let's go out and worship other gods', do not yield to him or listen to him. Show him no pity. Do not spare him or shield him. You must certainly put him to death. Your hand must be the first in putting him to death and then the hands of the people. Stone him to death because he tried to turn you away from the Lord your God.....Then all Israel will hear and be afraid, and no-one among you will do such an evil thing again." (Deuteronomy 13:6-11 NIV)*

Usually when Christian or Jewish friends comment, "People should be free to believe what they want,' I often cite the above passage with the words, "Yes, you are free to believe what you want as long as it doesn't entail killing me."

What I find particularly noteworthy in this text is the suggestion that the founding fathers of Judaism were not monotheistic because they are acknowledging the existence of other gods. The biblical authors don't write, "Kill all the crazies that are wearing a hammer around their necks in honor of a make believe god called Thor." Rather it says worshipping other gods, and we can trace this belief back to the Ten Commandments, whereby God says to Moses,"Worship no other gods before me". God first, other gods second, rather than, "There are no other gods".

And if you are looking for some further inspiration for performing acts of genocide and ethnic cleansing against your neighbours for worshipping Payton Manning instead of God Almighty look no further than this:

> *"If you hear it said about one of the towns the Lord your God is giving you to live in that wicked men have arisen among you and have led the people*

astray, saying, 'Let us go and worship other gods', then you must enquire, probe and investigate it thoroughly. And if it is true and it has been proved that this detestable thing has been done among you, you must certainly put the sword to all who live in that town. Destroy it completely, both its people and its livestock. Gather all the plunder of the town into the middle of the town square and completely burn the town and all its plunder as a whole burnt offering to the Lord your God." (Deuteronomy 13:12-16 NIV)

This passage paints the picture of a salivating sociopath watching from above, rubbing his hands together gleefully as those that express their freedom to follow other religious doctrine are mutilated in the streets with all their belongings torched as a token of worship to him.

It would be a harrowing exercise to calculate exactly how many villainous tyrants have interpreted the preceding passage as justification for murderous rampage?

I believe by now we have dismissed any misguided hope that the three Abrahamic religions are built on principles of racial and ethnic equality, human solidarity and peaceful coexistence. By shining the spotlight of truth on these dangerous biblical assertions, the bible, once again, becomes an indictment against itself. We must not delude ourselves any longer that these are religions of good, as the evidence presented thus far is proof to the contrary.

Violence is not only reserved for those that ignore God's commands or take his name in vain, but also those that disrespect his earthly representatives:

"Anyone arrogant enough to reject the verdict of the judge or of the priest who represents the LORD your God must be put to death. Such evil must be purged from Israel." (Deuteronomy 17:12 NIV)

Strange Laws of Marriage and Parenthood

It seems odd to me that God goes to some length to describe some fairly whacky and obscure laws in this chapter. One being in relation to marrying a captive woman:

"If you notice among the captives a beautiful woman and are attracted to her, you may take her as your wife. Bring her into your home and make her shave her head, trim her nails and put aside the clothes she was wearing when captured." (Deuteronomy 21:11-13 NIV)

So much for romance, huh? Arguably this could have been decreed by God with a little more romance with the inclusion of the words, "Subject to her being mutually attracted to you too". Just a little more thought here by God, such as the inclusion of the word 'consent', could have helped mitigate the justification that so many invading armies in later days used in systematically raping the conquered.

In the very next passage, God stipulates the ownership of first born children of a husband that is married with two women. I think I just heard a distant shout of 'woohoo' from Utah just now. God doesn't have a problem with polygamy anymore which contradicts his earlier commands:

> *"If a man has two wives and he loves one but not the other and both bear him sons but the firstborn is the son of the wife he does not love, when he wills his property to his sons, he must not give the rights of the firstborn to the son of the wife he loves in preference to his actual firstborn, the son of the wife he does not love." (Deuteronomy 21: 15-16 NIV)*

This seems highly problematic and complex. Why not just say "You can't have two wives"? Problem solved.

Moving onto parenthood, the Bible proves once more that it should never, ever be used as a reference guide for model child raising, as God dictates his disciplinary methodology for handling a rebellious son. Warning: Do not try this at home with your teenager, no matter how tempted you might be.

> *"If a man has a stubborn and rebellious son who does not obey his father and mother and will not listen to them when they discipline, his father and mother shall take hold of him and bring him to the elders at the gate of his town. Then all the men of the town shall stone him to death. You must purge the evil from among you." (Deuteronomy 21:18-21 NIV)*

What? Purge the evil from among you? How about not savagely killing your own son by throwing rocks at his head until his brains explode all over the dirt, because he was suffering a little teenage angst? For mine the only way to purge evil is to purge this kind of religious thought from our consciousness, so fuck you God!

The following law of marriage I do not want to include as merely a bulletpoint as it is exhibit #425 that religion is male gender constructed:

> *"If a man takes a wife and, after lying with her, dislikes her and slanders her and gives her a bad name, saying, 'I married this woman, but when I approached her, I did not find proof of her virginity,' then the girl's father and mother shall bring proof that she was a virgin to the town elders at the gate." (Deuteronomy 22:13-15 NIV)*

To make sure we are all on the same page here, the law is this: If you marry a woman and she turns out to be an absolute dud in the rack, then you can accuse her of being a 'slut' and humiliate her in front of her parents and the citizens of your town. A strange 'get out of jail card' for a man, as this follows the logic that a woman be a better performer in the bedroom if she were a virgin, as opposed to a woman who pole-danced at a Gentleman's club for a living. Hey God, as a matter of personal preference, please give me just twelve porn-starlets in heaven rather than seventy-two virgins.

Further, according to this law, if the bride's parents can produce evidence that their daughter was truly a virgin at time of wedding (how one does this I will never know!), then the husband is forced to pay a fine of five shekels of silver to his father-in-law and she must continue to be his wife and he is not permitted to divorce her. However, if her parents cannot prove her pre-marital purity:

> *"She shall be brought to the door of her father's house and there the men of the town shall stone her to death." (Deuteronomy 22:21 NIV)*

I am at a loss to describe the indefensible vulgarity of this male dominated law. Not only a despicable process for eradicating so-called evil, is it not enough to kill this hapless already traumatized woman, but to butcher her at her parent's doorstep.

The fingerprints of man (gender) are on this law too:

> *"If two men are fighting and the wife of one then comes to the rescue of her husband from his assailant and she reaches out and seizes the private parts, you shall cut off her hand. Show her no pity." (Deuteronomy: 25:11-12 NIV)*

Isn't it ironic that religious apologists talk about their religion being one of forgiveness, redemption and love? From Genesis to Deuteronomy we have seen absolutely no evidence of this, only evidence that if God were true, then he indeed hates us all.

God's Position on Raping a Woman

> *"If a man happens to meet a virgin who is not pledged to be married and rapes her and they are discovered, he shall pay the girl's father fifty shekels of silver. He must marry the girl, for he has violated her. He can never divorce her as long as he lives." (Deuteronomy 22:28-29 NIV)*

There's the slam dunk! How fortunate for the poor young lass that is brutally raped by a male attacker that she gains a husband out of it – the guy who raped her. Furthermore what of the penalty for the rapist? Fifty shekels, that's all? God commands in Leviticus that a man must be put to death for fucking a goat, but a payment of only a few dollars for raping a young girl? A woman's value is less than livestock in God's eyes. Women join me in raising your index finger skywards to show your protest at this alpha-dickhead in the clouds.

Other Laws

This truly wicked book of thuggish laws sets forth a number of equally ghoulish and absurd doctrines, with a majority of laws governing agriculture, including:

> *"Do not leave the body of someone you killed as an act of capital punishment on a tree overnight." (Deuteronomy 21:22 NIV)*
>
> *"If you see your brother's donkey fall over on the side of road, give him a hand." (Deuteronomy 22:4 NIV)*
>
> *"A man must not wear a woman's clothing, nor vice versa." (Deuteronomy 22:5 NIV)*
>
> *"If you come across a bird's nest on the side of the road and the mother is still with its young, you are not to take it." (Deuteronomy 22:6 NIV)*
>
> *"Do not plant two kinds of seeds in your vineyard." (Deuteronomy 22:9 NIV)*
>
> *"Do not wear clothes of wool and linen woven together." (Deuteronomy 22:11 NIV)*

I particularly like God's CSI methodology for solving a murder case, in which the Lord tells Moses that if a body is found slain, the suspect unknown and the jurisdiction unclear then the city elders are to measure the distance between the city gate and the body, the nearest city is to then bring a cow that has never been worked prior. The cow's neck is to be broken and its blood poured onto the murder site as atonement for the crime. God then commands the elders to recite the following at the scene:

> *"Accept this atonement for your people Israel, whom you have redeemed, O Lord, do not hold your people guilty of the blood of an innocent man." (Deuteronomy 21:8 NIV)*

Blessings and Cursings

The final and third sermon of Moses in Deuteronomy goes on to specify the blessings for the obedient and the curses for the disobedient. I am sure having come this far you are rightfully anticipating a little lopsidedness on the gain versus loss scale.

Moses tells the Israelites that the following blessings will come upon you if you obey your Lord your God:

> *"You will be blessed in the city and blessed in the country. The fruit of your womb will be blessed and the crops of your land and the young of your livestock... You will be blessed when you come in and blessed when you go out." (Deuteronomy 28:3-6 NIV)*

That's it really. That's what you get for a life of complete serfdom to a malevolent, capricious, celestial dictator. Maybe it's just me, but I'd be wanting a little more details as to 'what's in it for me' before I grovelled on my knees for eternity to this guy.

Compare the blessing against the list of curses for the disobedient and it becomes obvious that God prefers motivating with the stick, rather than with the carrot, as pages of maniacal tirades are forthcoming that spell doom for the wicked, as stated in Deuteronomy 28:15-68:

"You will be cursed in the city and cursed in the country."
"The Lord will plague you with diseases."
"The Lord will strike you with fever, inflammation, scorching heat and drought, with blight and mildew."
"The Lord will turn rain of your country into dust."
"The Lord will cause you to be defeated by your enemies."
"Your carcasses will be food for all the birds of the air."
"The Lord will afflict with you madness, blindness and confusion."
"You will be pledged to be married to a woman, but another will take her and ravish her."

(Who but a man could write this?)

"Your sons and daughters will be given as slaves to another nation."
"The Lord will afflict your knees and legs."

I think you get the point. One paragraph for the blessings you get for blinding obedience and multiple pages of wrath for disobedience.

Joshua to Succeed Moses

At one hundred and twenty years of age, Moses was becoming frail and of ill-health. God came down from the sky and sat at Moses' bedside and delivered him the news that he was dying and therefore it would not be him that led the Israelites into the Promised Land. God said to Moses:

"You shall not cross the Jordan. The Lord your God himself will cross ahead of you. He will destroy these nations before you and you will take possession of their land." (Deuteronomy 31:3-5 NIV)

Before taking off on his cloud God told Moses to anoint Joshua as his successor, to which he summoned him:

"(Joshua) Be strong and courageous, for you must go with this people into the land that the Lord swore to their forefathers to give them and you must go with this people into the land that the Lord swore to their forefathers to give them and you must divide it among them as their inheritance." (Deuteronomy 31:1-7 NIV)

God then spoke directly to his new charge, Joshua:

> *"Be strong and courageous, for you will bring the Israelites into the land I promised them on oath and I myself will be with you." (Deuteronomy 31:23 NIV)*

As Moses' final days approached he read a blessing to all the tribes of Israel, which finished with the words:

> *"Blessed are you, O Israel! Who is like you, a people saved by the Lord? He is your shield and helper and your glorious sword. Your enemies will cower before you and you will trample down their high places." (Deuteronomy 33: 29)*

Moses can't even bring himself to offer a message of peace on his deathbed, as he continues with the rhetoric of conquest. Which I guess is fair representation of the leadership of this vicious, fictitious character, on which the story of the Old Testament hangs.

Moses died at one hundred and twenty years of age in Moab and according to the bible:

> *"but to this day no-one know where his grave is." (Deuteronomy 34:6 NIV)*

Here ending the books of the Jewish Pentateuch. And what have we learnt via these books of God given laws? Well, in summary, we have learnt that God orders us to: kill anyone who worships a different god; kill anyone who worships idols; kill anyone who blasphemes; kill anyone who dishonours their parents; kill anyone who works on Saturday; kill anyone who commits adultery; kill any woman who has sex before marriage; kill anyone who steals a slave; kill anyone who has homosexual sex and wage genocidal war against any city or country that permits religious freedom.

Deuteronomy Body Count: 70,000

The genocide of Anakim = 5,000.

The eradication of the King of Heshbon's three cities = 5,000.

God ensured the defeat of the Bashanites and all citizens of Bashan's sixty cities were butchered = 50,000.

Cumulative Body Count: 31,718,001

The History Books

Chapter Six - The Book of Joshua

"Men never do evil so completely and cheerfully as when they do it from a religious conviction."
Blaise Pascal

The book of Joshua contains a history of the Israelites from the death of Moses to that of Joshua. After Moses' death, Joshua, by virtue of his previous appointment as Moses' successor, received from God the command to cross the Jordan River to receive the Promised Land. Unfortunately God had failed to inform the many then current occupants of the said territory and hence begins hundreds of years of conquest and ethnic cleansing. Whilst bearing in mind that the Promised Land referred to is hardly the awe-inspiring vegetation of New Hampshire in the fall, but is purely a sand filled wasteland hugging a tiny strip of the Mediterranean Sea.

The book essentially consists of three parts:

1. The history of the conquest of the land.
2. The allotment of the land to the different tribes.
3. The farewell addresses of Joshua, with an account of his death.

But what makes this book stand out is God's love for extermination, eradication and elimination of any country, city, or person that could potentially or actually impede the Israelite land grab. There is more bloodshed in this book than any other in the Bible, as this accounts for Joshua wiping out entire civilizations, men, women and babies, whilst following the Lord's orders. God said in Leviticus 19 that we should 'love our neighbours', it seems what he meant was 'love them as long as they don't occupy the land you want'.

I find it somewhat bemusing that Christians or Jews will debase Islam for 'atrocities' committed in the last thirty or so years but will not flinch when learning of the savage elimination of entire ethnic groups ordained by God on behalf of the Hebrews. Atrocities of the most gut-wrenching ever recorded in history.

The Lord Commands Joshua

After Moses had passed, God says to Joshua:

> *"Moses my servant is dead. Now then, you and all these people, get ready to cross the Jordan River into the land that I am about to give them – to the Israelites. I will give you every foot, as I promised Moses. Your territory will extend from the desert to Lebanon and from the great river, the Euphrates to the Great Sea on the west. No one will be able to stand against you all the days of your life. As I was with Moses, so I will be with you; I will never leave or forsake you." (Joshua 1:15 NIV)*

God tells Joshua to be strong and courageous and reminds Joshua that the Israelites stay true to the laws that Moses had given them via God. Joshua takes the required action and orders his officers to tell the people:

> *"Get your supplies ready. Three days from now you will cross the Jordan here to go in and take possession of the land the Lord your God is giving you for your own." (Joshua 1:10-11 NIV)*

Joshua now has his mission from God, and whilst it may seem more than a small logistical problem that that land be already occupied by other prospering societies, that is but a small bump in the road with God as your landlord. The Lord soon taketh and giveth.

The Walls of Jericho

Unfortunately for the men, women, and children of Jericho, God had determined that the land within the confines of the city walls, that they had resided on for probably hundreds if not thousands of years, was now to be allotted to his favorite human beings, and for this they would all soon be skewered by the Israelite swords.

Camped on the outskirts of the city of Jericho, Joshua sends out two spies who sneak in behind the city's fortified walls. The two spies take refuge with a Jericho prostitute named Rahab. Hey, if you are on a mission from God, why not rack up some 'entertainment' costs on his travel expense account?

It's not long before the King of Jericho is informed that some Israelite spies are within the confines of the city and he learns soon thereafter that the spies are with Rahab the prostitute. The King sends a message to the accommodating hooker:

> *"Bring out the men who came to you and entered your house, because they have come to spy out the whole land." (Joshua 2:2-3 NIV)*

Rahab sent a reply that yes the two Israelites had come to 'visit' her, wink wink, but they left the city before dusk and the closing of the city gates and that she had no knowledge of where they had fled to. However, she had hidden the two spies in the attic of her roof. Later that night she went up into the roof to speak with her harboured fugitives:

> *"I know that the Lord has given this great land to you and that great fear of you has fallen on us, so that all who live in this country are melting in fear because of you." (Joshua 2:9 NIV)*

Fearing for her life in what she is sure is a forthcoming attack on the city by the Israelites, she asks the Israelite spies to spare her life and that of her family in return for the kindness she displayed in offering them sanctuary from the King of Jericho. The spies agreed to make such a pact with her, "Our lives for your lives," they said. Meaning that they will agree to her plea if she helps them out of the city alive. The two clandestine operatives:

> *"This oath you made us swear will not be binding unless, when we enter the land, you have tied this scarlet cord in the window and have brought your father and mother, your brothers and all of your family into your house. If anyone goes outside the house (at the time we attack), then his blood will be on his own head." (Joshua 2:17-19 NIV)*

The spies successfully fled and reported back to Joshua that all the men of the land tremble in fear of the Israelites. Joshua then assembled his troops and readied to cross the River Jordan. Once at the river banks the water was flowing rapidly and they could not cross. That was until a little divine assistance, which, in the parting of the Red Sea style, miraculously stopped the flow of the entire river as soon as their feet touched the water's edge. With the Jordan no longer an obstacle, 40,000 Israelite soldiers armed for battle crossed over to the plains of Jericho in readiness for war.

After repeating his predecessor's maritime miracle, Joshua ordered each tribal leader to collect one stone from the riverbed as reminder to future generations that God had helped the Israelites cross the Jordan just as he had helped them cross the Red Sea, more than 40 years earlier.

Circumcision at Gilgal

If you can imagine, because I can't, 40,000 grown men being circumcised at the same time in the same place, then you are successfully imagining what took place in days prior to the attack on Jericho. 40,000 men having the protective sheaf of their penis carved off with flint knives, so that they would be 'clean' again and in honour of God's covenant. And according to the Bible, this is what necessitated this group genital mutilation:

> *"All those who came out of Egypt – all men of military age – died in the desert on the way after leaving Egypt. All the people that came out had been circumcised, but all the people born in the desert during the journey from Egypt had not." (Joshua 5:4-5 NIV)*

Can you imagine the guy standing way up the back laughing with his buddy, "Hey, I thought Abraham just said we had to cut off the protective layer of our cocks. He must have meant socks, eh?" What?

40,000 men mutilating their most treasured apparatus in preparation for war is just something that I can't even begin to put words to. I'm speechless – I have no speech. Except for my puerile default position in nicknaming this event the world's first 'Great Sausage Fest'!

The Fall of Jericho

Jericho was now on lockdown, in anticipatory fear that the Israelites would soon attack. The King of Jericho decreed that no individual was permitted to leave the city, nor was anyone granted entry into the city. As Joshua continued the military build-up on the city outskirts, God spoke to him:

> *"See, I have delivered Jericho into your hands, along with its king and its fighting men. March around the city once with all the armed men. Do this for six days. Make seven priests carry trumpets of ram's horns in front of the ark (of covenant). On the seventh day, march around the city seven times, with the priests blowing trumpets. When you hear them sound a long blast on the trumpets, make all the people give a loud shout; then the wall of the city will collapse and the people will go up, every man straight in." (Joshua 6:2-5 NIV)*

Only a half decent fictional writer could possibly come up with the idea that blowing trumpets and shouting at the top of your lungs could make a fortified city perimeter come tumbling down. This miraculous military operation to be performed after the troops had needlessly exhausted themselves by trudging around the city boundaries prior to the attack. It puzzles me why God being as powerful as he is, would order such trivialities when he had demonstrated time and time again that he has the power to make the walls come down himself. Is this how God keeps himself busy floating around the clouds all day, by inventing weird and mindless commands?

Joshua carried out God's bizarre pre-battle plan to its full extent and on the seventh day, the Israelite army got up at dawn and marched around the city seven times. On the seventh lap around the city, the priests blasted their trumpets and then on Joshua's command they all shouted.

The Bible doesn't say what it was they shouted but I will assume it was most likely, "Raaaahhh!"

"When the soldiers gave a loud shout, the wall collapsed; so every man charged straight in and they took the city. They devoted the city to the Lord and destroyed with the sword every living thing in it – men and women, young and old, cattle, sheep and donkeys." (Joshua 6:20-21 NIV)

It's terrific that God inspires such barbarism and bloodshed that includes the slaughtering of young children and if there is a message of peaceful coexistence in the Bible then we have not found any evidence of it so far. Oh well, they did save the lives of the prostitute, Rahab and her family, so that was a nice touch.

Victory at Jericho sealed the legitimacy of Joshua's leadership:

"...and his fame spread throughout the land." (Joshua 6:27 NIV)

Achan's Sin

After Jericho was successfully taken and its loot plundered, God becomes filled with rage when he learns that someone has taken some of the treasure that was set aside as offerings to him. And let it be known that nobody touches God's bounty without dire consequence and in retaliatory rage for the theft of his bling-bling, he punishes the entire Israelites by allowing their 3,000 men expedition force to get an ass-whipping in a city called Ai. Joshua asks God why he did not ensure victory for his chosen people against the Ai army. To which God replied:

"Israel has sinned; they have violated the covenant, which I commanded them to keep. They have taken some of the devoted things; they have stolen, they have lied, they have put them with their own possessions. This is why Israel cannot stand against its enemies." (Joshua 7:10-12 NIV)

Subsequently Joshua commands that he who is caught red-handed with God's silver and gold shall be destroyed by fire, along with everything that he owns.

Eventually a guy named Achan, from the tribe of Judah, confesses to his treason and directs Joshua to his hidden stash. Whereby it is revealed that Achan had illegally procured a robe, two hundred shekels of silver and a piece of gold.

Achan says he is sorry for his sins, but neither God nor Joshua are in any mood for forgiveness or acceptance of apologies, thus they take Achan together with his sons and daughters and his cattle and stone them to death before setting them all on fire. Tough justice. I guess sometimes sorry is never enough.

With the executions of Achan and his family, God is now pleased once more and he informs Joshua that he will help the Israelites destroy the city of Ai and all its inhabitants, based on a plan of ambush. God with a devilishly, sneaky strategy commands:

"Do not be afraid; do not be discouraged. Take the whole army with you and go up and attack Ai. For I have delivered them into your hands the King Ai, his people, his city and his land. You shall do to Ai and its King as you did with Jericho and its king, except that you may carry off their plunder and livestock for yourselves. Set an ambush behind the city." (Joshua 8:1-2 NIV)

Joshua took 30,000 of his best fighting men and sent them out with these orders:

"You are to set an ambush behind the city. I and all those with me will advance on the city and when the men (enemy) come out against us, we will flee from them. They will pursue us until we have lured them away from the city, then our army will rise up from ambush and take the city." (Joshua 8:4-6 NIV)

What happens next is not atypical of any of the preceding atrocities, as the Israelite's plan works to perfection and the city is taken. Except for the King of Ai, not a single Ai man, woman, or child is spared from a horrible death by the sword. 12,000 Ai residents were butchered on that day, which was not unlike a bad day on the Western Front of World War 1, and they had machine guns and hand grenades in 1916.

The captured King of Ai was brought handcuffed before Joshua. Joshua taking his cue from God drove a spear through the king and hung his body from a tree until evening.

"At sunset, Joshua ordered them to take down his body from the tree and throw it down at the entrance of the city gate. And they raised a large pile of rocks over it, which remains to this day." (Joshua 8:29 NIV)

The Sun Stands Still

The five Amorite Kings at the time included the Kings of Jerusalem, Hebron, Jarmuth, Lachish and Eglon. These kings bandied together to attack Gibeon, a city that had made a peace treaty with Joshua, as the Gibeonites feared the Israelites and did not want to fight them.

The Amorites set upon the Gibeonites. Outnumbered and outflanked, the Gibeonites sent a plea for help to Joshua, calling on him to honour their NATO like pact. Joshua mobilised his army and attacked the Amorites, taking them by complete surprise. The Amorites in panic and confusion fled:

"And as they fled before Israel on the road down from Beth Horon to Azekah, the Lord hurled down large hailstones down on them (Gibeonites) from the sky and more of them died from the hailstones than were killed by the swords of the Israelites." (Joshua 10:11 NIV)

God now using hail stones as ancient Scud missiles and the mythological bullshit of the story gets better with Joshua's army dominating the battlefield and the Gibeonites forlornly defending hopelessly for their lives, Joshua is worried that with nightfall approaching he won't be able to finish off the last remaining cornered enemy. With this in mind Joshua calls out to God for assistance to finish his grizzly task. He requests that God keep the sun in the sky to complete the annihilation. He asks God:

"O sun, stand still over Gibeon, O moon, over the Valley of Aijalon." (Joshua 10:12 NIV)

And as was requested, was delivered:

"The sun stopped in the middle of the sky and delayed going down about a full day. There has never been a day like it before or since, a day when the Lord listened to a man. Surely the Lord was fighting for Israel." (Joshua 10:13-14 NIV)

Joshua then tracked down the five Amorite Kings, who had fled the battlefield and were found hidden in a cave. In a cave! Christ, if only we had Commander Joshua as head of Afghanistan operations, we would have captured Osama Bin Laden by now.

Afterwards, the captured kings are brought to Joshua, who first humiliates them, then orders their death and has them impaled on long spears for public display. At sunset, the bodies are thrown back into the cave from which they hid and the entrance sealed.

Joshua's Genocidal Achievements

With God's divine will Joshua murdered thirty-one kings of the following cities and all of their inhabitants, including the elderly, women and children, so as to make way for Israelite occupation:

1. The king of Jericho, 2. The king of Ai, 3. The king of Jerusalem, 4. The king of Hebron, 5. The king of Jarmuth, 6. The king of Lachish, 7. The king of Eglon, 8. The king of Gezer, 9. The king of Debir, 10. The king of Geder, 11. The king of Hormath, 12. The king of Arad, 13. The king Libnah, 14. The king of Adullam, 15. The king of Makkedah, 16. The king of Bethel, 17. The king of Tappuah, 18. The king of Hepher, 19. The king of Aphek, 20. The king of Lasharon, 21. The king of Madon, 22. The king of Hazor, 23. The king of Shimron, 24. The king of Acshaph, 25. The king of Taanach,

26. The king of Meggido, 27. The king of Kedesh, 28. The king of Jokneam in Carmel, 29. The king of Dor, 30. The king of Goyim in Gilgal, 31. The king of Tirzah

The Allotment of The Promised Land to the Tribes of Israel

With the kingdoms of all of the aforementioned cities conquered and destroyed, it then became time to loot and pillage all property that remained and divide it amongst the victorious God's army. Thus God provided Joshua with instructions as to how the newly procured lands were to be divided amongst the twelve tribes of Israel, whilst also reminding him that there were still plenty more land to be taken.

The territory is divided by lot and each tribe's boundaries are described in some detail.

The Death of Joshua

Joshua died at the age of one hundred and ten and was buried in the land of his inheritance in the hill country of Ephraim, north of Mount Gaash.

Joshua Body Count: 12,031

The siege of Jericho = 2,000.

God butchers the Amorites = 1,000.

The Massacre of seven cities = 7,000.

God sees to the slaughter of the Hazorites = 1,000.

Slaughter at Anakim = 1,000.

Murder of the thirty one kings = 31.

Cumulative Body Count: 31,730,032

Chapter Seven - Book of Judges

"I admire the Pope. I have a lot of respect for anyone who can tour without an album."

Rita Rudner

The Book of Judges contains the history of Biblical judges (not to be confused with trial court judges), who helped rule and guide the ancient Israelites of their times. The main text discusses the five great judges, consisting of six stories each concerning a major judge and their struggles against an oppressive foreign overlord.

The stories concern the following battles:

1. Othniel vs. the King of Aram
2. Ehud vs. Eglon of Moab
3. Gideon vs. Midian
4. Jephthah vs. the Ammonites
5. Samson vs. the Philistines

It is the story of Samson that has captured most of western civilization's understanding of this book of the Bible, as the story of Samson is certainly one of fantastic fiction. Undoubtedly one of the great ancient herculean heroes and one that would have featured as a star of Marvel Comics had they published 2000 years ago.

The story has it that Samson, through the intervention of God, is granted super-human strength and paranormal physical size to combat his enemies and perform heroic feats unachievable by ordinary men, as we will soon discover.

"The woman gave birth to a boy and named him Samson. He grew and the Lord blessed him and the Spirit of the Lord began to stir him while he was in Mehaneh Dan." (Judges 13:24-25 NIV)

There is nothing written of Samson as a child, as the story of his life resumes with Samson expressing great lust and desire for a Philistine woman that he came across in his travels. Upon first laying eyes on her beauty, he tells his parents:

"I have seen a Philistine woman in Timnah; now get her for me as my wife." (Judges 14:2 NIV)

Judging (pun) by the above verse it is obvious that whilst Samson may have had the Fabio like physique to adorn the cover of a Mills and Boon cheesy romance novel, he would've fallen well short as one of their writers.

Samson's parents are appalled that from a selection of buxom Israelite beauties, all clean and worthy of an Israelite man, he would willingly choose to take a dirty Philistine woman to be his bride. His father subsequently offering a terse response:

"Isn't there an acceptable woman among your relatives or among all our people? Must you go to the uncircumcised Philistines to get a wife?" (Judges 14:3 NIV)

I'm not sure if this is a reference to this woman being a transvestite or just another example of biblical bigotry. Regardless Samson takes little notice of his father's racist objection and drags his parents to the town of Timnah to meet her and her family. But as they approached the vineyards on the outskirts of the town, a lion suddenly came roaring towards them:

> *"The Spirit of the Lord came upon him in power so that he tore the lion apart with his bare hands as he might have torn a young goat... Then he went down and talked with the woman and he liked her." (Judges 14:6-7 NIV)*

I love the beautiful simplicity of this passage. The Bible has just described an event so utterly physically improbable such as a man ripping apart an attacking lion with nothing but his bare hands. I once watched a contestant on 'World's Strongest Man' tear apart a telephone book, but not a bloody lion! Anyway, without any further elaboration of this super-human feat, the story promptly proceeds to say with comedic caveman-esq like effect, "Me Samson, me like hot chick!"

Reading this story, one gets the sneaky suspicion that the book's author may have found him or herself a nice little patch of psilocybin fungi ('magic mushrooms'), as the lion story concludes:

> *"Some time later when he went back to marry her, he turned aside to look at the lion's carcass. In it was a swarm of bees and some honey, which he scooped out with his hands and ate as he went along. When he rejoined his parents, he gave them some and they too ate it." (Judges 14:8-9 NIV)*

The full effects of the author's 'shroom consumption really starts to take hold as he gives an account for a bizarre wedding ceremony. Apparently in those days it was customary for the bridegroom to provide a feast for the all his groomsmen, in this case all were Philistines. At some stage in the afternoon family get-together, Samson stands on a table, so we can presume he was drunk as it is starting to sound all too familiar with some of my family gatherings, and asks a cryptic question to all thirty guests present:

> *"Let me tell you a riddle. If you can give me the answer within seven days of the feast, I will give you thirty linen garments and thirty sets of clothes. If you can't tell me the answer, you must give me thirty linen garments and thirty sets of clothes." (Judges 14: 10-13 NIV)*

Does Samson sound like the bad uncle at your Christmas gatherings?

The groomsmen agree they take him up on his wager and Samson asks the following riddle:

> *"Out of the eater, something to eat; Out of the strong, something sweet." (Judges 14:14 NIV)*

For three entire days his wife and the wedding party attempted to solve the riddle, but alas without any success. In frustration, they turned to her with the most heinous and excessive threat imaginable:

"Coax your husband into explaining the riddle for us, or we will burn you and your father's household to death. Did you invite us here to rob us?" (Judges 14:15 NIV)

Subsequently Samson's wife threw herself at him, sobbing with tears, demanding that Samson tell her the answer to the riddle, so that her friends would not burn her to death. Samson rejected her plea, telling her that he had not even told his parents the answer and he would not tell her.

Eventually Samson softened, after seeing his wife cry continuously for seven days and he gave her the answer. The two part answer being: honey and a Lion.

Samson's groomsmen ran to him with the answers, an answer they knew only because his wife had revealed it to them and demanded payment of the clothing he had promised as a reward for solving the riddle. Samson told them he would not pay, because they had not as agreed, figured it out for themselves. The gathering became furious with Samson for failing to honour his word, as they saw it. But a little divine intervention put paid to this conflict:

"Then the Spirit of the Lord came upon him in power. He went down to Ashkelon, struck down thirty of their men, stripped them of their belongings and gave their clothes to those that explained the riddle. Burning with anger, he went up to his father's house. And Samson's wife was given to the friend who had attended him at his wedding." (Judges 14:19-20 NIV)

The Lord still loves smiting innocents doesn't he? The poor old fellas in Ashkelon were killed by the spirit of God and they had nothing to do with the wager. Further, Samson's wife is discarded like trash because she revealed the answer to the riddle to her friends so that they would not kill her.

Samson then takes vengeance on the Philistines, for what it is not evidently clear, as it seems their only crime was to peak at an answer to a ridiculous riddle.

He returns to the home of his former wife, who he had passed onto one of his philistine friends. Samson appears at the door to his former father-in-law and states his intention to have sex with his ex, in her room. The former wife's father protests and says that she has been given away to one of Samson's friends and in an effort to placate the horny Samson, the father offers his other daughter to him in lieu:

"Isn't her younger sister more attractive? Take her instead." (Judges 15:2 NIV)

It's difficult to follow the logic of this story, but it seems as our stoned-storyteller is trying to convey that God, operating through Samson, was seeking to destroy the Philistines for whatever reason he could muster, as is evident with Samson's reply to the offer of the better looking younger sister:

"This time I have a right to get even with the Philistines; I will really hurt them." (Judges 15:3 NIV)

In a rage, Samson went out and caught three hundred foxes, tying them together in pairs by their tails. He then devises a plan to attach a torch to each pair of foxes and then sets them off running through the Philistines crops, which are naturally destroyed in the pursuing blaze. The town folk demand to know who was responsible for this malicious property damage and it is not long before the fingers are pointed at the former wife's father:

"Samson did this. Samson, the Timnite's son-in-law, because his wife was given to his friend." (Judges 15:6 NIV)

Well if you have read any of this book thus far, I am sure you can guess what happens next. The usual bloodshed and violence. The father-in-law and his daughter are set alight and burnt to death.

Samson enraged responds with the following personal declaration of war, before slaughtering countless number of Philistines:

"Since you've acted like this, I won't stop until I get my revenge on you." (Judges 15:7 NIV)

Soon word reaches Judah, the current leader of the Israelites, and Judah is pissed off that Samson has mercilessly attacked the Philistines in the manner in which he had. Judah concerned this would lead to a counter attack by the Philistines on the Israelites said to Samson:

"Do you realise the Philistines are rulers over us? What have you done to us?" (Judges 15:11 NIV)

Subsequently Samson agrees to surrender to Judah's army, under the condition that they will only pass him onto the Philistines and not harm him themselves. As the Philistines came towards Samson, the Spirit of the Lord came upon him in power and thus he was able to break free, the arm bindings dropped from his hands. Without weapon, he fortuitously finds a fresh jaw-bone of a donkey and uses this to kill a thousand Philistine soldiers. A thousand soldiers slain by a man with a donkey bone. Then Samson said:

"With a donkey's jaw-bone I have made donkeys of them. With a donkey's jaw-bone I have killed a thousand men." (Judges 15:16 NIV)

Based on this clever little poetic prose, in the midst of battle no less, we should credit Samson as the Godfather of rap.

As you can imagine, the act of killing a thousand men makes more thirsty work and Samson was parched as he scoured the battlefield. He looked to the heavens and cried:

> *"You have given your servant this great victory. Must I now die of thirst and fall into the hands of the uncircumcised?" (Judges 15:18 NIV)*

Sorry I don't get this. I have my fair share of bar room or football field brawls and never did it concern me whether or not my foe was sporting a hooded penis or not. Call me strange?

Anyway God fulfils Samson's plea by opening up the ground beneath his feet with a gushing, geyser of cool clean water to quench the thirst. Are there any marketing executives reading this? Because this makes for a great Budweiser beer commercial. Voice over prompt: "Just finished killing a thousand men with the jaw-bone of an ass and now feeling a little thirsty. [Cue: beer shooting up like a fountain from out of the ground] Then this Bud's for you! The nectar of the Gods!"

From this point in time, Samson led Israel for twenty years in the days of the Philistines.

Samson and Delilah

We are now introduced to the story of Samson and Delilah. The story has it that Samson ventured into the city of Gaza. The purpose of his trip was not for a little shopping, or sightseeing, or even just to catch up with an old friend. He was there to fuck a prostitute, which he successfully did and henceforth spent the night with her. Whispers quickly swept through the city that Samson was here and the men of Gaza surrounded the place and lay in wait for him all night at the city gate. The order went out that they would wait until he emerged at dawn, then kill him.

But Samson stayed with the prostitute only until the early evening, which suggests his bedroom stamina fell well short of his proclaimed fighting fitness. His strength did return thereafter though, as he was able to sneak out of the city safely by ripping apart the doors to the city gate with his bare hands.

Shortly after this event he fell in love with a woman from the Valley of Sorek, whose name was Delilah. However, Samson was unknowingly being set up for what was a sting operation. The Philistines had plotted with Delilah to mastermind Samson's doom. Once more another attempt by the Bible's authors to demonize women, matching the story of the original sin in the Garden of Eden.

The Philistines had said to Delilah:

"See if you can lure him into showing you the secret of his great strength and how we can over-power him so that we may tie him up and subdue him." (Judges 16:5 NIV)

Delilah, with the promise of financial reward from her puppet-masters, agreed and later that night she said to Samson:

"Tell me the secret of your great strength and how you can be tied up and subdued." (Judges 16:6 NIV)

Hello alarm bells! Hey, I love my wife, but I would never give her instructions as to how to kill me!

Samson confides in her that if she was to tie his arms together with fresh bow ribbons then this would render him powerless. Delilah informed the Philistines and several of their men waited for him to fall asleep that night. With his arms tied together and men hidden in the room, Delilah yelled out:

"Samson, the Philistines are upon you!" (Judges 16:9 NIV)

Samson startled was able to break free easily of the flimsy handcuffs and his would-be captors fled into the night. Then Delilah said to Samson:

"You have made a fool of me; you lied to me. Come now, tell me how you can be tied." (Judges 16:10 NIV)

This seems like a highly unnatural course of events, as there is no mention of Samson saying words to the effect of, "You treacherous cow, why would you deceive me so in order to have me killed!" None of that, just an incredulous wife accusing Samson of being a liar and angry that he didn't fall into the trap.

Samson then tells Delilah that if anyone were to tie him with new rope that had never been used before, then he would be as weak as any other man. Sure enough, on cue, Delilah waits for Samson to fall asleep, ties him up and shouts the same signal to the hiding Philistines. Once more, Samson breaks free of the ropes and his attackers run off into the night.

Delilah becomes even more pissed off and tells Samson that he has made a mockery of her, but still nothing from Samson that would suggest that at the very least he was displeased with his beloved.

She persists with the questioning and Samson fools her for a third time. Now, wouldn't you be getting the hell away from a woman that was so obviously trying to facilitate your downfall?

The Bible suggests that Delilah's probing for Samson's weakness went on for some time:

"With such nagging she prodded him day after day until he was tired to death. So he told her everything. 'No razor has ever been used on my head, because I am a Nazirite set apart to God since birth. If my head were shaved, my strength would become as weak as any other man.'" (Judges 16:17 NIV)

With this insight Delilah ran off to the Philistine authorities and urged them to come back once more, as she now was sure of Samson's secret. Later that night Samson fell asleep on her lap and she cut seven braids of his hair and immediately his strength left him. The men captured him on this fourth attempt and took him prisoner. Whereby they gouged out his eyes and took him to the city of Gaza.

"Binding him with bronze shackles, they set him to grinding in the prison. But the hair on his head began to grow again after it had been shaved." (Judges 16:22 NIV)

Two glaringly obvious points here, firstly why would the Philistines be so daft to allow Samson to grow his hair again after having finally figured out the way to subdue him, after having witnessed him kill a thousand of them with a donkey's jaw-bone? Secondly, if God chose Samson to be his servant providing him with such special super-human powers then why would he leave one of his own so exposed to such an obvious Achille's heel? Kryptonite was the only thing that could stop Superman and finding Kryptonite lying dormant on the ground posed a much greater logistical challenge than snipping a few strands of hair.

We will soon learn that the Philistines pay an enormous price for foolishly allowing Samson to re-grow his hair, as shortly after his imprisonment, the Philistine leaders assemble in a temple for a religious sacrifice to Dagon, one of their most important gods, for having delivered Samson into their hands. They summon Samson so that he may entertain them. Three thousand Philistines gathered under the roof to enjoy the carnival like atmosphere. However, now inside the temple, Samson, with his hair grown long again, asks the servant who is leading him to the temple's central pillars if he may lean against one of them.

"Then Samson prayed to the Lord, 'O Lord God, remember me, I pray thee and strengthen me, I pray thee, only this once, O God, that I may be at once avenged of the Philistines for my two eyes......Let me die with the Philistines!' Down came the temple on the rulers and all the people in it Thus he killed many more as he died than while he lived." (Judges 16:28-30 NIV)

After his death, Samson's family recovered his body from the rubble and buried him near the tomb of his father Manoah.

The fate of Delilah is never mentioned.

A Levite and His Concubine

This story is a duplication of that which is told of Lot and his daughters, in the Book of Genesis which further illustrates how mythology perpetuates and morphs throughout the ages, slightly tweaked along its whispered journey.

The author of Judges tells of an Israelite from the tribe of Levi whose concubine ran off because she had been unfaithful to him. It's only in the Bible where a concubine, aka 'booty call', can be guilty of being unfaithful. The concubine fled to her father's home in Bethlehem. But before long her Master followed in hope that he may convince her to return to his harem. Who says there is no romance in the Old Testament?

The Master located her family home and with hat in hand he pleaded with her father to release her back into his custody. The father and the Master became instant buddies and thus the young girl's fate was sealed, as her father agreed unconditionally to his new friend's request. They two men ate, drank, laughed and slept for the next five days before the Master departed with his concubine and two donkeys in tow.

The shortest journey home meant travelling through the city of Jebus (Jerusalem), but the Master was reluctant to stay there because the city was filled with Jebusites rather than Israelites. Therefore he opted to rest for the evening in Gibeah. As was custom in the day, travellers would stand in the city square hoping that a welcoming host would offer accommodation for the evening. As fate would have it an old man from the hill country of Ephraim would be the gracious and generous hotelier for this particular night and the master and his concubine followed him to his house.

Whilst the three of them were enjoying dinner a loud knock at the door interrupted pleasantries. A rabble of men had congregated in front of the entrance to the house. The men yelled out:

> *"Bring out the man who came to your house so we can have sex with him." (Judges 19:22 NIV)*

The host replied in the same incomprehensible and unforgivable manner in which Lot did:

> *"No, my friends, don't be so vile. Since this man is my guest, don't do this disgraceful thing. Look, here is my virgin daughter and his concubine. I will bring them out to you now and you can use them and do to them whatever you wish. But to this man, don't do such a disgraceful thing." (Judges 19:24 NIV)*

Further reinforcement in how lowly women rated on man's balance sheet in the eyes of God.

Judges Body Count: 6,500

Massacre of the Caanites = 2,000.

God sees to the slaughter of the Ammonites to Jephthah = 2,000.

Solomon kills 1,000 men with a donkey's bone.

Solomon kills at least 1,500 men with the destruction of the temple.

Cumulative Body Count: 31,736,532

Chapter Eight - The Book of Ruth

"God is love, but get it in writing."
Gypsy Rose Lee

As you may well guess, Ruth is the leading character in this rather short book consisting of only four chapters. Four chapters too long in my estimation, as this is a book of little comedic or intellectual value. Thus I will keep my synopsis succinctly brief.

In Hebrew, Ruth means 'mercy' and thus the story shows that God's grace, salvation and mercy extend beyond Israel to include all peoples. Which may be a blatant piece of God 'spin' propaganda to show his more compassionate side after he has performed genocide and barbaric acts of ethnic cleansing to any individual, tribe, city or nation that stood in the path of his beloved people to get what they need or want.

During the time of the Judges there was a famine across all the land. The narrative jumps straight into the story of an Israelite family from Bethlehem, the husband named Elimelech and his wife Naomi. They had two sons, Mahlon and Kilion and relocated their lives to Moab.

Once settled in Moab, both sons marry two Moabite women. Kilion marries Oprah. (Until now I never realized Oprah was a biblical name.) And Mahlon married Ruth. After ten years of residing in Moab, both Mahlon and Kilion die. The circumstances relating to their deaths are not recorded.

Naomi, the mother of Mahlon and Kilion, returns to Bethlehem with her two widowed daughter-in-laws, but soon after returning she urges Ruth and Oprah to head back to their own family under the care of their respective mothers. Oprah heeds Naomi's advice, but Ruth is adamant that she wants to stay in Bethlehem with Naomi:

> *"Don't urge me to leave you or to turn back from you. Where you will go I will go and where you stay I will stay. Your people will be my people and your God my God. Where you will die, I will die and there I will be buried.*

May the Lord deal with me, be it ever so severely, if anything but death separates you and me." (Ruth 1:16-17 NIV)

No matter how hard you try, you just can't get rid of some guests and Naomi reluctantly agrees to take Ruth under her care.

It is now the barley harvest season in Bethlehem and in order to support her mother-in-law and herself, Ruth goes to work in the fields. A field that is owned by a man named Boaz, a man that treats Ruth with grace and kindness because he has learnt of her loyalty to Naomi. As it turns out Boaz is a near relative of Naomi's husband's family and according to the local law he is required to marry Ruth, so that the family lineage can continue. Ruth doesn't really get a say in any of this, but in the final days leading up to the proposed union with Boaz, it is discovered that another man has the right of first option to marry Ruth. We don't learn the identity of this second fella but whoever he is we do know that upon him test-driving the human 'livestock' that is Ruth, he decides to exercise his right of first refusal and thus Boaz is given the all clear to marry her.

Boaz and Ruth exchange vows, which judging by the aforementioned text seems to be little more than a patriarchal ceremony to brand your personal stamp of ownership upon your new live possession. Shortly after, the newlyweds give birth to a son named Obed.

In the genealogy which concludes the story, it is made clear that Obed is the descendant of Perez the son of Judah and the grandfather of David.

As you can see the Book of Ruth is not the most enlightening or thrilling books of the Old Testament and accordingly we move forward.

Ruth Body Count: 0

Cumulative Body Count: 31,736,532

Chapter Nine - The Book of Samuel 1

"My mother said to me, 'If you are a soldier, you will become a general. If you are a monk, you will become the Pope.' Instead, I was a painter, and became Picasso."

Pablo Picasso

The Book of Samuel gets us back to the journey of fanciful fiction full of dramatic suspense that includes the story of Samuel's birth and rise to power. His abdication of the throne to Saul, who turns out to be a complete dud and failure and then onto the ascent of David beginning with his against all odds conquest over the giant Goliath. So let's begin.

The Birth of Samuel

A man from the country of Ephraim by the name Elkanah was married to two wives, Peninnah and Hannah. Possibly this is where the Mormons got their inspiration from! Anyway, Peninnah had sired a number of children for Elkanah, but Hannah had produced none. To Elkanah's credit he did not favour Penninah over Hannah and in fact he would provide more food for his childless wife as an act of compensatory empathy. This, however, obviously irked Penninah, as it is stated:

> *"But to Hannah he gave double portion (food) because he loved her and the Lord had closed her womb. And because the Lord had closed her womb, her rival wife kept provoking her in order to irritate her. This went on year after year. Whenever Hannah went up to the house of the Lord, her rival provoked her till she wept and would not eat." (1 Samuel 1:5-7 NIV)*

Again notice how it is the woman's fault. Maybe old Elkanah had the sperm count of a small garden pond and was therefore firing blanks. But this is the Bible and in this book history was written by the peniled sex. Thus blame everything on the ladies.

Hannah prayed continuously to God directly and through a priest named Eli. At the conclusion of one of Hannah's prayers, Eli having overheard her plea for a child, replied:

> *"Go in peace and may the God of Israel grant you what you have asked of him." (1 Samuel 1:17 NIV)*

The following morning it was said that Hannah no longer felt downcast, but did not know why. Later that night it was her turn on the bedroom roster to share the bed with her polygamous husband. After a quick romp she successfully conceived a child and nine months later gave birth to a son. Together they named him Samuel.

God Calls Samuel

As a boy, Samuel ministered the word of the God under the tutelage of the priest Eli. It was said that during these times the direct word of God was a rare occurrence and fewer and fewer men were experiencing him in dreams or visions. Hah, they think it was rare back then? It is even far rarer these days, with the exception of when Presidents want to go to war of course.

God's period of silence was broken, however, when he called out repeatedly to Samuel whilst he slept. Three times he was awoken by

God's thunderous voice from the clouds, but unsure if he was imagining things or not, he went back to sleep. Never being one to walk away from a challenge God tries a fourth time to get Samuel's attention and on this attempt does so successfully:

> *"See, I am about to do something in Israel that will make the ears of everyone who hears of it tingle. At that time I will carry out against Eli everything I spoke against his family – from beginning to end. For I told him that I would judge his family forever because of the sin he knew about; his sons made themselves contemptible and he failed to restrain them. Therefore, I swore to the house of Eli, 'The guilt of Eli's house will never be atoned for by sacrifice or offering'." (1 Samuel 3:11-14 NIV)*

God continued to look over Samuel, guiding him through adolescence until he was fit, ready and capable to lead his Israelite nation.

> *"And all Israel from Dan to Beersheba recognised that Samuel was attested as a prophet of the Lord... And Samuel's word came to all Israel." (1 Samuel 3:19-21 NIV)*

The Philistines Kick Some Israelite Ass

The Israelites and Philistines continue their tit-for-tat violence against one another. If you change just a couple of letters of the word Philistines, you get Palestine and 2000 years later we still have this quid pro quo shit fight from both sides.

On this occasion, however, the Israelites were handed a heavy defeat on the battlefield, with the loss of more than 4,000 of their men. Upon return from battle, the Israelite soldiers began questioning why it was that God had left them, to bring defeat upon his people. It was decided that during the next phase of fighting they would bring the Ark of the Covenant to the battlefield, as this would surely get their celestial coach juiced up and ready for a conquest.

The Philistines received advanced counter intelligence that the Israelites were planning to bring the Ark to battle the next morning and they duly began to shit themselves, which seems odd that they would be scared of a God they didn't believe in:

> *"A God has come into their camp. We're in trouble! Nothing like this has happened before. Woe to us! Who will deliver us from the hand of these mighty gods? They are the gods who struck the Egyptians with plagues in the desert." (1 Samuel 4:7-9 NIV)*

As the dawn unfolded, the Philistines figuratively harnessed themselves together to take the fight to the Israelites once more and despite their earlier stated fears they were victorious once again. More than 30,000 of Israel's men lay wasted because God wasn't paying any attention and those fortunate enough to survive the Philistine rout fled. In hasty retreat the Israelites abandoned the Ark of Covenant and it was captured by the enemy.

The Philistines Return the Ark

After the Philistines laid seize to the Ark, they moved it to a city called Ashdod and God was pissed! The Ark was to God, as the Vince Lombardi Trophy is to well, Vince Lombardi.

> *"The Lord's hand was heavy upon the people of Ashdod and the vicinity; He brought devastation upon them with tumors." (1 Samuel 5:6 NIV)*

Not surprisingly, the Ashdod civic leaders were super eager to get rid of the Ark. What is surprising is that the town of Gath agreed to have it moved there. Idiots! And God served up some of his old medicine and afflicted all citizens of Gath, young and old, with an outbreak of tumours. Yes Arnold Schwarzenegger's voice plays in my head every time I hear the word 'tumour'. "It's not a tumour!" See, I can't help myself.

Eventually the Philistines come to their senses and they opt to send the Ark back to Israel, care of donkey-mail, with immediate effect. The Philistines held the Ark for a total of seven months.

The Israelites Kick Some Philistine Ass

The Israelites took receipt of the Ark, plus some compensatory damages demanded by God of the Philistines. Samuel assembled all of Israel at Mizpah to celebrate the return of the Ark of Covenant. The Philistines Intel was on the money yet again and they attacked the Israelites there in an ambush strategy. Whilst Samuel was preparing an animal sacrifice for God, the Philistines chose this moment to unleash hell. But whilst Samuel was 'asleep at the wheel', God was wide awake and in a mood for some counter insurgency 'whoop-ass':

> *"That day the Lord thundered with loud thunder against the Philistines and threw them into such a panic that they were routed by the Israelites. The men of Israel rushed out of Mizpah and pursued the Philistines, slaughtering them along the way." (1 Samuel 7:10-11 NIV)*

Samuel led the recapture of all of Israel's territory that had been annexed by Philistine in the preceding years and with the Philistines reduced to a rabble the passage claims they never attacked Israelite territory ever again. But like a nervous seventeen year old, this call proves to be premature. Spoiler alert: The Philistines aren't done yet!

Israel Asks For a King

As Samuel grew old, it became apparent that both his sons were drunks and girly bar aficionados, and therefore unqualified to assume the leadership from him once he had passed. His boys were more interested in cards, women and booze, and had no designs on ruling:

> *"His sons did not walk in his ways. They turned aside after dishonest gain and accepted bribes and perverted justice." (1 Samuel 8:3 NIV)*

The elders of Israel conveyed their concerns to Samuel regarding his sons and urged Samuel to appoint a King to lead them instead. Samuel did not take kindly to this request, but like all good prophets he would seek God's advice before final deliberation on the matter, to which God replied:

> *"Listen to all the people are saying to you; it's not you they have rejected, but they have rejected me as their king. As they have done from the day I brought them out of Egypt until this day, forsaking me and serving other gods, so they are doing to you. Now listen to them; but warn them solemnly and let them know what the king who will reign over them will do." (1 Samuel 8:7-9 NIV)*

Samuel then went to the Israelites and echoed God's warning that a human king would lead them to ruin and that only God was fit to be the king of the Israelites. The elders, however, were stubborn and continued with their demand:

> *"We want a king over us. Then we shall be like other nations, with a king to lead us and to go out before us and fight our battles." (1 Samuel 8:20 NIV)*

Samuel could see there was no reasoning with his lot, and wasted no time in granting their God defying demand, and thus Israel would soon hereafter have a king for the first time in its history.

Samuel Anoints Saul as King

Saul was born the son of Kish, a member of the Benjamite tribe of Israel. It says that Saul was an impressive looking man who stood at least a foot taller than any of his fellow Israelites. A foot taller than all of them! As if he wasn't. (Sigh)

The narrative of Saul tells us of a story whereby Saul and his slave set out on a search and rescue mission for donkeys that were lost by Saul's father. A journey that seems extravagantly excessive for a couple of asses, as they wandered across several territories to find them. It is during the later stages of this hunt that Saul's slave recommends that they approach the 'man of God' in the nearby town, who could point them in the right direction. That man being Samuel of course. The two men enter the town and Samuel greets them.

Now the day prior to Saul's arrival in his town, Samuel had received a word from God:

"About this time tomorrow I will send you a man from the land of Benjamin. Anoint him leader over my people Israel; he will deliver my people from the hand of the Philistines. I have looked upon my people, for their cry has reached me." (1 Samuel 9:16 NIV)

This seems a little contradictory to earlier passages of the Book of Samuel for a couple of reasons. Firstly, Samuel had already led the Israelites to destroying the Philistines and the book stated that all the land had been reclaimed. But now God was insisting that he needed someone to deliver them from the Philistines. Again? Secondly, God had just told Samuel that he will abandon the Israelites if they chose a human king, but now he is saying that 'he will deliver my people'. This is one heck of a schizophrenic god!

As Saul continued his approach towards Samuel, God's voice boomed down from the heavens once more:

"This is the man I spoke to you about; he will govern my people." (1 Samuel 17 NIV)

Samuel spends a few moments trying to convince Saul that he has been chosen by God as the first King of Israel. You can imagine the look of utter bewilderment on Saul's face can't you? Here he was wandering around the desert in search of a couple of donkeys, lost and hungry. A stranger taps him on the shoulder and says, "Hey buddy, I just got off the phone with God and guess what, he wants you to be king". I am sure he never imagined that's how his day would have panned out when he got out of bed that morning.

Samuel obviously does a pretty good job in selling the gig to Saul, as he accepts the instructions to go a town called Gibeah. Samuel tells Saul that the following will take place upon his arrival at Gibeah:

"The Spirit of the Lord will come upon you in power and you will prophesy with them; and you will be changed into a different person. Once these signs are fulfilled, do whatever your hand finds to do, for God is with you." (1 Samuel 10:8 NIV)

As Samuel promises the above does occur and following the events at Gibeah, Samuel instructs all the tribes of Israel to meet at Mizpah. Shortly after, the Israelite towns were awash with speculation and rumours that the purpose of the meeting is to announce the new king, and the Israelites were delirious with anticipatory excitement.

Once all were gathered, Samuel h
he was hidden in, somewhat like t
the people stood with mouths
constituents. Proving the corpor
jobs. Samuel spoke:

> *"Do you see the man the Lor
> all people." (1 Samuel 10:2*

Then the Israelites shouted h

Saul Scores an Early Victory

A general named Nahash led the Ammonite a
town called Jabesh. The Israelites knowing they w
and outflanked by superior military force offered a pre-
But the ruthless Nahash would only accept surrender under t
that he may gouge out the right eye of every citizen of the town. What

News reached Saul promptly and with an enraged temper he took tw of his oxen and cut them to pieces. The bits of flesh he gave to his staff with the message:

> *"This is what will be done to the oxen of anyone who does not follow Saul or Samuel (into battle)." (1 Samuel 11:7 NIV)*

The next day Saul organised his army into three divisions and in the early hours of the morning they broke into the Ammonites camps and exterminated them all, a bloodbath that lasted until the middle of the day. The Ammonites chose the wrong Hebrew to fuck with.

The Israelites rejoiced together and celebrated for many days the victory of Saul and his kingship was confirmed. Enabling the ageing Samuel to retire to the background to see out his final days.

Saul Proves To Be a Dud

Saul's early victory proved to be his last and this young wunderkind lost a number of military engagements that infuriated the retired Samuel and more importantly gave God the utter shits. The figurative straw being Saul's failure to follow God's command to the full extent by showing mercy to the defeated Amalekites, a story that echoes earlier tales of vengeful ethnic annihilation.

God orders Saul to destroy the last remaining Amalekites for what they did to the Israelites soon after they fled Egypt:

> *"Now go, attack the Amalekites and totally destroy everything that belongs to them. Do not spare them; put to death men and women, children and infants, cattle and sheep, camels and donkeys." (1 Samuel 15:3 NIV)*

at it again. No stopping this guy is there?
as commanded by God and all Amalekites were killed
ssion completed? Wrong. Saul had allowed the cattle to
ey were in good condition and could provide food and
s people. Which seems like a sound decision by any
t of rationality. Well didn't God get his 'y-front knickers' in a
this belligerent act of disobedience, because nothing pisses God
e than the survival of innocent bystanders. God promptly
ned the dutiful Samuel and said to him:

> *am grieved that I have made Saul king, because he has turned away from me and has not carried out my instructions." (1 Samuel 15:11 NIV)*

amuel tracked Saul down and lambasted him for not completely destroying everything that was Amalekite and informed him that his kingship would come to an end soon, telling him:

> *"You have rejected the word of the Lord and the Lord has rejected you as king over Israel." (1 Samuel 15:26 NIV)*

Saul just found out the hard way that his new boss, God, was not looking for the virtues of compassion, or mercy as part of the job description.

Samuel Taps David for the Job

God tells Samuel to quit beating himself up over the decision to anoint Saul as king and get on with the task of finding a replacement and pronto. God leads Samuel to a man from Bethlehem who goes by the name of Jesse. This man Jesse had eight sons and God suggests to Samuel that one of these eight will be the new king, but offers no more insight than that.

Samuel finds Jesse, tells him of God's will and obligingly the father parades seven of his sons for Samuel to inspect. Samuel unimpressed by the appearance of any of the boys says to Jesse, "Are these all the sons you have?" Jesse replied that he had one other son, but he was the youngest and was busy tending to the sheep. Samuel states that he will not leave until he has had the opportunity to view the eighth and youngest child.

Moments later, in walked young David, small in stature and ruddy in appearance. But then the Lord's voice came in over the mythical PA system, "This is the one. Rise and anoint him."

The heir apparent had been chosen and soon the name David would be the greatest among all Jews.

David and Goliath

Saul was still in charge, during this transition period whilst David was still a boy and Saul was eager to meet with the King-elect, he was very impressed with David and took an immediate liking to him.

In the background, of this meeting, the Philistines were assembling for war in Judah. Saul received news of the enemy's military mobilization and in response he moved the Israelites to the Valley of Elijah. The two opposing camps were divided by a valley, with the Philistines perched on one hill and the Israelites on the other.

The Philistines had a secret weapon in the form of a nine foot tall giant, his name Goliath. (Yes it does state the equivalent of nine foot tall in the narrative.) Goliath sported a bronze helmet and wore a coat of scaled armour and if you were to envisage a fighter as depicted in the movie 'Gladiator' then you are not far off picturing Goliath's battle ready outfit.

"On his legs he wore a bronze greaves and a bronze javelin was slung on his back. His spear shaft was like a weaver's rod and its iron point weighed six hundred shekels. His shield bearer went ahead of him." (1 Samuel 17:6-7 NIV)

No doubt the sight of a nine foot man armed to the max scared the bejesus out of the 4'5" average height Israelites on the other side of the valley. Sensing their fear, Goliath step forward and shouted across to the ranks of the Israel:

> *"Why do you come out and line up for battle? Am I not a Philistine and you are the servants of Saul? Choose a man and have him come down to me. If he is able to fight and kill me, we will become your subjects; but if I overcome him and kill him, you will become your subjects and serve us. This day I defy the ranks of Israel! Give me a man and let us fight each other." (1 Samuel 17:8-10 NIV)*

On hearing this cock-sure taunt backed by his huge physical presence, that has him a good foot taller than the Guinness Book of Records holder for world's tallest man, caused the Israelites to brown their pants. Rightfully, they were terrified.

Goliath continued to harangue the Israelites with the same challenge every morning and every evening for forty consecutive days. And the Israelites had no man amongst them that was willing to offer himself as Goliath fodder. Up to this point David had not been on the front line, as he was back helping with supplies, but on the forty first morning David came to say hello to his brothers that were facing this daunting monster of a man every day. Whilst visiting the front line, David heard Goliath throw down his challenge and was dismayed that not a single Israelite was brave enough to stand up to the Philistine. David asks the men standing near him:

> *"What will be done for the man who kills this Philistine and removes this disgrace from Israel? Who is this uncircumcised Philistine that he should defy the armies of Israel?" (1 Samuel 17:26 NIV)*

Again if I was to fight a nine foot behemoth, I'd hardly be bothered by what model penis he was sporting, but hey each to their own I guess. Regardless, David approached Saul and expressed his eagerness to fight Goliath, but Saul rejected:

> *"You are not able to go out against this Philistine and fight him; you are only a boy and he has been fighting men from his youth." (1 Samuel 17:33 NIV)*

David pleaded his case stating that he had killed lions and bears that stalked his sheep, with his bare hands. His logic being that if he could kill a wild vicious animal then an uncircumcised man would be a synch. Saul gave into David's persistence and told him that the Lord would be with him.

Saul dressed David in his own armour, but due to the fact that David was just a boy his elder's garb fell off his diminutive frame, so he took it all off. Refusing to even use Saul's heavy sword, David began fumbling through the dirt to in search of just five smooth stones. Once found he placed the stones in his shepherd's bag and approach Goliath ready for battle.

Goliath was ready and waiting, but was shocked to learn that the Israelites had chosen just a small boy to challenge him. Goliath became incensed in the belief that the Israelites were mocking him. Goliath, thumping his chest, called out to David:

> *"Come here and I'll give your flesh to the birds of the air and the beasts of the field." (1 Samuel 17:44 NIV)*

David now standing in front of Goliath who was nearly triple his height, said to the Philistine:

> *"You come against me with sword and spear and javelin, but I come against you in the name of the Lord Almighty, the God of the armies of Israel, whom you have defied. This day the Lord will hand you over to me and I'll strike you down and cut off your head. Today I will give the carcasses of the Philistine army to the birds of the air and the beasts of the earth and the whole world will know that there is a god in Israel. All those gathered here will know that it is not by the sword or spear that the Lord saves; for the battle is the Lord's and he will give all of you into our hands." (1 Samuel 17: 45-47 NIV)*

Goliath, upon hearing such an audacious prediction from this diminutive lad, almost fell backwards laughing but when the laugher stopped it was replaced by furious anger and the giant moved forward to attack David, but the little fella had a plan. He reached into his pouch that contained the stones, placed one within the leather holder of his slingshot and as the Philistine giant got within swatting distance, David launched the stone and it lodged into the forehead of Goliath killing him instantly. One stone - one kill! David stood above the fallen giant, grabbing him by his mane of hair, and then severed his neck so that he held his victim's head aloft in victorious celebration.

The Philistines witnessing their hero defeated, quickly fled in retreat and the war was won. David was subsequently promoted to a high rank within the army.

But Saul's fondness for David soon evaporated, as he became consumed with jealousy upon their successful homecoming. The locals of their town rushed the streets with singing and dancing. And as they danced they sang:

"Saul has slain his thousands and David his tens of thousands."
(1 Samuel 18:7 NIV)

Saul became incensed that a boy would be credited with greater accomplishment by the Israelites over their King. And if God can't get over the pitiful emotion of jealousy what hope had Saul? And this jealousy gnawed away at Saul like a festering wound, but he remained scared of David because he knew full well that God was by David's side.

Saul then plots to kill David and tries unsuccessfully on numerous occasions. One plot involved Saul convincing his own son Jonathon to perform the treacherous deed, but Jonathon was fond of David and he could not go through with it. On another attempt Saul took matters into his own hands and whilst David was playing his harp, Saul grabbed his spear in an effort to pin David to the wall with it, but at the last second David saw him coming and eluded death once again.

David continued to grow in stature and played key parts in various other battles and with this success came the increased adoration of the Israelites, and the scorn of Saul who is now hell-bent on destroying the future king.

Saul had returned home from slaying more Philistines and was told that David was camped in the Desert of En Gedi, so David took more than 3,000 of his men with the intention to murder David there. At this point God forewarned him of Saul's intentions and he hid in a cave. As Saul entered the cave, David crept up behind Saul unnoticed and as he was about to drive his weapon into the back of his one-time mentor, he could not allow himself to go through with it and he allowed Saul to live sparing his life. Saul threw himself to the ground and wept, saying:

"You are more righteous than I. You have treated me well, but I have treated you badly...the Lord gave me into your hands, but you did not kill me. When a man finds an enemy, does he let him get away unharmed? May the Lord reward you well for the way you treated me today. I know that you will surely be king and the kingdom of Israel will be established in your hands." (1 Samuel 24:17-20 NIV)

Saul's humility and grace did not last long, as he continued to hunt down David in the days, weeks and months that followed. David growing tired of continually running from Saul decides to take 600 of his men and move into the land of the Philistines, rationalizing that Saul would never think to look for him there. Thus David and his two wives packed their bags, (It's good to be the king!) and settled in a town called Gath. When Saul learnt that David had fled to Gath, he no longer hunted him.

In Israel versus Philistine battle 43, or so it would seem, the Philistines smash the Israelite army that is led by Saul. Saul's sons are killed in action and he too is critically wounded by an arrow. Fearing that the Philistines will have their way with him with their uncircumcised penises, he draws out his own sword and falls on it, ending his life and his reign over Israel.

Samuel 1 Body Count: 4,000

God puts a spell on the Philistine army that forces them to kill one another = 1,000.

God commands Saul to kill every single Amalekite citizen = 2,000.

God ensures another defeat of the Philistines = 1,000.

Cumulative Body Count: 31,740,532

Chapter Ten - Book of Samuel 2

"No mention of God. They keep Him up their sleeves for as long as they can, vicars do. They know it puts people off."

Allan Dennett

With the death of Saul, David is now officially the new King of Israel and in a further display of decency he calls for a national week of mourning for the fallen, flawed king and his son Jonathon. David wrote a lament that was to be read to all citizens of Israel:

"How the mighty have fallen. Saul and Jonathon – in life they were loved and gracious and in death they were not parted. The weapons of war have perished." (2 Samuel 1:19-27 NIV)

All the tribes of Israel gathered at Hebron to rejoice in the rise of David to king. The people said to him:

> *"We are your own flesh and blood. In the past, while Saul was king over us, you were the one who led Israel on their military campaigns. And the Lord said to you, 'You shall shepherd my people Israel and you shall become their ruler'." (2 Samuel 5:1-2 NIV)*

David was thirty years of age when he became king of Israel.

David Conquers Jerusalem

David led his men to the city walls of Jerusalem, whereby they were warned that they would never have the military strength and resources to overthrow the Jebusites who resided there, as their army was far superior. Despite this warning the Israelites took siege of the city with little more than renegade resistance offered by the Jebusites and David took up residence in the fortress and then somewhat narcisticcally renamed Jerusalem as the City of David. Well why not really?

> *"David was becoming more and more powerful, because the God Almighty was with him." (2 Samuel 5:10 NIV)*

The King of Tyre sent building materials including cedar, stone and workers to build a palace for David within the city. David was obviously basking in his success and status and like any good rockstar would, he takes dozens of sex slaves from the city and makes them his own. Before long he has dozens of sons and daughters, with multiple wives.

Whilst David was busy enjoying the sexual fruits of his toil, the Philistines were always busy in the background just itching for another fight with the Israelites. There should be a picture of a Philistine under persistence in the dictionary, because these guys just never quit. Meanwhile, whilst David was 'balls deep' amongst his harem he receives a memo that the Philistines had amassed their forces at the Valley of Rephaim. David then escalates the matter to God and God replies with a Patton-like strategy:

> *"Do not go straight up, but circle around behind them and attack them in front of the balsam trees. As soon as you hear the sound of marching in the tops of the balsam trees, move quickly, because that will mean the Lord has gone out in front of you to strike the Philistine army." (2 Samuel 5:23-24 NIV)*

David did as ordered by his celestial Commander in Chief and the Philistines were carved up in their thousands, as God struck them down all the way from Gibeon to Gezer.

The Ark Is Brought To Jerusalem

The Ark was brought from Abinadab to Jerusalem and the Israelites celebrated with full gusto upon sight of the Ark entering the city. They danced wildly in the streets and no one partied harder than King David on this day, in what can only be described as a bizarre demonstration of rejoice by a king, as David removed all his clothing and danced naked amongst the entire populace of the city. For a moment I tried to imagine Queen Elizabeth doing same, but promptly deleted that troubling mental image from my mind.

Saul's daughter Michal is the only one it seems that took offence to the sight of a naked, dancing king with his pecker flying all over the place and she let rip with a verbal barrage for his indignant display, which prompted the following terse response from David:

> *"It was the Lord who chose me rather than your father or anyone from his house when he appointed me ruler over the Lord's people Israel – I will celebrate before the Lord." (2 Samuel 6:21 NIV)*

So nah Michal, take that!

God's Promise to David

As David settled into his new extravagant digs at the palace, God being the proudly jealous god, sent a message to David via Nathan the prophet. A message that in essence has God lodging an envious complaint. God's jealous gripe is that he is displeased that David should have such a luxurious dwelling whilst the God's Ark was confined to a modest tent, being the Tent of Meeting. In a stunning announcement of proclaimed injustice God who can't even bear to describe how his feelings are so hurt directly to David's face, uses Nathan to pass on the following messenger:

> *"Are you the one to build me a house to dwell in? I have not dwelt in a house from the day I brought the Israelites up out of Egypt to this day. I have been moving from place to place with a tent as my dwelling." (2 Samuel 7:8-9 NIV)*

God again reminds David that it was he that brought the Israelites out of Egypt, and that God had made David a great man, and now that the Israelites were prospering it was time for his people to build him a throne in his honour. And should David build such a temple then God will ensure David's throne lasts forever. Later, we will see this as another broken promise.

David's Victories and War Crimes

With God's promise covering David's back, David was unstoppable and delivered a royal ass kicking to all and sundry that was so bold as to stand in his way.

He defeated the Philistines again. I am not sure what was left of these people, but they kept coming back for more punishment. He then crushed the Moabites and in an inventive show of perverse cruelty he tied cord to all their captured soldiers, placing them in a straight line. He then proceeded to hack every two out of three Moabite prisoners to death with his own sword, allowing every third standing man to live so that they would tell of David's ferociousness to their own people.

In an effort to restore Israelite control along the banks of the Euphrates River, he slayed twenty thousand of the King of Zobah's troops. And when the Arameans came to the assistance of Zobah, he struck down another twenty thousand men. This followed the annihilation of eighteen thousand Edomites in the Valley of Salt.

David's legend and reputation as a champion warrior were sealed when he rounded up forty thousand Ammonites at Helam, sparing not a single life. All nations of the Middle East were now in fear of David and God's chosen people.

God Murders David's Child

In this chapter we find an odd piece of dialogue between God and one of his prophets Nathan. God expressing his fury with David, due to the fact that David had killed Uriah the Hittite with the sword of an Ammonite, before taking Uriah's wife to be one of his own alongside the other dozens of wives and sex slaves that he already had. Let it be said that David had the virility and stamina of Hugh Hefner in his prime, as this guy had a sexual appetite that was seemingly insatiable. Anyway, God is not happy and this is the messages he gives Nathan to pass on to David:

> *"Out of your own household I am going to bring calamity upon you. Before your very eyes I will take your wives and give them to one who is close to you and he will lie with your wives in broad daylight. You did it in secret, but I will do this thing in broad daylight before all of Israel." (2 Samuel 12:11-12 NIV)*

Now we can add the label 'voyeuristic pervert' to the long list of wicked titles that based on the events of the Bible to this point are deservedly God's. It takes a depraved mind to invent a punishment that prescribes one of your best friends shagging your multitude of wives, concubines, groupies and slaves in the middle of the street, in the middle of the day, so that all your neighbours can witness this act voluntarily or otherwise. Who comes up with this stuff albeit for God? As an extreme social-liberal, I have absolutely no moral problem with consenting adults performing whatever farfetched sex acts that the mind can conjure, but I certainly am not going to throw my life into one of religious serfdom to worship the owner of this act.

Back to the punishment itself, it would seem to me that God's retribution on David has exceeded the act of the crime. I'd be happy to call it even anyway, but not God. God still wants to dish it out and he does so by murdering the child that David had fathered with Urriah's wife. Nathan says to David:

> *"The Lord has taken away your sin. You are not going to die. But because by doing this you have made the enemies of the Lord show utter contempt, the son born to you will die."* (2 Samuel 13-14 NIV)

David does much protesting to God to beg for the sparing of his son's life, but God shows no such compassion or mercy and his son dies in his arms.

Samuel 2 Body Count: 8,001

God sees to the defeat of the Philistines, this time to David = 1,000.

God inflicted a three year famine on Israel because he was unhappy with Saul's kingship = 7,000.

God kills David's son = 1.

Cumulative Body Count: 31,748,533

Chapter Eleven - The Book of Kings 1

"To err is human; to blame it on somebody else is even more human."
John Nadeau

David's Sons Position Themselves To Take The Throne

The opening chapter begins with the continuation of David's 'pantsman' like ways, with the first chapter commencing with David now well advanced in age. And due to age related illnesses and presumably syphilis, he is bed stricken, which considering the bedroom is where he did his best work, it wasn't a bad place for the king to be.

Lying in bed suffering from what is described as symptoms of a fever, one of his servants says:

> *"Let us look for a young virgin to attend the king and take care of him. She can lie beside him so that our lord the king may keep warm." (1 Kings 1:2 NIV)*

For some reason this passage just produced the abhorrent image of an elderly German tourist riding around the beach of Pattaya, Thailand with an underage girl attached to his ageing hairy sweaty torso.

In the background of his touted bedroom hi-jinx is a power struggle of two sons to position themselves as heir to David's throne. His son Adonijah elicits some sporadic support and begins a whisper campaign that he is the natural heir apparent, but his assumed acts quickly draws condemnation from those close to his father David. Nathan offers a cautionary 'heads up' to his rival brother's (Solomon) mother:

> *"Have you not heard that Adonijah has become king without our lord David's knowing of it." (1 Kings 1:11 NIV)*

Solomon's mother, Bathsheba, wastes no time in getting in front of this rumour to head Abonijah's political campaign off at the pass, as she goes directly to David with a plea that he keep his promise for her son:

> *"My Lord, you yourself swore to me that Solomon would be king after you and he will sit on your throne. But now Adonijah has become king and you, my lord the king, does not know about it...My lord the king, the eyes of all Israel are on you, to learn from you who will sit on the throne of my lord the king after him. Otherwise, as soon as the lord the king is laid to rest with his fathers, I and my son Solomon will be treated as criminals." (1 Kings 1:17-21 NIV)*

With this news of a bloodless coup imminent, David gets his weary legs out of bed, stumbling over his concubines and takes the required action to ensure that his favoured son, Solomon is anointed his successor.

Under oath David made the following proclamation to Solomon's mother Bathsheba:

"As surely as the Lord lives, who has delivered me out of every trouble, I will surely carry out today what I swore to you by the Lord, the God of Israel: Solomon your son shall be king after me and he will sit on my throne in my place." (1 Kings 1:29-30 NIV)

With Solomon officially ratified as heir apparent, Abonijah shits himself that his brother will come after him to kill him for treachery, but Solomon spares him, with the order:

"If he shows himself to be a worthy man, not a hair on his head will fall to the ground; but if evil is found in him he will die." (1 Kings 1:52 NIV)

Abonijah's life is spared for now.

David was now on his deathbed and he summoned Solomon to his side, to give him his keys to the palace:

"I am about to go the way of all the earth. So be strong, show yourself a man and observe what the Lord your God requires: Walk in his ways and keep his decrees and commands, his laws and requirements, as written in the Law of Moses, so that you may prosper in all you do and wherever you go and the Lord may keep his promise to me:" (1 Kings 2: 2-4 NIV)

David finished off his dying words of wisdom with an order to kill a few guys that had crossed him under his kingship and with the final 'Godfather' like vendetta leaving his lips, his life had passed and his forty year reign over Israel had come to a close.

Solomon was now king of Israel. And he did not waste time in continuing the family business of murder, rape and plunder with his first order carried out being the execution of his brother Abonijah, where he is gorged with the tip of the sword in a field on the outskirts of town.

Two Prostitutes, a Baby and a Bigger Brain

Solomon made an alliance with the Pharaoh King of Egypt, by marrying his daughter. Even if she were fat and ugly, what does it matter when you are the king of Israel? You are going to end up with a dozen, possibly hundreds of wives anyway, so why not make a pact with your one time enemy by taking his daughter in marriage. No brainer decision by my estimation.

Returning to the City of David with his bride, he falls asleep the same night and God appears to him in a dream. The dialogue of this REM state conversation has God asking Solomon:

"Ask for whatever you want me to give you." (1 Kings 3:5 NIV)

With echoes of the hit 60s TV comedy 'I dream of Jeanie', Solomon has an opportunity to wish for anything his heart desires - a new cart, or a new horse; a new dreidal or a new harp; or a harem filled with gorgeous babes. Cleverly he does not fall for God's little game of mind-fuck and he replaces material gain for that of cerebral enlightenment. Solomon's modest reply to God's tempting offer:

"O Lord my God, you have made your servant king in place of my father David. But I am only a little child and do not know how to carry out my duties. Your servant is here among the people you have chosen, a great people, too numerous to count or number. So give your servant a discerning heart to govern your people and to distinguish between right and wrong." (1 Kings 3:7-9)

God was pleased with this response. Pleased that Solomon had not requested the trappings of power, prestige or wealth. Pleased that is humble request was that only of wisdom. Accordingly God filled Solomon's head with wisdom. Doesn't really mention how, but I imagine he blew in his ear, with a little breath a sophisticated young lady might give when cooling her soup. In addition to his new and improved brain, God rewarded Solomon with an abundance of gold and usual trappings of success, as he was very pleased.

"Moreover I will give you what you have not asked for - both riches and honour - so that in your lifetime you will have no equal among kings." (1 Kings 3:13 NIV)

It wasn't long before Solomon was in a position to test drive his new brainpower, as two prostitutes soon after approached him with a veritable conundrum:

"My lord, this woman and I live in the same house. I had had a baby while she was there with me. The third day after my child was born, the woman also had a baby. We were alone; there was no one in the house by the two of us. During the night this woman's son died because she lay on him. So she got up in the middle of the night and took my son from my side while I was asleep. She put him by her breast and put her dead son by my breast. The next morning, I got up to nurse my son - and he was dead! But when I looked at him closely in the morning light, I saw that it wasn't the son I had borne." (1 Kings 3:17-21 NIV)

The other woman promptly claimed the other was lying and the new king could not be sure who really was telling the truth and who the living child's real mum was. The smaller brained Solomon might have struggled with a solution to this tricky one man judicial case, but the new and improved Solomon came up with a stroke of genius. Drawing his sword out, he raised it above the baby's head and just as he was about to slice the baby in two, so that both claimants could at least keep half a baby each, the true mother of the child yelled out:

> *"Stop. Please my lord, give her the living baby! Don't kill him!" (1 Kings 3:26 NIV)*

Whilst the phoney mum, horrifically, demanded Solomon continue with his one-half is better than none ruling. As such Solomon knew that the real mother was the one who was prepared to forfeit her child, in preference to losing him to the sword and the baby was given to the rightful mother.

> *"When all Israel heard the verdict the king had given, they held the king in awe, because they saw that he had wisdom from God to administer justice." (1 Kings 3:28 NIV)*

Solomon's Wisdom Grows

> *"God gave Solomon wisdom and very great insight and a breadth of understanding as measureless as the sand of the seashore. Solomon's wisdom was greater than the wisdom of all men of the East and greater than all the wisdom of Egypt." (1 Kings 4:29-34 NIV)*

Further the Bible claims that with his wisdom came fame throughout all nations. His brilliance exemplified in his ability to know three thousand proverbs and five thousand songs. Which suggests that should we transplant your everyday teenage radio junkie 3,000 years back in time, then their brilliance would be admired too. However, today we do set a higher standard for revering human endeavor.

Solomon Builds The Temple

In the four hundred and eightieth year after the Israelites had come out of Egypt and in the fourth year of Solomon's leadership, Solomon began to build a temple for the Lord after the prodding from a friend named Hiram from Tyre. Entirely constructed out of slave labour, the temple is certainly the most lavish monument ever dedicated to God by the Israelites to date. The Book of Kings specifies the dimensions, furnishings, materials in lengthy detail and also includes a narrative from God to Solomon:

"As for the temple you are building, if you follow my decrees, carry out my regulations and keep in my commands and obey them, I will fulfill through you the promise I gave your father. And I will live among the Israelites and will not abandon my people Israel." (1 Kings 6:11-13 NIV)

The above is just another example of God moving the goal-posts of servitude and obedience, he already has several covenants with Israel and one in place with Solomon, but now he has to tie it to this newly built temple too. Must be part of his divine plan to keep us jumping from foot to foot, so we never become fat and content.

At the same time he was building this Temple for the Lord, he had also begun construction of his palace. A palace so vast and opulent that it would take thirteen years to complete.

The Ark of Covenant was moved to the Temple upon its completion, which kick started a month long festival for all of Israel. The celebration included an absurd and perverse number of animal sacrifices and it states in the Bible:

"The entire assembly of Israel that gathered about him before the ark, sacrificing so many sheep and cattle that they could not be recorded or counted." (1 Kings 8:4-5 NIV)

The Temple is judeo-christianity's first ever church or synagogue.

At this gruesome opening ceremony, Solomon stood before the assembly and gave a long winded ribbon-cutting speech, a speech that nevertheless lays the foundation for the first ever official place where people can come to pray to God, therefore establishing the Temple as the first ever synagogue. Solomon's prayer of dedication to God, read before Israel:

"May your eyes be open towards the Temple night and day, this place of which you said, 'My Name shall be there,' so that you will hear the prayer your servant prays towards this place. Hear from heaven, your dwelling-place and when you hear, forgive." (1 Kings 8:28-30 NIV)

The Lord Appears To Solomon

At the conclusion of Solomon's opening address for the Temple and the completion of the Palace, God appeared to Solomon in a dream, like he had appeared to him at Gideon earlier. God's words to Solomon:

"I have heard the prayer and plea you have made before me; I have consecrated this temple, which you have built, by putting my Name there for ever. My eyes and my heart will always be there." (1 Kings 9:3 NIV)

God continued with a warning to Solomon, a warning that would come back to haunt Solomon in the next chapter:

"If you or your sons turn away from me and do not observe the commands and decrees I have given you and go off to serve other gods and worship them, then I will cut off Israel from the land I have given them and will reject the Temple I have consecrated for my Name. Israel will then become a byword and an object of ridicule among all peoples." (1 Kings 9:6-7 NIV)

Solomon Accumulates Gold, Wives and Concubines

Solomon's empire stretched from the Euphrates River to Egypt and with this great land annex came the usual symbols of success, 'bling-bling' and girls. His annual revenue in gold alone was more than twenty two metric tons. A phenomenal income, but more impressive was his accumulation of bed-mates. Solomon had over seven hundred wives and more than three hundred concubines. Numbers that would make even Julio Iglesias blush.

"King Solomon loved many foreign women besides Pharaoh's daughter – Moabites, Ammonites, Edomites, Sidonians and Hittites." (1 Kings 11:1 NIV)

The fall of man is blamed once again on women, as the author explains that Solomon's wives were responsible for leading him astray in the worship of other gods and idols. His disobedience doesn't sneak past the always vigilant God and he summons Solomon for a little face-time to work things out:

"Since this is your attitude and you have not kept my decrees, which I commanded you, I will most certainly tear the kingdom away from you and give it to one of your subordinates." (1 Kings 11:11 NIV)

But just as you and I are now bracing for God's predictable merciless ass-whipping as penance for Solomon's straying, God shows a soft-heart, although with delayed comeuppance forewarned, as he continues:

"For the sake of David your father, I will not do it during your lifetime. I will tear it out of the hand of your son." (1 Kings 11:12 NIV)

Regardless Solomon died shortly after anyway, cause of death is not listed, but it says he ruled over Israel for forty years. And if I had a penny for every time the number forty appeared in the Bible just to this point, then I'd have quite a few pennies.

The Kingdom Divided

Rehoboam succeeded his father Solomon and judging by the scriptures he was a rebellious little shit that took no notice of older and wiser men than himself, rejecting their counsel for that of his much younger peers. His foolhardiness led him to one or two poor judgements and the Israelites soon denounced him as their king:

"What share do we have in David, what part in Jesse's son? To your tents, O Israel! Look after your own house, O David." (1 Kings 12:16 NIV)

This seemingly innocuous poetical call of mutiny resulted in a nation rising up against their new commander and he was chased down by the unruly mob but once cornered, King Rehoboam managed to escape the lynching by fleeing on chariot. Israel was not in rebellion against the house of David and they promptly sought a new king. The Israelites wasted no time in anointing Jeroboam the new king of Israel. Jeroboam is identified as the son of Nebat and had once rebelled against Rehoboam's father Solomon.

King Jeroboam was now the king of all Israel, excluding Judah which remained loyal to the house of David and thus Rehoboam. But this meant that the kingdom was now divided against itself.

Jeroboam led the Israelites, excluding Judah of course, down a slippery slope away from the word of God and towards paganism in fear that his subjects would one day realise they had made a mistake in overthrowing Rehoboam and ultimately the house of David. His logic being that if he could lead them to a new and improved religious doctrine then the Israelites would remain loyal to him. The scripture confirms this with a conversation between Jeroboam and himself:

"The kingdom is now likely to revert to the house of David. If these people go up to offer sacrifices at the temple of the Lord in Jerusalem, they will again give their allegiance to the lord, Rehoboam king of Judah. They will kill me and return to King Rehoboam." (1 Kings 12:26-27 NIV)

Taking his own advice, he went out and constructed two golden calves, then set out to convince the Israelites that it was far easier and much closer to home to worship at the altar of the golden calves as opposed to travelling all the way to Jerusalem to pray at the Temple. Jeroboam then placed one golden calf in a town called Bethel and the other in Dan and many Israelites travelled far and wide to worship these new idols. Jeroboam didn't stop here with this quest to construct new religious infrastructure, as he set out building shrines on all surrounding mountain tops and made priests out of anyone that was willing. Would it be too silly a joke to say that God was being 'calved' up by Jeroboam's self-serving antics? [Editor's note: Yes!]

Obviously God was not pleased and hatched a scheme to cause the downfall of Jeroboam, a God-led coup that would be telegraphed to Jeroboam via a prophet named Ahijah. A prophet that also moonlighted as a medical practitioner. At this time Jeroboam's son became ill and Jeroboam ordered his wife to take their son to see Doctor Ahijah in a nearby town. Prior to the arrival of Jeroboam's son, God made a call to Ahijah and forewarned him of his soon-to-be visitor, as Jeroboam had instructed his wife to conceal her identity. As Jeroboam's wife knocked on the door to appear before Ahijah, Ahijah answered:

"Come in, wife of Jeroboam. Why the pretence? I have been sent to you with bad news. Go, tell Jeroboam that this is what the Lord, the God of Israel, says, 'I raise you up from among the people and made you a leader over my people Israel. I tore the kingdom away from the house of David and gave it to you, but you have not been like my servant David, who kept my commands and followed me with all his heart, doing only what was right in my eyes. You have done more evil than all who lived before you. You have made yourself other gods, idols made of metal; you provoked me to anger and thrust me behind your back.'" (1 Kings 14:6-9 NIV)

Forthwith is God's punishment for Jeroboam:

"Because of this, I am going to bring disaster on the house of Jeroboam. I will cut off from Jeroboam every last male in Israel – slave or free. I will burn up the house of Jeroboam as one burns dung, until it is all gone. Dogs will eat those belonging to Jeroboam who die in the city and the birds of the air will feed on those who die in the country. The Lord has spoken." (1 Kings 14:10-11 NIV)

God is not done yet, as he clears his throat for the treatment of Jeroboam's innocent child and using the prophet as his microphone says to Jeroboam's wife:

"As for you, go back home. When you set foot in your city, the boy will die." (1 Kings 14:12 NIV)

God was truly furious with not just Jeroboam alone, but also with Israel in its entirety and he decided to turn his back on Israel for now.

Jeroboam passed away, after he reigned over Israel for twenty two years and Nadab, his son, succeeded him as king. Two years into Nadab's term as king of Israel, Asa was king of Judah. Nadab, like his father Jeroboam, also did evil in the eyes of the Lord. God wasted no time in interceding with the current course of events and had a man by the name of Baasha step forward and slay Nadab in a Philistine town called Gibbethon. God was pleased with the thuggish work of Baasha and duly crowned him the new king of Israel, whilst Asa was in his third year as king of Judah – with the two houses of Israel still divided.

As soon as Baasha took the throne he butchered Jeroboam's entire family, according to God's orders:

> *"He did not leave Jeroboam anyone that breathed, but destroyed them all, according to the word of the Lord given through his servant Ahijah the Shilonite – because of the sins Jeroboam had committed and had caused Israel to commit and because he provoked the Lord, the God of Israel, to anger." (1 Kings 15:29-30 NIV)*

During the reigns of Baasha as king of Israel and Asa as king of Judah - the two houses waged war on each other. It is written that Baasha's reign lasted twenty four years and was ended by God. The Lord choosing to smite Baasha for following the same idol worshipping as his predecessors Jeroboam, which is a little hard to believe isn't it? I mean c'mon, Baasha watched on as God destroyed Jeroboam's kingdom and assumed the position of Dear Leader as the direct beneficiary of God's wrath and fury. So why on earth would Baasha cease to believe and worship in the God of Abraham, whom he obviously had a good working relationship with up to now, to toddle off to praise the feet of competitor Gods. This is just cocky-pop, as my Grandfather would say. To add a further dollop of crap to this unbelievable story - God, in all his wisdom, decides to appoint Baasha's son as the new king of Israel. What? Surely Baasha's son was worshipping the same alternative God as his father, as this does normally occur in families, for example children of Jewish parents, are unlikely to become Islamic in the most part. And furthermore, this probability had already been proven true with the appointment of Jeroboam's son, Nadab, as king. This is one dim-witted God we are talking about; no doubt the same God that thought it necessary to design men with nipples.

Sure enough God was forced to put a hit on Baasha's son, Elah and he organised one of Elah's generals to carry out the coup de tat. And one evening whilst Elah was drunk, his head of the military slashed his throat and then in accordance with God's orders he murdered Elah's entire family. His name was Zimri and in the twenty-seventh year of Asa's reign over Judah, he became the new king of Israel. Zimri's reign lasted just seven days, as he was also killed by God for following in the footsteps of Jeroboam. God had the throne of Israel working like a turnstile and as such Ahab became the new king.

The Valley of Elijah

Ahab married a woman by the name of Jezebel. A name that has become symbolic throughout the ages as a derogatory term for a sexually promiscuous woman. With Jezebel as his wife, she and Ahab encouraged pagan worship of Baal., a local god responsible for natural climatic events such as rain, thunder and lightning. And as such they displeased God almighty with their actions. Thus, enter a simple man named Elijah, who makes his entry into the Bible without any hoopla. In fact very little is known of Elijah, as the text includes no reference of his background or origins.

The backdrop to this story is that the king and queen of Israel had set out to kill or exile all prophets of the God of Israel and replace them with prophets of Baal. During this time God offers protection for Elijah outside of Israel. After forty days and forty nights taking refuge in a small valley to the east of Jordan, God whispers to Elijah to return to Israel to offer Ahab a challenge. The challenge being to tempt Ahab in pitting 450 of Baal's prophets against 400 of God's on top of Mount Carmal, in a contest to prove the existence of their respective god.

The rules and playing conditions of the contest included that both teams build a respective altar made of wood, with two slaughtered oxen placed on each. The winner of this challenge would be the team whose BBQ themed altar lit on fire using prayer as the only igniter. The Baal team won the coin toss and elected to start. Their 450 prophets danced and sang loudly around the altar, but after many hours it would not light. As the hours passed by their desperation grew and they began shouting wildly at the sky with their swords drawn upwards, but still no fire.

It was Team God's turn to pursue victory and with that Elijah stepped towards the altar and placed twelve stones down, each stone representing one of the twelve tribes of Israel. A few cries of, "O Lord, O Lord, O Lord," and abracadabra Elijah had himself a fire with God sending down a fireball directly on to the hotplate. The prophets of Baal flee in terror and Elijah seizes the moment to demand that they be put to death. But Queen Jezebel becomes enraged that this 'nobody' would order such a thing against her chosen prophets and demands that Elijah himself be executed.

Elijah flees for his life to Beersheba in Judah. At some stage on the run, he falls asleep under a juniper tree and whilst in a deep slumber and angel touches him on the shoulder and tells Elijah to wake up and eat. Upon wakening he finds that the angel has brought quite a picnic hamper of all sorts of goodies. Elijah eats all its contents, and then falls back to sleep. The angel wakes him a second time and recommends that he eat some more as he has a long journey ahead of him. Elijah continues on his flight of safety for a further forty days and forty nights to Mount Horeb, where he seeks shelter in a cave. Whilst seeking refuge in the cave, God's voice was heard by Elijah, "What are you doing here Elijah?" asked God

Elijah replied:

"I have been very zealous for the Lord God Almighty. The Israelites have rejected your covenant, broken down your altars and put your prophets to death with the sword. I am the only one left and now they are trying to kill me too." (1 Kings 19:10 NIV)

God said:

"Go out and stand on the mountain in the presence of the Lord, for the Lord will pass by." (1 Kings 19:11 NIV)

Cool, a holy fly-by promised. But God being the prankster he is, sent a tornado, then an earthquake, followed by a fire. God was not in any of those natural occurring events and at the conclusion of the rumbling and flames, and in complete paradox to the preceding phenomena God spoke again in a wee small voice, telling Elijah to return to Damascus with the orders to anoint Hazael as king of Syria and Jehu as king of Israel, whilst he (Elijah) himself is to be replaced by Elisha.

Elijah has no difficulty in finding his new attendant, Elisha, locating him in his field ploughing with twenty four oxen. Elijah informs Alisha that he has been assigned a mission from God and the pair set out to fulfill their heavenly master's orders.

Meanwhile Ben-Hadad, king of Aram, planned an attack on Israel, warning that he will kill all men, women and children of Israel if they did not surrender. The Aram king gave three such warnings, before mobilising his vast army in readiness to launch Operation Rolling Thunder V1, but God sent down a messenger to pass on a telegram from his heavenly holiness to the king of Israel, Ahab. God's telegram read:

"Do you see this vast army? I will give it into your hand today and then you will know that I am the Lord." (1 Kings 20:13 NIV)

Ahab summoned 7,000 of his best soldiers and sprung a surprise attack on the Arameans whilst they drank booze in their tents on the eve of their would-be attack on Israel. The Arameans suffered huge losses and fled on horseback into the night.

The prophet returned to visit Ahab, the Israelite King and passed on another warning from God:

"Strengthen your position and see what must be done, because next spring the king of Aram will attack you again." (1 Kings 20:22 NIV)

King Ben-Hadad of the Arameans, evolved a new strategy to expose what he believed to be the Israelite weakness, that weakness being that the Jewish God only had power to assist the Israelites if they fought on the hills. The prophet passed on this vital piece of military intelligence to Ahab, saying:

"Because the Aramenans think the Lord is a god of the hills and not a god of the valleys, I will deliver this vast army into your hands and you will know that I am the Lord." (1 Kings 20:28 NIV)

For the next seven days the opposing armies camped opposite each other before throwing their full military might at one another. God true to his word ensured that the Israelites ran up a huge total on the scoreboard, inflicting more than 100,000 dead Arameans on day one of the battle. A fair effort considering the Israelite army only totalled a mere 7,000!

King Ben-Hadad is taken prisoner-of-war by Ahab and begs for his mercy. In his plea for self-preservation he offers Ahab a treaty that meant that Israelites could have access to the commercial districts of Damascus to sell their goods, if his life be spared. Ahab signs the surrender treaty and allows Ben-Hadab to walk away a free-man.

Well God wasn't happy with this pact between the two rival kings and dished out one of his all too familiar unforgiving death sentences, with further implication for the Israelites sometime in the near future:

"You have set free a man I had determined should die. Therefore it is your life for his life, your people for his people." (1 Kings 20:42 NIV)

This is God's reward for forgiveness, clemency and mercy? The punishment of death!

Vineyard of Naboth

For the moment anyway, Ahab is placed on figurative death row and continues to reign over Israel. But Elijah encounters Ahab again, after Ahab had acquired a blue chip piece of real estate, a vineyard, by murder.

Ahab's villainous plot required the conspiring of his wife Jezebel, who writes to the owner of the vineyard, Naboth of Jezreel. But Naboth refuses to sell the vineyard on the basis that God had told him not to sell his land. That pesky God even works hard to put commercial deals to death.

Ahab becomes disillusioned that he will not get to own the piece of property he so deeply desired and spends the next seven days sulking in his bedroom, even refusing to eat. But the feisty Jezebel writes to all of the town's elders and priests, using Ahab's letterhead and forged signature. Her letter claims that Naboth had committed a great number of sins and crimes, all of which were false accusations. But the town elders believe the claims and have poor old Naboth stoned to death, thus enabling her husband, Ahab, to acquire his dream property without hindrance.

God calls on his prophet Elijah to confront Ahab with a question and a simultaneous prophecy:

"Have you not murdered a man and seized his property? In the place where dogs licked Naboth's blood, dogs will lick up your blood – yes, yours!!" (1 Kings 21:19 NIV)

Elijah then adds some of his own venom to God's decree and via his own accord he adds that not only will his entire kingdom reject his authority, but that his wife, Jezebel, will be eaten by dogs by the gates of Jezreel. Ahab drops to his knees in cold sweated fear and pleads for forgiveness and offers his penance. God with a softening heart, decides to spare Ahab, but keeps the death option open for his wife and son, Ahaziah.

Ahab continued as king of Israel, but in a third battle against the Arameans, Ahab was struck between the protective shields of his armour by an arrow wielding marksman and died on the battlefield as a result of his wounds. His body was brought back to Samaria, where he was dressed for burial and just as God had prophesized, dogs licked up his blood that had fallen from his body.

Kings 1 Body Count: 1,000

The town of Baasha was destroyed by God = 1,000.

Cumulative Body Count: 31,749,532

Chapter Twelve - Book of Kings 2

"If you're a preacher, you talk for a living, so even if you don't make sense, you learn to make nonsense eloquently."

Andrew Young

With Ahab's son, Ahaziah, in Israel's throne, his first act as new commander in chief was to set out a small platoon to hunt and kill the prophet Elijah. But Ahaziah underestimated, as President G.W. Bush would have said, God's role and power in assisting Elijah. As such Elijah called down from heaven two fireballs to incinerate the first of two patrols. When the third patrol locates Elijah, the prophet agrees to meet with Ahaziah, where he gave his prophecy in person:

"Is it because there is no God in Israel for you to consult that you have sent messengers to consult Baal-Zebub, the God of Ekron? Because you have done this, you will never leave the bed you are lying on. You will certainly die!" (2 Kings 1:16 NIV)

And just as prophesized, King Ahaziah went to bed and never woke up. And because Ahaziah had no son, Joram became the new king of Israel in the second year of Jehoram's reign over Judah.

Elijah Taken Up To Heaven

The story of Elijah's ascension to heaven is interesting in so far as it is unique for several reasons. Firstly, this is the first time in the Bible that tells of a prophet's rise into heaven, as Moses, Abraham and all those after them died like mortal men and were buried as mere mortals. However, Elijah who had appeared on the Biblical scene with little or no fanfare, his background unknown, is elevated to the sky above in quite a miraculous fashion. With Elijah and his lieutenant Elisha by his side, the two approached the river Jordan. Yes get ready for another body of water parting. Like Moses with his staff, Elijah strikes the water with his mantle and the river divides allowing both men safe passage to the other side. Once on dry ground again, a chariot and horses on fire appear before Elijah. Elijah casually steps aboard and his whisked away into heaven in a whirlwind. As Elijah takes his horse flight to join God, his mantle falls to the ground for Elisha to pick up.

Elisha as The New Prophet

There is some fantastic comedy within this passage of the Bible, as it attempts to tell of the mythical biography of the prophet Elisha. His first achievement was to convert polluted drinking water that was killing the crops of a local town, into a crystal clear drinkable solution by throwing a pinch of salt over his shoulder into a nearby waterhole. And then as he was walking along the road to the town of Bethel a bunch of rebellious teenagers came running up to Elisha and jeered him with the following hysterical taunts:

"Go on up, you baldhead! Go on up, you baldhead!" (2 kings 2:23 NIV)

Elisha with his feelings hurt, called on God for some tender loving care and with that two grizzly bears emerged suddenly from out of the woods and mauled the forty-two youths to death.

Surely a warning to any others that you put your life in your own hands by humming the tune of the Advanced Hair commercial to any bald-headed blokes that frequent your pub.

The Two Houses of Israel Unite To Fight Moab

Mesha the king of Moab had a contract to supply the king of Israel with one hundred thousand lambs and with the wool of one hundred thousand rams, but after Ahab had died and had been succeeded by Joram as the new king of Israel, Mesha refused to honour the terms and conditions and thus rebelled against Israel. The king of Israel, on war footing, called on Jehoshaphat the king of Judah for his support and the formation of a new Jew alliance. Jehosphaphat replied obligingly:

> *"I will go with you. I am as you are, my people as your people, my horses as your horses." (2 kings 3:7 NIV)*

The two kings decided the best route for attack was via the Desert Edom, but after seven days of marching, the men and horses were out of water and near death. Facing one of the biggest military blunders in Biblical history, the king of Judah cried out:

> *"Is there no prophet of the Lord here, that we may enquire of the Lord through him?" (2 Kings 3:11 NIV)*

Now I find this absolutely comical. I can't help but imagine two kings on horseback surrounded by thousands of their finest soldiers suffering from severe dehydration and the only course of action is the sitcom-like first aid call of, "Help! Is there a prophet in the house?" Until now the Kings of Israel had always had a direct line to God but now only a messenger would suffice. Now that's funny!

The cry was heard and Elisha was summoned to the general's tent. The two kings asked for some two-way communication with God to save them from their seemingly inevitable plight. Elisha replied that he would not speak until a harpist was playing him some tunes. I swear I am not making this up. Whilst the harpist played a catchy little number, Elisha said:

> *"This is what the Lord says: Make this valley full of ditches. You will see neither wind or rain, yet this valley will be filled with water and you, your cattle and your other animals will drink. This is an easy thing in the eyes of the Lord; he will also hand Moab over to you. You will overthrow every fortified city and every major town. You will cut down every good tree, stop up all the springs and ruin every good field with stones." (2 Kings 3: 15-19 NIV)*

Sure enough, the next morning, water began flowing and the land filled with water. The soldiers and animals replenished themselves and prepared once more for battle. However, the Moabites had assembled a powerful army and were ready to attack the Israelites at their camp. The Moabites had received false intelligence that the Israelites, being divided into two houses of Judah and Israel respectively, had begun turning on each other and thus the Moab attack was sounded. But the Israelites were unified and with God's help they slaughtered the Moabites in their thousands and just as Elisha had telegraphed the Israelites did not cease their plundering until every Moab crop was covered in stone and every tree uprooted. The few remaining Moabites surrendered and returned to far off distant lands to never be heard of again.

Succession of Failed Kings

Failed king after failed king followed for Israel for the next several hundred years, the only highlight from God's perspective being the violent death of the wicked Jezebel, who was thrown from a tall building with her blood splattering across the footpath. Her body set upon by the Israelites, leaving her skull and her hands as the only remains. Additionally, God was pleased that the ministers of the pagan god Baal were all slaughtered by Jehu, the king of Israel at that time, who led a platoon of soldiers to hack them to death with machetes. Jehu ordered:

> *"Go in and kill them; let no one escape" (2 Kings 10:25 NIV)*

The Israelite soldiers hurled their butchered remains into the street, then proceeded to destroy every artifice of the Baal temple and shrine, before burning the site to the ground. The god of Baal had been defeated by God's chosen warriors.

Joash then followed as king of Israel, his single achievement being the repair of the Temple in Jerusalem, by money raised by offerings and tithes, which took more than fifteen years of labour.

The Last King of Israel

Inheriting a failed legacy from his forebears, Hosea was the final king of Israel, but God had had enough. His disappointment of the Israelites and frustration that the kings could not lead the chosen people away from worshipping other Gods to total observance of the commandments was eventually too much for the heavenly father to take. And he allowed Assyria to invade and conquer Israel, because his people had provoked his anger.

> *"Therefore the Lord rejected all the people of Israel; he afflicted them and gave them into the hands of plunderers, until he thrust them from his presence." (2 Kings 17:20 NIV)*

The Two Kingdoms Fall

Henceforth, all the people of Israel were taken from the promised land into exile. The Northern Kingdom (Israel), was taken into Assyria's captivity in 722 BC and one hundred and thirty six years later the Southern Kingdom (Judah) into Babylon's control.

The two Israelite kingdoms remained in exile for the next forty to fifty years.

Babylon Destroys the Temple

The king of Babylon was Nebuchadnezzar and upon marching triumphantly into the city of Jerusalem to glorify his defeat of the Southern Kingdom he chose the destruction of the Jewish temple to be his victory signature. He set the temple ablaze raising it to the ground. The Babylonians looted anything of value such as the bronze pillars and all the bronze articles used in ceremonial service. The city itself was also totally destroyed, with every house set alight and the city walls pulled down. God had punished his chosen people good and proper.

Kings 2 Body Count: 20,000

God inflicts a seven year famine on the Israelites as punishment for disobedience = 20,000.

Accumulative Body Count: 31,769,532

Chapter Thirteen & Fourteen - Book Of Chronicles 1 & 2

"I was thinking about how people seem to read the Bible a whole lot more as they get older; then it dawned on me, they're cramming for their final exam."
George Carlin

Thankfully we won't spend much time dissecting this book as it doesn't really offer much that we haven't heard already in the respective books of Samuel and Kings. It is just a recount of those stories adding some crudely constructed genealogy to help make certain events come out right. For purpose of brevity Chronicles may be summarize into its four components:

- Chapters 1-10 of Chronicles 1 refers in most part to genealogy, concluding with the House of Saul and Saul's rejection by God, which sets the stage for the rise of David.
- Chapters 11-29 of Chronicles 1 present a history of David's reign.

- Chapters 1-9 of Chronicles 2 provide a history of the reign of King Solomon, son of David.
- Chapters 10-36 of Chronicles 2 is an account of the kings of Judah to the time of the Babylonian exile and concluding with the call by Cyrus the Great for the exiles to return to their land.

Whilst we don't really learn anything new in this book, what is interesting is the flagrant contradictions this book makes in attempting to reconcile the stories of the preceding books. Here are but a few examples.

King David asked Joab to count his fighting men that could be made ready for battle. In the Book of Samuel:

"Joab reported the number of fighting men to the king: In Israel there were eight hundred thousand able-bodied men who could handle a sword." (2 Samuel 24:9 NIV)

Whereas Chronicles adds a further 300,000 to the number, it reads:

"Joab reported the number of fighting men to David. In all Israel there were one million one hundred thousand men who could handle a sword." (1 Chronicles 21:5 NIV)

In the Book of Samuel God threatens David, via a prophet, with the prospect of famine for failing to keep his people on the path of worship:

"So God went to David and said to him, 'Shall there come upon you seven years of famine in your land?'" (2 Samuel 24:13 NIV)

Whereas Chronicles shows a four year differential:

"So God went to David and said to him, 'This is your choice: Three years of famine, three months of being swept away before your enemies, with their swords overtaking you, or three days of plague in the land, with the angel of the Lord ravaging every part of Israel?'" (1 Chronicles 21:12 NIV)

There is some corroboration to the heinous end of this story however, with both books claiming that God killed seventy thousand men of Israel with a plague as a result of his ill-temper.

When David triumphantly brought the Ark back to Jerusalem the respective authors of Samuel and Chronicles offer opposite claims. With Samuel writing that the Ark was returned to the city after the Philistines had been defeated, whereas Chronicles chapters13 and 14 records that the Ark was brought back to the city before the battle against the old foe.

The life of King Ahaziah is contradicted between the Book of Kings and Chronicles. Kings claim that Ahaziah took reign over Jerusalem at the youthful age of twenty-two, whereas Chronicles writes:

"Ahaziah was forty-two years old when he became king."
(2 Chronicles 22:2 NIV)

These accounts may seem picky but a careful inspection of the Books of Samuel and the Books of Kings laid down side by side against Chronicles highlights dozens of numerical discrepancies. Discrepancies that further prove the fallibility of the Bible.

Chapter Fifteen & Sixteen - Book Of Ezra & Nehemiah

"If there is no Hell, a good many preachers are obtaining money under false pretences."
William Sunday

These two books tell of one of the most important events in Jewish history, the return to Jerusalem from exile in Babylon in 536 B.C

It is also of historical importance that this moment in history marked the first time whereby the Israelites no longer referred to themselves as such anymore, but adopted the name 'The Jews'. Signalling the end of the divided houses of Israel and Judah.

The period covered by both books is approximately 100 years, starting with the compassionate decision of the king of Persia, Cyrus to release the Jews back to their homeland after seventy years in captivity. Although the Bible claims that the Lord persuaded the Persian king to do so.

The author numbers the Jews of all returning tribes, with the total being 42,360 men, women and children. Not including 7,337 slaves, 737 horses, 245 mules, 435 camels and 6,720 donkeys.

It is important to note that whilst the Jews were freed, they were still ruled by Persia, but were given authority to rebuild their society and culture in peace.

Rebuilding of the Temple

When the Jews returned to Jerusalem they each contributed gold and silver proportionately to their respective wealth, to help lay the foundations to make Israel a strong nation once more. A larger percentage of this fund was to be used to rebuild the Temple in Jerusalem that the Babylonian's had destroyed more than seventy years prior.

The rebuilding of the Temple took twenty years and its completion marked celebrations of enormous nationalistic proportions. The Jews were united, their temple now finished and God was pleased. And thus the best way the Jews, through past experience, knew to please God, was through blood sacrifice:

> *"For the dedication of this house of God they offered a hundred bulls, two hundred rams, four hundred male lambs and, as a sin offering for Israel, twelve male goats, one for each of the tribes of Israel." (Ezra 6:17 NIV)*

That's a lot of dead animals!

Ezra Comes To Jerusalem

Ezra, although not technically a prophet according to the Jews, was known as a man of God, but more specifically as a man well versed in God's laws. His God mission was to restore national identity and to right the wrongs of all the failed kings of Judah and Israel. The Bible describes him as such:

> *"Ezra was a teacher well versed in the Law of Moses, which the Lord, the God of Israel, had given." (Ezra 7:6 NIV)*

Ezra's power to lead the Jews was ratified by the Persian king Artaxerxes, who wrote:

> *"And you, Ezra, in accordance with the wisdom of your God, which you possess, appoint magistrates and judges to administer justice to all the people of Trans-Euphrates – all who know the laws of your God. And you are to teach any one who do not know them. Whoever does not obey the law of your God and the law of the king must surely be punished by death, banishment, confiscation of property, or imprisonment." (Ezra 7:25-26 NIV)*

Ezra believed that the purity of Jewish blood had been polluted by intermarriages between Jews and non-Jews, i.e. racist bastard! This multiculturalism, he stated, had led the Jews away from God, during the seven hundred year period of the kings, towards pagan god worshipping et cetera. Ezra believed the best way for the Jewish people to start over again and regain God's trust and favour, was to eradicate all husbands or wives not of pure Jewish blood. In his address to tribal elders at the Temple, Ezra spoke:

> *"You have been unfaithful; you have married foreign women, adding to Israel's guilt. Now make confession to the Lord, the God of your fathers and do his will. Separate yourselves from the peoples around you and from your foreign wives." (Ezra 10:10-11 NIV)*

The elders were in unanimous agreement and the new Israel was built on a platform of blatant racist ideology.

Chapter Seventeen - Book of Esther

"I'm Jewish. I don't work out. If God had wanted us to bend over, He would have put diamonds on the floor."
Joan Rivers

This book is somewhat of an anomaly in the Bible, as it does not directly deal with God, or even mention a single word of God in its passages. Rather the book is the story of a Jewish orphan girl who is adopted by a Persian family and through her charm and good looks becomes the Queen of Persia through her marriage to King Xerxes in 480 B.C.

The Persian Empire at this time stretched all the way from the Nile to India and after another victorious military campaign, the Persian elite celebrated the glory and splendour of their king by throwing a 180 day long banquet in the king's palace, whereby guests drank free flowing wine from gold goblets. At this time King Xerxes was married to Vashti and in his drunken state, he summoned her to the main ballroom to dance provocatively, imagine Shakira meets Jenna Jamieson, for all the guests. But the Queen denied her husband's tawdry request, as she did not want to perform a titty dance for all and sundry. The king became enraged and called for her before the high court, ending their marriage there and then. The Court granted the marriage termination on the grounds that Persian noblemen were becoming concerned their wives would also deny their husband's requests to strip naked in front of their guests. There is some sound logic!

The King wasted no time in searching for a substitute bride and called to his personal attendants:

> *"Let a search be made for beautiful young virgins for the king. Let the king appoint commissioners in every province of his realm to bring all these beautiful girls into the harem at the citadel of Susa. Let them be placed under the care of Hegai, the king's eunuch, who is charge of the women; and let beauty treatment be given to them. Then let the girl who pleases the king be queen." (Esther 2:2-4 NIV)*

Hey one has to admit that it is pretty darn funny and cunningly practical that the king appointed Hegai, bereft of testicles, to be the one responsible for the vetting process for a bunch of hot chicks.

Hegai eventually rounded up several dozen of the world's sexiest women and kept them in the confines of the king's palace to be pampered and cared for, so they would look their very best on the day that the king would make his choice. It's good to be the king, right?

Hegai, the ball-less one, took particular interest in Esther and treated her most favourably over the other concubines in the king's harem. Hegai went out of his way to provide Esther with extra body exfoliations, beauty treatments and upper lip hair removal. And this process of beautification took more than one year, before Hegai believed the women to be adequately presentable for the king. The twist in this story, is that Hegai had no idea that Esther was of Jewish origin.

The Plot to Kill Xerxes

On the night that it was finally Esther's turn to perform and present for the king, she must have put on some show because the king was instantly besotted with her and wasted no time in crowning her the new Queen of Persia. The king, like Hegai, unknowing of her dirty little Jewish secret.

The Persian father who had adopted Esther from a very young age was a man by the name of Mordecai. And on the evening that followed the wedding ceremony, Mordecai overheard two of the king's guards talking of a plot to assassinate Xerxes. Mordecai quickly informed his adopted daughter, Queen Esther, who in turn informed her husband. The guards were arrested and hung to death the next morning.

The Jews Are Persecuted

Shortly after, the King elevated a man by the name of Haman to a seat higher than all other nobles in the land. During this ceremony Mordecai refused to bow before Haman. The guards seized Mordecai and interrogated him. During this Vegas style 'backroom' questioning session the interrogators were able to ascertain that the Queen was of Jewish descent and this information made its way back to Haman. Now, Haman did not want to embarrass the king who had treated him favourably, so Haman took a more Machiavellian like approach and suggested that it was the Jewish people causing problems for the Persians. He said to Xerxes:

> *"There is certain people dispersed and scattered among the peoples in all the provinces of your kingdom whose customs are different from those of all other people and who do not obey the king's laws; it is not in the king's best interest to tolerate them. If it pleases the king, let a decree be issued to destroy them and I will put ten thousand talents of silver into the royal treasury for the men who will carry out this business." (Esther 3:8-9 NIV)*

The king listened to Haman and replied with unconditional support:

> *"'Keep the money', he said, 'and do with the people as you please.'" (Esther 3:11 NIV)*

Military patrols were sent in dispatches to all corners of the kingdom to annihilate every Jew woman, child and man, young and old. And a law was put in place immediately to ratify this murderous edict.

Mordecai went to Esther to convince her to dissuade the king from carrying through the order to exterminate the Jews in Persia, but Esther initially refused to believe her husband to be that villainous. To which Mordecai pleaded:

> *"Do not think that because you are in the king's house that you alone of all the Jews will escape. For if you remain silent at this time, relief and deliverance for the Jews will arise from another place, but you and your father's family will perish. And who knows but that you have come to royal position for such a time as this? (Esther 4:13-14 NIV)*

Esther heeded the words of wisdom and warning and sent Mordecai with a message to disperse to all the Jews urging that they pray and fast for three days. And at the end of the third day she would do all in her power in attempting to stop the king's Jewish extermination plan, even if it meant losing her life.

As promised, she made her approach to her husband, the King and said she needed to ask a special favour of him. The King, still basking in the honeymoon glow of newlyweds, replied that he would give her half of the kingdom if that was her wish. Esther replied that rather than tell of her wish there and then on the spot, that she instead would prefer to ask the King at the conclusion of a banquet she was intending to host the following evening. Esther made a point of asking her husband that Haman be invited as an honorary guest.

Whilst Esther made preparations for the banquet, the King learnt that it was Mordecai that tipped Esther off about the planned coup of the two guards. The King wanted to demonstrate his gratitude by honouring Mordecai, Esther's adopted father, at the banquet. This news reached Haman that Mordecai would be in attendance as a guest at the banquet and he was utterly disgusted that a Jew would be honoured by the King and plotted to bring Mordecai's downfall. On the second day of the banquet, the King turned to his wife and asked her:

> *"When Esther, what is your partition? It will be given to you."*
> *(Esther 7:2 NIV)*

Esther replied:

"If I have found favour with you, O King and if it pleases your majesty, grant me my life – this is my petition. And spare my people – this is my request. For I and my people have been sold for destruction and slaughter and annihilation. It

we had merely been sold as male and female slaves, I would have kept quiet, because no such distress would justify disturbing the king." (Esther 7:3-4 NIV) The slavery of her people would not have warranted the Queen to bother her husband about?

Anyway, the king asked if there was anyone in particular she had in mind that posed a risk for her and her people. To which Esther answered:

"The adversary and the enemy is Haman."

Haman had been out manoeuvered and knowing his fate he begged for his life, but the King elected to appease his wife's wish and in a twist of irony he had Haman hung on the gallows that Haman had intended to execute Mordecai on.

The Oppressed Become The Oppressors

The same day the King issued a new edict that granted the Jews freedom from persecution. No Jew was to be harmed from this day on. For the Jews this was a time of joy, gladness and honour.

The edict further granted the Jews the right to destroy and annihilate anyone that intended bad things against them, thus as soon as the celebrations of freedom had subdued, the Jews went on a campaign of revenge killing. If you have seen the new Quentin Tarantino movie *Inglorious Basterds,* in which the movie's plot is based on a renegade pack of Jewish militia who inflict reciprocal cruelty on captured Nazi soldiers in the name of vengeance then this will frame the goings-on in this story. The citadel of Susa, was the first to come under Jewish attack and there they slaughtered five hundred men by the sword. By the time they had killed all those that hated the Jews, the number dead equalled more than seventy-five thousand. The blood lust continues.

Again a reminder that the Bible is more weighted towards revenge and anger rather than forgiveness and grace.

The Books of Poetry

Chapter Eighteen - Book of Job

"Expecting the world to treat you fairly because you are good is like expecting the bull not to charge because you are a vegetarian."
Dennis Wholley

The Book of Job is written as an ancient poem and tells of the misfortune of a character by the name of Job. In fact the great English poet, Lord Tennyson, called it, "The greatest poem, whether of ancient or modern literature".

The book, via this narrative, attempts to explain why bad things happen to good believers.

Job is named as a man that lived in a place called Uz, a man that lived a morally perfect life, feared God and denied evil. Job was married, but his wife's name is not disclosed by the author. He sired seven sons and six daughters. The prologue to this story includes an audit of Job's agricultural balance sheet listing his assets as seven thousand sheep, three thousand camels, five hundred oxen, five hundred donkeys and a vast number of human slaves.

"He was the greatest man among all people of the East." (Job 1:3 NIV)

Job was so righteous that he would perform animal sacrifices not out of guilt that he or his children had sinned, but as a pre-emptive measure in the event that they might have unknowingly sinned against God. Job was the poster boy for goodly, godly living and the author goes to some great pains to demonstrate this. However, Job's world soon gets turned upside down when a wager is made between God and Satan. Yes I too asked the obvious question, why didn't God just shoot Satan at the heavenly blackjack table, right there and then, rather than enter into a high stakes game of betting with a man's life? The only answer to that question can be that nothing has really made any sense to this point in the Book, so why change now?

The story has it that Satan hitched a ride with a few of God's angels to meet God face-to-face. God is surprisingly startled by the arrival of his uninvited guest and says:

"Where have you come from?" (Job 1:7 NIV)

Now doesn't this belie the claim that God is omniscient? Because if God was so, then surely he would have stated: "Hi Satan I saw you coming up the driveway, now what do you want?"

Nevertheless, Satan answered:

"I have come from roaming the earth and going to and fro in it." (Job 1:7 NIV)

Strangely, God still does not reply with words such as, "Oh I see and what is it that you want now?" Rather, he interjects with an out of context introduction of this character named Job:

"Have you considered my servant Job? There is no one on earth like him; he is blameless and upright, a man who fears God and shuns evil." (Job 1:8 NIV)

Satan immediately seizes on the opportunity to throw down a challenge to God and replies that Job worships God only because he is successful, with a loving and healthy family and vast wealth. Satan further asserts that if disaster struck Job, then his faith in God would surely wane. As you can see this is fast becoming a pissing-contest between the two polar opposite mythical forces and God succumbs to Satan's implied gambit:

"Very well, then, everything he has is in your hands, but on the man himself do not lay a finger." (Job 1:12 NIV)

Disaster Strikes

The following day after Satan and God had spat into their own respective palms and shook hands to seal the wager, poor old hapless Job was enjoying dinner in his living room, when one of his servants suddenly burst through the doors all panic stricken to inform his master that a nearby tribe had attacked all the donkeys, oxen and slaves and now all were dead from the sword of the Sabeans. Interestingly the author claims that this servant passing on the dreaded news is the only surviving, but then the very next paragraph states:

"Whilst he was still speaking, another of his servants came and said, 'The fire of God fell from the sky and burned up the sheep and the servants and I am the only one who has escaped to tell you.'" (Job 1:16 NIV)

The contradiction doesn't stop here, as a third servant enters Job's living room to tell him that three raiding parties from a nearby town stole all his camels and killed all his servants, except of course for the one passing this message. And then there is more:

"Yet another servant came and said, 'Your sons and daughters were feasting and drinking wine at the oldest brother's house, when suddenly a mighty windswept in from the desert and struck the four corners of the house. It collapsed on them and they are dead and I am the only one who has escaped to tell you.'" (Job 1:18-19 NIV)

With all his livestock, his human stock and now his family dead within minutes, Job stripped off all his clothes threw himself to the ground in grief and also in worship and said:

> *"Naked I came from my mother's womb and naked I shall depart. The Lord gave and the Lord has taken away; may the name of the Lord be praised." (Job 1:20 NIV)*

Thus the origin of the phrase, 'The Lord giveth and the Lord taketh'. Although Stephen King, prolific horror author and movie producer, summarized it best when he was once asked of the story of hapless Job:

> *"When his life was ruined, his family killed, his farm destroyed, Job knelt down on the ground and yelled up to the heavens, 'Why God? Why me?' and the thundering voice of God answered, 'There's just something about you that pisses me off.'"*

Half-time score: God 1 – Devil 0

Job had passed his first test of tribulation and continued to worship God despite his suffering, but Satan was still up for a fight and flew up to Heaven once more to lay down a challenge for a second round of betting.

The Second Test

Again Satan's arrival in Heaven catches God off-guard, as God asks, "Where did you come from?" Seems to me that a few mall cops may be handy to prevent such easy access to the kingdom. Satan ups the ante with the following dare:

> *"Skin for skin! A man will give all he has for his own life. But stretch out your hand and strike his flesh and bones and he will surely curse you to your face." (Job 2:4-5 NIV)*

God accepted this double-downed bet and Satan flew back to earth to unleash painful sores all over Job's body, from the top of his head to the soles of his feet. The author overlooking the fact that he had earlier stated that the conditions of this wager between God and Satan were that Job was not to be physically harmed. Anyway, Job's wife witnessing her husband's anguish, pleads with him to forsake this God he still worships because in worshipping him they have lost everything, their property and their family. Read this passage again and you can see that it is just another charge against women as evil temptresses. But Job maintained his faith and had passed the second test.

The Three Friends

When Job's three friends, Eliphaz, Bildad and Zophar, saw how much their good friend Job was suffering, they travelled to his house to offer comfort and solace. But upon finding Job huddled in the ashes of his home covered in pus filled sores, they barely recognised their defeated friend. In somewhat black comedy fashion the three friends tore of their clothes, wept aloud and sprinkled dirt on their foreheads in effort to share Job's pain. I have had some down moments in my life too, but if three of my friends turned up to my house and stripped naked whilst sprinkling dirt on themselves this would cheer me up somewhat. Nevertheless the three friends of Job sat silently with him for yes you guessed it, seven days and seven nights.

On the eighth day of this communal silence, Job finally was the first to speak and with tears streaming down his face he cursed the day he was born and said:

> *"May the day of my birth perish and the night it was said, 'A boy is born!' That day – may it turn to darkness; may God above not care about it; may no light shine upon it. May darkness and deep shadow claim it once more." (Job 2:3-5 NIV)*

> *"What I have feared has come upon me; what I dreaded has happened to me. I have no peace, no quietness; I have no rest, but only turmoil." (Job 2:25-26 NIV)*

But the three friends were in agreement that surely Job must have sinned so as to warrant this punishment. As Eliphaz rebuked:

> *"Consider now: Who being innocent, has ever perished? Where were the upright ever destroyed? As I have observed, those who plough evil and those who sow trouble reap it. At the breath of God they are destroyed." (Job 4:7-9 NIV)*

Thus begins a monotonous claim versus counter-claim between Job and his buddies, with each maintaining their certitude that Job must have done something to displease God to earn such wrath. But Job continued to defend his unblemished record of righteousness, whilst also wishing that God just put him out of his misery by ending his life:

> *"Oh, that I might have my request, that God would grant what I hope for, that God would be willing to crush me, to let loose his hand and cut me off." (Job 6:8-9 NIV)*

> *"I despise my life; I would not live forever. Let me alone; my days have no meaning." (Job 7:16 NIV)*

In Job's desperate moment of self-pity, Bildad and Shuhite echoed what Eliphaz had said to Job earlier:

> *"Your words are a blustering wind. Does God pervert justice? Does the almighty pervert what is right?" (Job 8:3 NIV)*

Some friends, huh? Further implying that Job is paying for sins he or his family had committed, albeit unwittingly, because it was unthinkable to his friends that a righteous man would be treated so ill by the God they all worshipped.

Finally after another thirty-two chapters of back and forth between Job and his friends, God appears before Job to provide him the comfort he is seeking, as God says to Job:

"Brace yourself like a man; I will question you and you shall answer me." (Job 40:7 NIV)

God then explains to Job why he has suffered, in an extremely verbose manner than resembles that of a drunkard, his explanation being that the righteous are so strong that they can withstand any dark hour, because faith in God is all they require to withstand hardships. This is the lesson he was trying to teach Job, that bad things happen to good people but faith will pull you through. This is a fine teaching, but I'd like to see a follow up chapter on why good things happen to bad people, probably even more so in my personal experience and understanding of historical events.

Job replies to God:

"I know that you can do all things; no plan of yours can be thwarted. Surely I spoke of things I did not understand, things too wonderful for me to know. My ears have heard of you but now my eyes have seen you. Therefore I despise myself and repent in dust and ashes." (Job 42:4-6 NIV)

The Story's Ending

God was unhappy with the advice that Job's friends had given him and so ordered the slaughter of seven bulls and seven rams in his honour to pay for their errs.

Job then prayed for the redemption of his friends and then God rewarded Job for his faithfulness by making him twice as rich as he was before the start of all this. Which goes to say that God believes money and wealth to be more important than the lives of his children, because God did nothing to bring back to life Job's sons and daughters murdered as a result of God's gambling habits.

Job Body Count: 60

God allowed Satan to kill all of Job's ten children plus all his servants which is guessed to have been at least fifty = 60.

Cumulative Body Count: 31,749,342

Final Old Testament Body Count: 31,749,592

It's interesting to note that Satan's body count is only 60 and he needed God's permission to achieve that, whilst God's death toll is almost 32,000,000 by conservative estimates.

Chapter Nineteen - Book of Psalms

"A good sermon should be like a woman's skirt: short enough to arouse interest but long enough to cover the essentials."
Ronald Knox

Without doubt Psalms is the most beloved book of the Old Testament by Jews and Christians alike. The Hebrew title of this book is the Book of Praises, which indicates that the contents include songs of worship, praise and prayer – a total of 150 psalms or songs are included.

The Book of Psalms is so indelible to the Jewish experience that many read this book from start to finish on a weekly or monthly basis, as it is viewed in Jewish tradition as a tool for gaining God's favour.

Similarly, Christians equally refer to this book to heighten the religious experience through song and in the early centuries of the Church it was expected that any candidate for the position of bishop would be able to recite the entire book from memory, something they often rote learned during their time as monks.

As to who authored this book, modern biblical scholars often attribute the works to various authors from different time periods throughout Israel's history, ranging from the time of David (approx. 1100-900 BCE) to the inter-testamental period (300-50 BCE).

Whilst reading Psalms 22, and 23 take a note of some of the phrases and keep in mind when we review the biography of Jesus in the New Testament. Some of these phrases are used to construct his life's story.

Psalm 22: Why Have You Forsaken Me

"My God, my God, why have you forsaken me?
"Why are you so far from saving me, so far from the words of my groaning?
"O my God, I cry out by day, but you do not answer, by night and am not silent.
"Yet you are the enthroned as the Holy One;
"You are the praise of Israel. In you our fathers put their trust;
"They trusted and you delivered them.
"They cry out to you and you were saved; In you they trusted and were not disappointed.
"But I am a worm and not a man, scorned by men and despised by the people.
All who are see me mock me; they hurl their insults, shaking their heads:
"He trusts in the Lord; let the Lord rescue him. Let him deliver him, since he delights in him.

"You brought me out of the womb; you made me trust in you even at my mother's breast. From birth I was cast upon you; from my mother's womb you have been my God.
"Dogs have surrounded me; a band of evil men has encircled me, they have pierced my hands and my feet. I can count all my bones; people stare and gloat over me. They divide my garments among them and cast lots for my clothing."

Psalm 23: The Lord is My Shepherd

"The Lord is my shepherd, I shall not be in want.
"He makes me lie down in green pastures, he leads me beside quiet waters, he restores my soul.
"He guides me in paths of righteousness for his name's sake.
"Even though I walk through the valley of the shadow of death,
"I will fear no evil, for you are with me;
"Your rod and your staff they comfort me.
"You prepare a table for before me in the presence of my enemies.
"You anoint my head with oil; my cup overflows.
"Surely goodness and love will follow me all the days of my life,
"And I will dwell in the house of the Lord forever."

Some other better known Psalms include the following:

Psalm 51: Have Mercy On Me O God

"Have mercy on me, O God,
"According to your unfailing love; according to your great compassion blot out my transgressions.
"Wash away all my iniquity and cleanse me from my sin.
"For I know my transgressions and my sin is always before me.
"Against you, you only, have I sinned and done what is evil in your sight, so that you are proved right when you speak and justified when you judge.
"Surely I was sinful at birth, sinful from the time my mother conceived me.
"Surely you desire truth in the inner parts; you teach me wisdom in the inmost place.
"Cleanse me with hyssop and I shall be clean; wash me and I shall be whiter than snow.
"Let me hear joy and gladness; let the bones you have crushed rejoice. Hide your face from my sins and blot out my iniquity.
"Create in me a pure heart, O God and renew a steadfast spirit within me. Do not cast me from your presence or take your Holy Spirit from me.
"Restore to me the joy of your salvation and grant me a willing spirit, to sustain me.

"Then I will teach transgressors your ways and sinners will turn back to you. Save me from your bloodguilt, O God, the God who saves me and my tongue will sing of your righteousness. O Lord, open my lips and my mouth will declare your praise.
"You do not delight in sacrifice, or I would I bring it; you do not take pleasure in burnt offerings. The sacrifices of God are broken spirit; a broken and contrite heart, O God, you will not despise.
"In your good pleasure make Zion prosper; build up the walls of Jerusalem. Then there will be righteous sacrifices, whole burnt offerings to delight you; then bulls will be offered on your altar."

What a terrible and psychologically damaging notion to convince children, to convince even well-functioning adults, that we are born in sin. Even as a foetus we are sinful and thus we must throw ourselves at the feet of this sky god to repent for sins we committed in uteri.

Psalm 137: By The Rivers of Babylon

"By the rivers of Babylon we sat and wept when we remembered Zion.
"There on the poplars we hung our harps, for there our captors asked us for songs, our tormentors demanded songs of joy; they said, 'Sing us one of the songs of Zion!'
"How can we sing the songs of the Lord while in a foreign land? If I forget you O Jerusalem, may my right hand forget its skill.
"May my tongue cling to the roof of my mouth if I do not remember you, If I do not consider Jerusalem my highest joy.
"Remember O Lord, what the Edomites did on the day Jerusalem fell.
"'Tear it down', they cried, 'Tear it down to its foundations!'
"O Daughter of Babylon, doomed to destruction, happy is he who repays you for what you have done to us – he who seizes your infants and dashes them against the rocks."

That last paragraph sure is a doozy. The Israelites whilst in exile in Babylon, are hoping that God will repeat his Egypt baby killing performance and that last sentence is as blood thirsty as any piece of literature I have ever read.

Chapter Twenty - Book of Proverbs

"The secret of a good sermon is to have a good beginning and a good ending, then having the two as close together as possible."
George Burns

The book of Proverbs is referred to as wisdom literature. The book does not tell a story but is rather a collection of one to two paragraph quotable quotes for one seeking a path of God-endorsed righteousness. The authorship of the book is not for certain, but the book itself claims to be the writings of Solomon, Agur the Oracle and Lemuel the Oracle.

In a way the book reads like a letter, written in bullet point form, from a dad to his son on the ways to live his life. Literally hundreds of one sentence proverbs for attaining wisdom with recurring themes that include: fearing God; shunning evil; rewards for living a righteous life; the folly of foolishness; the curse and temptation of wickedness; the fruits of laziness; advice for dealing with a nagging wife; the sin of beer and wine; the healing qualities of beer and wine; and recommendations for disciplining your slaves.

Interestingly the feminine gender of our species is given a pleasant token gesture, in that 'wisdom' is spoken of as a woman. Scholars cite the reason for this is that the Hebrew (chokmah) and Greek word (sophia) are of feminine origins. In the first of the thirty-one chapters this is evident:

> *"Wisdom calls aloud in the street, she raises at the head of the noisy streets she cries out, in the gateways of the city she makes her speech." (Proverbs 1:20-21 NIV)*

To be completely fair there are some brilliant pieces of writing in this book and quotations that truly can be used as guidance for living a good life. Some of the better ones include:

> *"Blessed is the man who finds wisdom, the man who gains understanding, for she is more profitable than silver and yields better returns than gold." (Proverbs 3:13-14 NIV)*

> *"The man of integrity walks securely, but he who takes crooked paths will be found out." (Proverbs 10:9 NIV)*

> *"When pride comes, then comes disgrace, but with humility comes wisdom." (Proverbs 11:2 NIV)*

> *"He who seeks good finds goodwill, but evil comes to him who searches for it." (Proverbs 11:27 NIV)*

> *"A fool finds no pleasure in understanding but delights in airing his own opinions." (Proverbs 18:2 NIV)*

But with my dark hair now showing speckles of silver as a symptom the ageing process and an inheritance from my mother, I am particularly fond of this passage:

> *"Grey hair is a crown of splendor; it is attained by a righteous life." (Proverbs 16:31)*

The grace that women are given in Proverbs does not last long however, as a return to the permeating theme that women are evil temptresses with evil intent to lure men into wicked ways is narrated from the fifth chapter. Offering this warning to all red-blooded males:

> *"For the lips of an adulteress drip honey and her speech is smoother than oil; but in the end she is bitter as gall, sharp as a doubled edged sword. Her feet go down to death; her steps lead straight to the grave. She gives no thought to the way of life; her paths are crooked, but she knows it not." (Proverbs 5:3-6 NIV)*

In chapter seven a passage is told of a young righteous man lured into the wanting loins of a married lady, with the message being that women are so evil that even the taken ones will try to budge you off the road to holy pursuit:

> *"With persuasive words she led him astray; she seduced him with her smooth talk. All at once he followed her like an ox going to slaughter, like a deer stepping into a noose, till an arrow pierces his liver like a bird darting into a snare, little knowing it will cost him his life." (Proverbs 7:22-23 NIV)*

Some of the stranger or at least somewhat humorous proverbs include:

> *"It is better to live in the desert than with a quarrelsome and ill-tempered wife." (Proverbs 21:19 NIV)*

> *"Wine is a mocker and beer a brawler; whoever is led astray by them is not wise." (Proverbs 20:1 NIV)*

Chapter Twenty-One - Book of Ecclesiastes

"Heaven won't take me, and Hell is afraid I will take over."
Bumper Sticker

A first glance of this book and it reads like a man wallowing in self-pity as evident by the author's opening paragraph:

"Meaningless! Meaningless! Utterly meaningless! Everything is meaningless." (Ecclesiastes 1:2 NIV)

The book claims to be the work of Solomon, but most scholars are of consensus that the writer be a descendent of Solomon, with the authorship guessed to be approximately 250 B.C.

On this issue of authorship, the New Bible Dictionary writes the following:

"Although the writer says that he was king over Israel (1:12) and speaks as though he were Solomon, he nowhere says that he is Solomon. The style of the Heb. is later than Solomon's time."

There are two significant messages this book tries to convey, one being that despite all earthly pleasures available to man man will only find true pleasure and happiness in worship of God. The second concerns death and mortality, with the author going so far as to say that the dead are dead and that there is no afterlife or resurrection. Thus the ultimate message is quite a sobering one for believers of Judaism or Christianity, that being that a meaningless life is followed by nothing but an eternity spent in the dirt (grave).

"A live dog is better off than a dead lion! For the living know that they will die, but the dead know nothing; they have no further reward and even the memory of them is forgotten. Their love, their hate and their jealousy have long since vanished; never again will they have a part in anything that happens under the son." (Ecclesiastes 9:5-6 NIV)

If you were thinking that the Old Testament was a path to Heaven, well you can readjust that mindset because Ecclesiastes makes it undisputedly clear that a lifetime of worship will reward us with absolutely nothing in the afterlife. Dead is dead!

The author tries to persuade us that the only pleasure worth pursuing is the pleasure derived from worshipping God and that the following pursuits will provide no pleasure at all:

Wisdom: *"For with much wisdom comes much sorrow; the more knowledge, the more grief." (Ecclesiastes 1:18 NIV)*

Pleasures: *"I bought male and female slaves. I acquired men and women singers and a harem as well – the delights of the heart of man." (Ecclesiastes 2:7-8 NIV)*

Work: *"I hated all the things I had toiled for under the sun, because I must leave them to the one who comes after me." (Ecclesiastes 2:18 NIV)*

Wealth: *"Whoever loves money never has money enough; whoever loves wealth is never satisfied with his income. This too is meaningless." (Ecclesiastes 5:10 NIV)*

Included in Ecclesiastes is a poem that many book and movie titles and song lyrics have drawn their inspiration from:

"There is a time to be born and a time to die,
"a time to plant and a time to uproot,
"a time to kill and a time to heal,
"a time to tear down the and time to build,
"a time to weep and a time to laugh,
"a time to mourn and a time to dance,
"a time to scatter stones and a time to gather them,
"a time to embrace and a time to refrain,
"a time to search and a time to give up,
"a time to tear and time to mend,
"a time to be silent and a time to speak,
"a time to love and a time to hate,
"a time for war and a time for peace."
(Ecclesiastes 3:1-8 NIV)

Chapter Twenty-Two - Song of Songs

"Most of us spend the first six days of the week sowing wild oats, then we go to church on Sunday and pray for a crop failure."
Fred Allen

This book is a love song between two characters, Solomon and his maid, a Shulamite woman. Before you get swept away by the romance of this song, as did singers Kate Bush and Sinead O'Connor who drew inspiration from here, remember that Solomon had seven hundred wives and three hundred concubines. This was a man who had a lot of love to hand around.

The song reads as dialogue between Samson and his maid, with a few interjections from some random women of Jerusalem. The book is one of the shortest of the Bible consisting of a mere 117 verses, as it depicts the courtship through to consummation of a fledgling romantic affair.

The authorship whilst claiming to be that of Solomon himself, is more likely to be that of an anonymous third-party and begins with the maid declaring her infatuation:

"Let him kiss me with the kisses of his mouth – for your love is more delightful than wine. No wonder the maidens love you! Take me away with you – let us hurry! Let the King bring me into his chambers." (Song of Songs 1:2-4 NIV)

You can't blame her for wanting to get her knickers off in quick time when she was competing for his attention against 1000 other of his women.

Solomon replies:

"I liken you, my darling, to a mare harnessed to one of the chariots of the Pharaoh. Your cheeks are beautiful with ear-rings, your neck with strings of jewels." (Song of Songs 1:9-10 NIV)

The maid obviously takes no insult in being likened to a horse and replies with subtle sexual provocation:

"While the king was at his table, my perfume spread its fragrance. My lover is to me a sachet of myrrh resting between my breasts." (Song of Songs 1:12-13 NIV)

Admittedly this song is filled with beautiful imagery throughout and little wonder it has inspired many song writers throughout history all the way back to Bach. To paraphrase this book would certainly not do justice to its poetry and thus I will leave you with one of my personal favourite verses:

"How beautiful you are, my darling! Oh how beautiful! Your eyes behind your veil are doves. Your hair is like a flock of goats descending from Mount Gilead. Your lips are like a scarlet ribbon; your mouth is lovely. Your temples behind your veil are like the halves of a pomegranate. Your neck is like the tower of David, built with elegance. Your breasts are like two fawns of a gazelle that browse among the lilies. All beautiful you are, my darling; there is no flaw in you." (Song of Songs 4:1-7 NIV)

The next time you arrive late home from the pub you can do worst than to modify the words of this song to your own situation and attach them to a bunch of roses. Whatever misdemeanour you have committed in the eyes of your wife, cannot withstand this kind of prose that typically makes women go weak at the knees.

Books of The Prophets

"If God dropped acid would he see people?"
Bumper Sticker

It has been said that the aforementioned books of poetry, that include Psalms and Proverbs, reflect the period known as the golden age of the Israelite nation, whereas the books of the prophets belong to the dark ages of God's chosen people. A period of time that saw the two kingdoms, Judah and Israel, divided into separate monarchies before eventually falling into captivity (exile) at the hands of the respective Babylonian and Assyrian empires.

As we will review in the coming sixteen chapters, there are a total of sixteen prophets, four of which are considered the 'major' prophets and the remaining twelve as the 'minor'.

God instituted the office of the prophet to communicate his message to the respective kings, with his primary duty being to remind the people of his time to walk the righteous walk. In this sense you can more or less think of the prophet as your high school hallway monitor, who ensured you were never late to class, guided you to the right doorway and snitched on you if you mucked about with your prankster buddies.

The period of the prophets covered approximately five hundred years from the tenth to fifth century BC.

I must admit I do love the books of the Prophets. Arguably the only men of the Old Testament that displayed an appreciation and understanding of social justice, as they protested against corruption and unfair treatment. And they didn't just protest via scribbling away on a few pieces of papyrus. They protested through street demonstrations, making them the Biblical ancestors of famous street performer David Blaine. The prophet Isaiah walked the streets naked to get his point across; Jeremiah walked the streets with a wooden yoke around his neck to symbolise his warning that the Israelites would soon be captives of neighbouring enemies as punishment for turning their backs on God; Ezekiel slept on the street for 430 consecutive days eating nothing but bread and human faeces.

Let us now learn the teachings and warnings of the prophets.

Chapter Twenty-Three - Book of Isaiah

"The gods are fond of a joke."
Aristotle

The first book of the prophets is that of Isaiah who wrote of his communication with both God and the Israelites of Judah in the final years prior to the exile into Babylon, whilst Israel was already in exile to Assyria.

Isaiah prophesized during the period of the kings of Judah that included the reigns of Uzziah, Jotham, Ahaz and Hezekiah. An interesting factoid is that Isaiah includes exactly sixty-six chapters, that being the same number as the Bible.

Prophecy Against Judah

During the reign of kings Uzziah and Jothan, Isaiah continually preached that the kingdom of Judah was on path to follow the destructive fate of Israel and this is reflected in Isaiah's first telegram from God which reads:

> *"For the Lord has spoken: I reared children and brought them up, but they have rebelled against me. The ox knows his master, the donkey knows his manger, but Israel does not know, my people do not understand. Ah, sinful nation, a people loaded with guilt, a brood of evildoers, children given to corruption! They have forsaken the Lord; they have spurned the Holy One of Israel and turned their backs on him." (Isaiah 1:2-3)*

He adds worldly emphasis to his warning with:

> *"The daughter of Zion is left like a shelter in a vineyard, like a hut in a field of melons, like a city under siege. Unless the Lord Almighty had left us some survivors, we would have become like Sodom, we would have been like Gomorrah." (Isaiah 1:8-9 NIV)*

Before adding symbolic warning by walking naked for a continual period of three years amongst the people of Judah. The message being that if Judah followed Israel's wicked ways they too would end up naked as prisoners in exile.

But Isaiah is quick to remind the kingdom of Judah that God will protect their way of life if they continue to follow his laws, forsake other Gods or Idols and pursue the righteous path, whilst simultaneously offering a not so subtle reminder of what fate awaits if they choose the wrong option:

> *"Though your sins are like scarlet, they shall be as white as snow; though they are red as crimson, they shall be like wool. If you are willing and*

obedient you will eat the best from the land; but if you resist and rebel, you will devoured by the sword." (Isaiah 1:18-20 NIV)

King Ahaz

Despite Isaiah's promise of God's intervention for disobedience the house of Judah continued to follow in the wayward footsteps of its sister kingdom Israel and evidently his prophetic words fell on deaf ears.

Matters continued to deteriorate in Judah in the eyes of God with the death of Uzziah and Jotham and the arrival of Ahaz as new king. Ahaz was an open idolater and followed many pagan traditions which really pissed off God and therefore Isaiah. In the background Assyria was readying itself to invade Judah and with a much superior military King Ahaz panicked that doom was surely heading his way. God summoned Isaiah to offer encouragement to Ahaz that he would protect the Judahan army and people. The message from God to Ahaz via Isaiah read:

"Be careful, keep calm and don't be afraid. Do not lose heart… If you do not stand firm in your faith, you will not stand at all." (Isaiah 7:4-9 NIV)

Ahaz's faith in God was flimsy at best and he sought the comfort of praising other idols in his place. Isaiah growing impatient told Ahaz in what is a stand out passage for Christians as false evidence that Isaiah foretold the arrival of Jesus Christ, that God would provide a sign of his power:

"Therefore the Lord himself will give you a sign: The virgin will be with child and will give birth to a son and will call him Immanuel. He will eat curds and honey when he knows enough to reject the wrong and choose the right, the land of the two kings you dread will be laid to waste. The Lord will bring on you and on your people and on the house of your father a time unlike any since Ephraim broke away from Judah – he will bring the king of Assyria." (Isaiah 7:14-17 NIV)

The above passage, as we will see, will become ammunition for the Jesus crew later in the New Testament. All this jibber-jabber of meta-physically impossible virgin births, a story told countless times throughout numerous ancient civilizations did little to impress or sway Ahaz, and as promised by God, the Assyrians invaded and took capture of Judah, with God sounding the trumpet for the enemy:

"Prepare for battle and be shattered! Devise your strategy but it will be thwarted; propose your plan, but it will not stand." (Isaiah 8:9-10 NIV)

God continues to call on Ahaz to fear him and bow to his power, whilst Isaiah continues with the foretelling of a messianic like child:

"For to us a son is given and the government will be on his shoulders. And he will be called Wonderful Counsellor, Mighty God, Everlasting Father, Prince of Peace." (Isaiah 9:6 NIV)

Christians interpret these passages as Isaiah's prediction of the birth of Jesus Christ, whilst Jews believe it to be the promise of a new king to deliver Israel back to the promised land in unity. Depending on what side of the fence you sit, you are free to interpret this meaning in whatever way you will.

Payback on The Babylonians

A common theme of the Bible is that God permits nations to inflict carnage on his chosen people when he deems that their behaviour deserves punishment, but in all instances the conquerors are smashed in swift God-led retribution upon such time that Israel corrects itself.

This is continued with Isaiah's prophecy of Babylon's doom whom the house of Israel are captive to. The prophet does not attempt to cover God's baby killing lust when he says:

"Whoever is captured will thrust through; all who are captured will fall by the sword. Their (Babylons') infants will be dashed to pieces before their eyes; their houses will be looted and their wives ravished." (Isaiah 13:15-16 NIV)

God not only endorsing infanticide but also rape. The claim for the Bible being a moral compass continues its slippery slide.

Further adding to the forecast of Babylon's demise:

"Babylon, the jewel of kingdoms, the glory of the Babylonians pride, will be overthrown by God like Sodom and Gomorrah. She will never be inhabited or lived in through all generations; no Arab will pitch his tent there, no shepherd will rest his flocks there." (Isaiah 13:19-20 NIV)

Isaiah adds that God's favour will then return back to Israel.

Death of Ahaz

In Isaiah 14:28 we read that King Ahaz died and in his place Hezekiah took reign over Judah. His kingdom began one of the most poignant periods of Israel's history. Assyria was a nation on the rise and had conquered Samaria during this period and thus with the winds of victory at her back the Assyrians were as determined as ever before to invade Judah in the fourteenth year of King Hezekiah's reign.

The king of Assyria sent his diplomatic envoy to Jerusalem to negotiate a deal that would offer the Israelites an honourable surrender and hence sparing needless bloodshed. The message from Assyria was direct and simple, "Surrender now or we will destroy you. As you can see our vast military out numbers yours!" King Hezekiah was defiant and informed the envoy that God was on his side and if Assyria attempted to attack then they would be at the mercy of an angry god.

The reply from Sennecherib, the king of Assyria was just as terse:

> *"Do not let the god you depend on deceive you when he says, 'Jerusalem will not be handed over to the king of Assyria'. Surely you have heard the kings of Assyria have done to all the countries, destroying them completely?" (Isaiah 37:10-11 NIV)*

Hezekiah could see the Assyrian troop built up from the fortified walls of the city and he became worrisome. His prayer to God for support reads:

> *"O Lord Almighty, God of Israel, enthroned between the cherubim, you alone are God over all kingdoms of earth. You have made heaven and earth...It is true, O Lord, that the Assyrian kings have laid waste all these peoples and their lands. They have thrown their gods into the fire and destroyed them, for they were not gods but only wood and stone, fashioned by human hands. Now, O Lord, deliver is from his hand, so that all kingdoms on earth may know that you alone, O Lord, are God." (Isaiah 37:16-20 NIV)*

God loves nothing more than his people denouncing his competitor gods and thus he was pleased with Hezekiah. God's gleeful reply to Hezekiah's prayer was precisely what the king was hoping for, as God said:

> *"He (king of Assyria) will not enter this city or shoot an arrow here. He will not come before it with shield or build a siege ramp against it. I will defend this city and save it, for my sake and for the sake of David my servant." (Isaiah 37:33-35 NIV)*

The following morning God sent down one of his angels and 85,000 Assyrian soldiers were 'mysteriously' found dead in their tents. The king of Assyria was the only survivor and he wasted no time in fleeing the scene, only to be hunted down by God who ordered his own sons to slay him with his own sword whilst he prayed to a foreign god.

Hezekiah Becomes Ill

Following God's slaughter of the threatening Assyrians, Hezekiah became sick and on his death bed, he prayed to God to spare his life as he felt he still had things to accomplish. To support his plea Hezekiah reminded God that he had been a righteous follower and had done his best to steer the Israelites away from the competitor gods in the region. God heard his prayer and replied:

> *"I have heard your prayer and seen your tears; I will add fifteen years to your life." (Isaiah 38:5 NIV)*

Following Hezekiah's miraculous return to health courtesy of Doctor God, neighbouring Babylon sent an envoy carrying gifts and a letter from the king of Babylon. Hezekiah welcomed the Babylonian diplomats and was most flattered that they would be so concerned for his health. During their visit Hezekiah showed the Babylonians all corners of his palace including his collection of gold, art and fine antiques. Shortly after their departure, Isaiah arrived on Hezekiah's doorstep and enquired as to whom the visitors were. The king answered that they were from Babylon, bearing gifts and he had provided them with a royal tour of his mansion. Then Isaiah said to Hezekiah:

> *"Hear the word of the Lord Almighty. The time will surely come when everything in your palace and all that your fathers have stored up until this day, will be carried off to Babylon. Nothing will be left, says the Lord. And some of your descendents, your own flesh and blood who will be born to you, will be taken away and they will become eunuchs in the palace of the king of Babylon." (Isaiah 39:5-7 NIV)*

Comfort in Exile

As the book of Isaiah is part history, part prophecy and part fairytale, it is somewhat non-sequential. As chapter 40 commences Isaiah's writings attempt to offer comfort to the kingdoms of Judah and Israel that are now in exile to Babylon and Assyria. We don't learn anything of the invasion and conquest in this book, only of Isaiah's objective to reassure God's people that the Lord has not forsaken them and he will intervene soon to rescue them out of bondage as he had done so in Egypt in the time of Moses.

> *"But you, O Israel, my servant, Jacob, whom I have chosen, you descendents of Abraham my friend, I took you from the ends of the earth, from its farthest corners I called you. I said, 'You are my servant'; I have chosen you and have not rejected you. So do not fear, for I am with you; do not be dismayed, for I am your God. I will strengthen you and help you; I will uphold you with my righteous right hand." (Isaiah 41:8-10 NIV)*

Isaiah further attempts to inspire the Israelites with a prediction of what God will do to their captors when the moment should come:

> *"All who rage against you will surely be ashamed and disgraced; those who oppose you will be nothing and perish. Though you search for your enemies, you will not find them. Those who wage war against you will be nothing at all." (Isaiah 41:11-12 NIV)*

Isaiah reminds Israel that the reason for their captivity is that God wanted it this way to teach them a lesson for acting foolishly in worshipping other Gods. God's message via his prophet is made clear: if you worship others

I will forsake and doom you, but if you obey me fully then I will love you. Wow talk about conditional love.

> *"I form the light and create darkness. I make peace and create EVIL. I the LORD do all these things." (Isaiah 45.7 NIV)*

God then promises Israel via Isaiah that Babylon will fall and Israel will once again become a great nation and sends a chilling warning to their captors:

> *"Sit in silence, go into darkness; Daughter of Babylonians; no more will you be called queen of kingdoms. I was angry with my people and desecrated my inheritance; I gave them into your hand and you showed them no mercy… Disaster will come upon you and you will not know how to conjure it away. A calamity will fall upon you that you cannot ward off with a ransom; a catastrophe you cannot foresee will suddenly come upon you." (Isaiah 47:5-11 NIV)*

Surely it is fair to ask where was God when his people were being ushered into the gas chambers by the Nazis? It seems the Babylonians treated the Israelites far kinder than the Germans. Fair question isn't it?

Israel Freed

God reminds the Israelites that only through obedience to him can they be guaranteed freedom and independence, with his usual tone of self worship God says:

> *"I am the Lord your God, who teaches you what is best for you, who directs you in the way you should go." (Isaiah 48:17 NIV)*

On the condition that they agree to stay on God's ordained path he frees them, telling them to stand up and walk out of Babylon:

> *"Leave Babylon, flee from the Babylonians! Announce this with the shouts of joy and proclaim it." (Isaiah 48:20 NIV)*

God Makes Some Bold Promises

An obvious euphoric God delirious with joy that his people have opted to follow his ways again, knowing they have learnt a valuable lesson in captivity gets a little adrenalin rush and begins to waffle out some incredible promises, including this doozy:

> *"Never again will there be in it an infant who lives but a few days, or an old man who does not live out his years; he who dies at a hundred will be thought of as a mere youth." (Isaiah 65:20 NIV)*

Chapter Twenty-Four - Book of Jeremiah

"You talk to God, you're religious.
God talks to you, you're psychotic."
Doris Egan

This book contains arguably the most ghastly sermon from God anywhere in the Bible. It is one in which he whets the appetite for cannibalism. God far from happy with Israel and Judah's worship of him promises the following if they continue to disobey him:

> *"I will make them eat the flesh of their sons and daughters and they will eat one another's flesh during the stress of the siege imposed on them by the enemies that seek their lives." (Jeremiah 19:9 NIV)*

God of love and kindness? He is the antithesis of such.

Jeremiah was born into a priestly family that resided on the outskirts of Jerusalem, his father an elder and teacher of the word of God. Unexpectedly, to Jeremiah anyway, God plucked this unlikely teenager from obscurity to be his chosen messenger to the people of Judah. Jeremiah's surprise is evident in this interchange between God and the young lad, with God calling to him:

> *"Before I formed you in the womb I knew you, before you were born I set you apart; I appointed you as prophet to the nations." (Jeremiah 1:5 NIV)*

No doubt startled by God's calling, Jeremiah replied in shock:

> *"Ah, Sovereign Lord. I do not know how to speak; I am only a child." (Jeremiah 1:6 NIV)*

God assured Jeremiah that he would put his words in the youth's mouth when the time came and that people would listen because of the wisdom that came forth. And God wasted no time in getting his newly appointed messenger into action and advised him that the Babylonians were preparing to attack the city from the north and that his holiness was permitting the siege because Jerusalem had forsaken him:

> *"They will come against her surrounding walls and against all the towns of Judah. I will pronounce my judgments on my people because of their wickedness in forsaking me, in burning incense to other gods and in worshipping what their hands have made." (Jeremiah 1:15-16 NIV)*

God promises to protect his new disciple and orders him to proclaim the following message to all of Jerusalem:

"I remember the devotion of your youth, how as bride you loved me and followed me through the desert, through a land not sown. Israel was holy to the Lord, the firstfruits of his harvest; all who devoured her were held guilty and disaster overtook them." (Jeremiah 2:2-3 NIV)

The above verse from God is just the opening shot of what is a several pages long litany of charges against Israel. Some of God's more poetic charges include:

"You have defiled the land with your prostitution and wickedness. Therefore the showers have been withheld and no spring rains have fallen. Yet you have the brazen look of a prostitute; you refuse to blush with shame." (Jeremiah 3:2-3 NIV)

Jeremiah urges the kingdom of Judah to change its way or they too will follow their sister monarchy into captivity. Like Isaiah he resorts to street performances to underscore his message. Jeremiah walked the streets with a wooden yoke around his neck as a symbolic warning that captivity awaits. But the elders and priests of Jerusalem accused Jeremiah of talking rubbish and dismissed him. And thus Judah continued to sin in the eyes of the space daddy which irked God to the point of furious rage. God had this message to pass through Jeremiah to Judah:

"The days are coming when people will no longer call it Topeth or the Valley of Ben Hinnom, but the Valley of Slaughter, for they will bury the dead in Topeth until there is no more room. Then the carcasses of this people will become food for the birds of the air and the beasts of the earth and there will be no-one to frighten them away. I will bring an end to the sounds of joy and gladness and to the voices of bride and bridegroom in the towns of Judah and the streets of Jerusalem, for the land will become desolate." (Jeremiah 7:32-34 NIV)

Ask yourself if the above words are that of a cool, calm and collected overseer or that of a hot-tempered, maniacal lunatic? And if that is not enough to whet your appetite then how about this for an endorsement of cannibalism?

The Israelites had become so pissed off with Jeremiah's forecasts of pending doom that they hatched a plot to murder the young prophet, but God provided him with advance warning and he escaped with his life. Jeremiah thanked the lord saying that he had been unknowingly, *"led like a lamb to slaughter"*. Which is where this phrase originates. In retaliation God promises to slaughter the plotters and also their sons and daughters.

Jeremiah continues his preaching to the Israelites, reminding them to obey all of God's commandments, because failure to do so would lead to their destruction. If this is sounding repetitive already, then read the Bible itself to see how monotonous this to and fro actually is. On one particular occasion Jeremiah prophesized the destruction of the city within the presence of the city's priests and they seized him for blasphemy with many demanding his execution:

"This man should be sentenced to death because he has prophesized against this city. You have heard it with your own ears." (Jeremiah 26:11 NIV)

Jeremiah defended his actions claiming he only spoke on behalf of God and that if they decided to kill him then they will have the blood of an innocent man on their hands and God would act swiftly to punish them. Jeremiah must have laid bare a convincing argument because they decided against any punitive action and furthermore they chose to hear what else God had to say through him.

Jeremiah had now earnt the respect of the elders and he was asked to send a letter to the Israelite exiles residing in Babylon under captivity, on behalf of Judah. The letter was ordained by God, of course, and reads as instructions for mounting a quiet resistance against the Babylonian captors:

"Marry and have sons and daughters; find wives for your sons and give your daughters in marriage, so that too may have sons and daughters. Increase in number; do not decrease." (Jeremiah 29:6 NIV)

This operation to breed like bunnies also came with a promise from God. A promise that stated that if the Israelites showed remorse for their wicked ways in serving other gods and returned to obey the laws of the covenant, then their captivity would end after seventy years.

As Jeremiah had promised on numerous occasions the Babylonians attacked Jerusalem and its people fell into captivity. This attack was, of course, sanctioned by God, as he said to his people in a gleeful tone:

"Do not deceive yourselves, thinking, 'The Babylonians will surely leave us.' They will not! Even if you were to defeat the entire Babylonian army that is attacking you and only wounded men were left in their tents, they would come out and burn this city down." (Jeremiah 37:9-10 NIV)

Jeremiah was thrown in prison accused of deserting as the Babylonians began to amass their armies to lay siege on Jerusalem, he remained in custody until the day the city was captured. Which took place in the ninth year of Zedikah's reign over Judah, which is estimated to have been 588 B.C.

After eighteen months of siege King Zedikah and his soldiers fled from the city, as they knew they were no match for the approaching Babylonians. The city fell without much of a fight and the invading army chased Zedikah and his soldiers to the plains of Jericho, where they were captured and brought before Nebuchadnezzar king of Babylon. The victorious king used swift vengeance and had Zedikah's two sons slaughtered in front of him, their bodies laid at his feet, before he was himself was blinded and carried away in chains to Babylon.

Nebuchadnezzar then called for the destruction of the royal palace in Jerusalem and for all the surviving Israelites within to be taken into exile. Word reached the Babylonian king that the prophet Jeremiah remained in custody within the city gates and thus commanded a small platoon to find him with instructions not to harm him. Within a day of this search and rescue mission, they found the young prophet bound in chains walking amongst his fellow captives. The commanding Babylonian officer read the following order to Jeremiah:

> *"The Lord your God decreed this disaster for this place. And now the Lord has brought it about; he has done just as he said he would. All this happened because you people sinned against the Lord and did not obey him. But today I am freeing you from the chains on your wrists. Come with me to Babylon, if you like and I will look after you; but if you do not want to, then don't come. Look, the whole country lies before you; go wherever you please." (Jeremiah 40:2-4 NIV)*

I find this quite bizarre that the king of Babylon would release an Israelite prophet of a god that he, the king, did not believe in or worship. It is bizarre rhetoric that makes absolutely no sense and is quite clearly a strip of adhesive to fill in the gaps of the story. Furthermore, Jeremiah, despite Nebuchadnezzar's generous offer, continued to cry out against Babylon and prophesized their eventual doom. Whilst not excluding the Egyptians and Assyrians from his lambast.

The bible does not mention Jeremiah's death, but scholars believe that he died somewhere in Egypt.

Chapter Twenty-Five - Book of Lamentations

"When I do good, I feel good; when I do bad,
I feel bad, and that is my religion"
Abraham Lincoln

The author of this book is widely accepted to be that of Jeremiah, although it does not claim to be so in any of the passages. This book includes five poems pertaining to the period of Israel's exile to Babylon and Assyria. They are poems of sorrow that articulate Israel's pain in refusing God, but

accepting of his punishment they belie
them. They are his chosen ones after all. N

First Poem

"How deserted lies the city, once so full of people! H who once was great among nations! She who was provinces has now become a slave. Bitterly she weeps at her cheeks. Among all her lovers there is none to comfort her. have betrayed her; they have become her enemies." (Lamentations

"Her foes have become her masters; her enemies are at ease. The Lo brought her grief because of her many sins. Her children have gone exile, captive before foe." (Lamentations 1:5 NIV)

Second Poem

"Without pity the Lord has swallowed up all the dwellings of Jacob; in his wrath he has torn down the strongholds of the Daughter of Judah. He has brought her kingdom and its princes down to the ground in dishonour." (Lamentations 2:2 NIV)

"The Lord is like an enemy he has swallowed up Israel. He has swallowed up all her places and destroyed her strongholds. He has multiplied mourning and lamentation for the Daughter of Judah." (Lamentations 2:5 NIV)

"The Lord has rejected his altar and abandoned his sanctuary. He has handed over to the enemy the walls of her palaces; they have raised a shout in the house of the Lord as on the day of an appointed feast." (Lamentations 2:7 NIV)

Third Poem

Highlights the pain of slavery.

"He has made my skin and my flesh grow old and has broken my bones. He has besieged me and surrounded me with bitterness and hardship. He has made me dwell in darkness like those long dead." (Lamentations 3:4-6 NIV)

"To crush underfoot all prisoners in the land, to deny a man his rights before the Most High, to deprive a man of justice – would not the Lord see such things?" (Lamentations 3:34-36 NIV)

f Ezekiel

rite for it;
live for it."

behalf whilst they lived
day and night, as they
. forsaken them and also
said love was easy right?
the fall of the Northern
eventual collapse of the
87 B.C. Heartbreakingly
laid flat and its Temple
chains and had returned
to an era of slavery, in Egypt. Hence they needed a prophet and not one to just remind them of their wrong-doings, but one who could offer them hope, hope to survive these troubled times. That hope came in the form of Ezekiel.

Shit Sandwich

An easy way to remember Ezekiel is as the dude that God forced to eat shit sandwiches for 430 consecutive days, this grotesque protest ordered by God to symbolize the prophesized fall of Jerusalem. How so you ask? God ordered Ezekiel to build a model of Jerusalem made of clay, then to lay on his side on the street facing towards the model. God says to Ezekiel:

> *"Lie on your left side and put the sin of the house of Israel upon yourself. You are to bear their sin for the number of days you lie on your side. I have assigned the number of days as the years of their sin. So for 390 days you will bear the sin of the house of Israel." (Ezekiel 3:20 NIV)*

God then tells Ezekiel that he is to turn onto his right side of his body whilst lying on the street next to model Jerusalem for a further 40 days, to represent the number of years of Judah's sin against God.

During this 430 day long street protest God says to Ezekiel that he must feed himself bread made from lentils, barley and beans. But here comes the kicker:

> *"Eat the food as you would a barley cake; bake it in the sight of the people, using human excrement for fuel. In this way the people of Israel will eat defiled food among the nations where I drive them said the Lord." (Ezekiel 4:12-13 NIV)*

I bet your Pastor didn't tell you this story in Church? What kind of megalomaniac would force one of his chosen prophets to do such a ghastly act for 18 consecutive months? The answer: God!

Pulp Fiction

For many of us the first time we heard of the book of Ezekial was mention of it in the movie 'Pulp Fiction' where Samuel L. Jackson's character would recite Ezekiel 25:17 prior to assassinating his victim:

> *"The path of the righteous man is beset on all sides with the iniquities of the selfish and the tyranny of evil men. Blessed is he who in the name of charity and good will shepherds the weak through the valley of darkness, for he is truly his brother's keeper and the finder of lost children. And I will strike down upon those with great vengeance and with furious anger those who attempt to poison and destroy my brothers. And you will know that my name is the Lord when I lay my vengeance upon thee."*

As a matter of fact a good dose of Hollywood fiction was applied to the above script as the actual passage of Ezekiel 25:17 reads:

> *"I will carry out vengeance on them and punish them in my wrath. Then they will know that I am the Lord, when I take vengeance on them."*

But credit to Quentin Tarantino for adding his skill of dramatization to what is a somewhat obscure passage in the Bible.

Bible Porn

The cheesy adult film scriptwriters in San Fernando Valley would have trouble matching this piece of horny prose:

> *"There she lusted after her lovers whose genitals were like those of donkeys and whose emission was like that of horses. So you longed for the lewdness of your youth, when in Egypt your bosom was caressed and your young breasts fondled." (Ezekiel 23:20-21 NIV)*

Makes you wonder why Christians have such an aversion to sex, because God's prophets fricken love the raunchy stuff.

Vision of God and Heaven

The opening chapter of Ezekiel begins with the prophet experiencing an obvious hallucinogenic vision of God, as he writes:

> *"The heavens were opened and I saw visions of God... I looked and I saw a windstorm coming out of the north - an immense cloud with flashing lightening and surrounded by brilliant light. The centre of the fire looked like glowing metal and in the fire was what looked like four living*

creatures. In appearance and their form was that of a man, but each of them had four faces and four wings...Their faces look like this: Each of the four had the face of a man and on the right side each had the face of a lion and on the left the face of an ox; each also had the face of an eagle. Such were their faces." (Ezekiel 1:1-11 NIV)

Four faced creatures? What the fuck was this guy smoking? And as his heavenly tour report proceeds it becomes even more fantastic.

"The appearance of the living creatures was like burning coals of fire of like torches. Fire moved back and forth among the creatures; it was bright and lightening flashed out of it. The creatures sped back and forth like flashes of lightening." (Ezekiel 1:13-14 NIV)

Ezekiel then tells of a voice out of nowhere, a voice that sounds like God, although he has never heard God speak before. With the sounding of this strange voice, the winged creatures fluttering off lightning bolts with four heads, ceased to move. And then God spoke to Ezekiel:

"Son of man, stand up on your feet and I will speak to you. I am sending you to the Israelites, to a rebellious nation that has rebelled against me; they and their fathers have been in revolt against me to this very day." (Ezekiel 2:3 NIV)

God then hands Ezekiel a scroll containing words of lament and mourning on either side of the document. Unfortunately, Ezekiel doesn't describe God's penmanship, but God in true secret agent fashion does command his prophet to eat the scroll immediately after reading it. God promises him that the scroll is quite nourishing and Ezekiel says

"So I ate it and it tasted as sweet as honey in my mouth." (Ezekiel 3:3)

I hope you are having a giggle, because I am on the floor right now.

Warning to Israel

God is pissed and makes it clear to Ezekiel in no uncertain terms that death awaits those who do not repent their sins, cease their wickedness and return to worshipping him. God underlines this instruction that their blood will be on Ezekiel's head if he is unable to lead the Israelites back to his heavenly master.

God lists a number of actions that will result in their deaths:

"If you warn a wicked man and he does not turn from his wickedness or from his evil ways, he will die for his sin."

"When a righteous man turns from his righteousness and does evil, he will die."

God also informs Ezekiel that he has put a some kind of voodoo spell on his prophet which makes Ezekiel's tongue stick to the roof of his mouth when God is not ready for any telegrams to be passed to his people, but will release his tongue at the appropriate time. I have worked for some tough bosses in my time, but this guy takes the prize.

God then spills out passages of doom for Ezekiel to relay to the Israelites. A promise that the following will be their fate if they have not learnt their lessons for worshipping other gods:

> *"I will bring a sword against you and I will destroy your high places. Your altars will be smashed; and I will slay your people in front of your idols. I will lay the dead bodies of the Israelites in front of their idols and I will scatter your bones around your altars. Wherever you live, the towns will be laid waste and devastated… Your people will fall slain among you and you will know that I am the Lord." (Ezekiel 6:3-7 NIV)*

Chapter after chapter Ezekiel writes that he has been instructed by God to illustrate what the end of days for the Israelites looks like if they refuse to bend to God's will. God's motivational modus operandi is not all stick though as he does dangle the carrot of freedom just out in front of the Israelite's gaze:

> *"I will gather you from the nations and bring you back from the countries where you have been scattered and I will give you back the land of Israel again." (Ezekiel 11:17 NIV)*

We find that God's love of violent retribution is not just confined for the sinner but also for those that he believes are guilty by association. Which means that if your cousin murdered a man, then because you are distantly related you are guilty of the crime too, even if you weren't even in the country at the time of the crime or had never spoken with this relative. You are still guilty of their sins. Thank Christ we don't base our judicial systems on this irrational, insane logic.

> *"If a country sins against me by being unfaithful and I stretch out my hand against it to cut off its food supply and send famine upon it and kill its men and their animals, even if these three men – Noah, Daniel and Job – were in it, they could save their own sons or daughters by their own righteousness." (Ezekiel 14:12-14 NIV)*

Oh and in case you had forgotten God was an uncontrollably jealous, vengeful bastard, he is always there to remind you:

> *"I will bring upon you the blood vengeance of my wrath and jealous anger." (Ezekiel 16:38 NIV)*

Like the prophet Jeremiah, Ezekiel prophesizes that God will destroy Babylon, Moab, Assyria, Ammonm, Philistia, Tyre, Sidon and Edom before returning the Israelites back to their promised land. Ezekiel writes of a vision in which God shows him the building plans for the reconstruction of the

Temple in Jerusalem and also provides Ezekiel with instructions as to how the new land is to be divided amongst the Israelites post-independence.

Chapter Twenty-Seven - Book of Daniel

"I do not feel obliged to believe that the same God who has endowed us with sense, reason, and intellect has intended us to forgo their use."
Galileo Galilei

Daniel was born to a family of high rank and nobility within the city of Jerusalem and was only sixteen years of age when the Babylonians took siege of the city in 587 B.C. The Babylonians killed many of the Israelites that held offices of high position but king Nebuchadnezzar decreed that handsome young men with physical attributes and an aptitude for learning and from families of nobility would be reserved a special place in the king's palace to study Babylonian culture, literature and language. This indoctrination would last a period of three years and the best of the brightest would take up high positions within government.

Immediately Daniel stood out from the other lads, as he refused to dine on the kings' luxurious food and wine in which his fellow Babylonian Studies undergrads scoffed on. And thus Daniel grabbed the immediate attention of God hovering somewhere above. Daniel claimed the food to be impure and not suitable for an Israelite devoted to his God and he cunningly defended his rejection of the king's food offerings with claims that a poor diet would not be conducive to learning. Instead Daniel suggested that a diet of vegetables and water would facilitate better study habits. The king agreed to put Daniel's recommended diet to the test and half of the select Israelite boys remained on the kings' diet and the other half on Daniels. After ten days it became apparent that Daniel's diet team were in far better physical and mental condition and from that point on Brussels' sprouts and water was their dinner. You can imagine how popular Daniel was amongst the others can't you? As popular as a cold sore on a first date I think!

God began to speak to Daniel in visions and dreams from this point forward and the king was astonished at the young Israelite's wisdom and foresight.

"In every matter of wisdom and understanding about which the king questioned him, he found him ten times better than all the magicians and enchanters in his whole kingdom." (Daniel 1:20 NIV)

In the second year of king Nebuchadnezzar's reign the king had trouble sleeping and he experienced many dreams. These dreams made the king restless and he summoned for his best magicians, astrologers and sorcerers to interpret his visions. The magic men and the voodoo scientists failed to offer the king a satisfactory explanation and he ordered their executions. The king then called for Daniel and three of his learned buddies to ease the king's restlessness, but Daniel had heard that the star gazers had been placed on death row for failing to satisfy their king. This made Daniel terribly nervous and there is no better moment for prayer time than when you are close to shitting your pants and thus Daniel called out to the sky Dictator:

> *"Praise be to the name of God for ever and ever; wisdom and power are his. He changes times and seasons; he sets up kings and desposes them. He gives wisdom to the wise and knowledge to the discerning. He reveals deep and hidden things." (Daniel 2:20-22 NIV)*

Daniel was summoned by the guards and brought before the king. Daniel asked that the magicians and sorcerers be spared should he be able to provide a satisfactory interpretation of the king's dream, to which the king agreed. God then spoke through Daniel and said that his dream represented the future. The king's dream included a statue and a rock carved out of a mountain, carved out by hands that were not human, to which Daniel with God as his Svengali said:

> *"The God of heaven will set up a kingdom that will never be destroyed, nor will it be left to another people. It will crush all those kingdoms and bring them to an end, but it will itself endure forever. This is the meaning of the of the vision of the rock cut out of a mountain, but not by human hands – a rock that broke the iron, the bronze, the clay, the sliver and the gold to pieces." (Daniel 2:44-45 NIV)*

The king was impressed and lavished praise and gifts upon Daniel for this insight, although the dream interpretation was a not so covert message that God was coming to destroy Babylon and in its place make Israel a mightier nation than it had ever been before.

Not too long after the king had a second dream and called for Daniel to interpret it for him. Daniel this time adopted a little more straight talk and thus pulled no punches in explaining to the king that his reign and his kingdom was coming to an end. The king scoffed at this interpretation and didn't give it any further thought until one year later whilst walking on the roof of his palace, he said aloud:

> *"Is not this the great Babylon? I have built this royal residence, by my mighty power and for the glory of my majesty." (Daniel 4:30 NIV)*

As the above words were leaving his mouth, God spoke to the king from somewhere high above:

"This is what is decreed for you, King Nebuchadnezzar: Your royal authority has been taken from you. You will be driven away from people and will live like wild animals; you will eat grass like cattle. Seven times will pass by for you until you acknowledge that the Most High is sovereign over kingdoms of men and gives them to anyone he wishes." (Daniel 4:31-32 NIV)

God's words came true for Nebuchadnezzar immediately and he was driven away from his people and ate grass like cattle. Nebuchadnezzar not only walked away from his throne, but devoted the rest of his life to worshipping the God of the Israelites.

In his place Nebuchadnezzar's son, Belshazzar, became new king of Babylon. To celebrate his ascension to the throne Belshazzar threw a huge banquet party in his own honour. Present were more than a thousand guests including his numerous wives and concubines. The honoured guests drank wine from gold goblets that had been looted from the Temple of God in Jerusalem and as they drank they gave thanks to the many pagan gods they worshiped such as the God of gold and the God of silver.

The festive atmosphere was abruptly interrupted by the appearance of a human hand, a hand suspended in mid air, unattached to a human body. This floating hand began to write a cryptic message on the wall nearest to the lamp stand in the royal palace. And this is where the expression the 'writing on the wall' originates.

The new king, visibly shaken, offered the prize of a gold chain if anyone could interpret what had been written. One of the king's servants informed him that whilst his father Nebuchadnezzar was king he often used the Israelite Daniel to interpret mysteries for him and hence Belshazzar wasted no time in summoning Daniel.

Daniel, not mincing words, reminded the new king that it was God that gave his father the power to rule over his people and it was God that stripped him of his throne because he became arrogant and proud and failed to thank God for his power. This is why he was sent out into the long grass, so to speak. Daniel's words to the king:

"You have set yourself up against the Lord of heaven. You had the goblets from his temple brought to you and your nobles, your wives and your concubines drank wine from them… Therefore he sent you this inscription." (Daniel 5:23-24 NIV)

The inscription on the wall contained four words:

MENE, MENE, TEKEL, PARSIN

The Bible says the above words mean the following:

Mene: God has numbered the days of your reign and brought it to an end.

Tekel: You have been weighed on scales and found wanting.

Parsin: Your kingdom is divided and given to the Medes and Persians.

Later that same night Belshazzar, king of Babylon, was found murdered is his bed and Darius the Mede took over the reins of the kingdom at the age of sixty-two.

Daniel's Dream

Like the preceding books of the prophets, I urge you return to this passage at the conclusion of reading the Book of Revelations, as this serves as another inspiration for later plagiarism.

Daniel tells of a dream he had one night whilst Belshazzar was still alive:

> *"In my vision at night I looked and there before me were the four winds of heaven churning up the great sea. Four great beasts, each different from the others, came up out of the sea. The first was like a lion and it had the wings of an eagle. I watched until its wings were torn off and it was lifted from the ground so that it stood on two feet like a man and the heart of a man was given to it." (Daniel 7:2-4 NIV)*

Daniel then describes the bizarre physical features of the first and second beasts with the later two straight out of a 60s horror movie:

> *"This beast looked like a leopard. And on its back it had four wings like those of a bird. This beast had four heads and it was give authority to rule. After that, in my vision at night, I looked and there before me was a fourth beast – terrifying and frightening and very powerful. It had large iron teeth; it crushed and devoured its victims and trampled underfoot whatever was left. It was different from all the former beasts and it had ten horns." (Daniel 7:6 NIV)*

Remember that the concept of Hell, an eternal suffering is nowhere to be found in the Old Testament, but from these dreams and writings it is obvious that the early Christian church of Paul drew on these passages to create the concept of a destination for the damned.

And for the benefit of the last chapter of this book, I offer another of Daniel's visions for your reference:

> *"As I was thinking about this, suddenly a goat with a prominent horn between his eyes came from the west, crossing the whole earth with out touching the ground... The goat became very great, but at the height of his power his large horn was broken off and in its place four prominent horns grew up towards the four winds of heaven." (Daniel 8:5-8 NIV)*

The End Times

Daniel's final chapter promises end times and for the first time in the Old Testament the promise of resurrection and after-life is suggested.

> *"There will be a time of distress such as had not happened from the beginning of nations until then. But at that time your people – everyone whose name is found written in the book will be delivered. Multitudes who sleep in the dust will awake: some to ever-lasting life, others to shame and everlasting contempt. Those who are wise will shine like the brightest of the heavens and those who lead many to the righteousness, like the stars for ever and ever." (Daniel 12:1-4 NIV)*

Chapter Twenty-Eight - Book of Hosea

"Some things have to be believed to be seen."
Ralph Hodgson

The Book of Hosea is the first of twelve books of the 'minor' prophets, not minor in terms of inferior to Isaiah, Jeremiah, Ezekiel, or Daniel, but minor in terms of the amount of material written.

Hosea was a prophet sent by God to prophesize to the Jews of the Northern Kingdom of Israel and he did so during the period of Jeroboam II's reign in approximately 700 B.C. This is a significant moment in Middle Eastern history as this is also the period when Rome was beginning to establish itself in the region, thus a period of great political and social instability.

Hosea has often been referred to as the Jeremiah of the Northern Kingdom, remembering that Jeremiah prophesized to those in the Southern Kingdom of Judah.

The opening passage of Hosea begins with God commanding Hosea to marry a prostitute named Gomer. Hosea does not love her, but God being God made it clear that this was not a negotiation. Hosea obeys and marries this woman of ill repute and she bears him two sons and a daughter. God in his usual pissy tone orders Hosea to name his first as so:

> *"Call him Jezreel, because I will soon punish the house of Jehu for the massacre of Jezreel and I will put an end to the kingdom of Israel. In that day I will break Israel's bow in the Valley of Jezreel." (Hosea 1:4-5 NIV)*

Hosea eventually falls in love with the woman God has pre-arranged for him, but then becomes heartbroken when she runs off to continue plying her ass for cash at the 'Boom Boom Room' in Bethel. Hosea cries on God's shoulder:

> *"Their mother has been unfaithful and has conceived them in disgrace. She said, 'I will go after my lovers, who give me my food and my water, my wool and my linen, my oil and my drink.'"* (Hosea 2:5 NIV)

God tells Hosea to lift up his droopy chin and go forth to lure his prostitute wife back to him:

> *"Go, show your love to your wife again, though she loved by another and is an adulteress. Love her as the Lord loves the Israelites, though they turn to other gods and love the sacred raisin cakes."* (Hosea 3:1 NIV)

God just help himself to a little jealous filled jab at the Israelites, but now he is envious of the people he created and the people he chose to be his favourites because they love raisin cakes?

Hosea obeys his invisible master and goes on a shopping spree purchasing silver and grain. He then goes down the brothel she performs tricks at, pulls her outside for a chat and on hands and knees begs for her to return to him, with the offering the aforementioned gifts, but on the proviso:

> *"You are to live with me for many days; you must not be a prostitute or be intimate with any man and I will live with you."* (Hosea 3:2-3 NIV)

Here endeth this strange love story, as the remainder of Hosea's writings echo that of the major prophets, as he too prophesizes the downfall of Israel because they now worship other gods.

> *"Hear the word of the Lord, you Israelites, because the Lord has a charge to bring against you and who live in the land: There is no faithfullness, no love, no acknowledgment of God in the land."* (Hosea 4:1 NIV)

Hosea forewarns that the end of their kingdom is near and because of their idol worshipping they can count on God not coming to save them unless they change their ways.

Chapter Twenty-Nine - Book of Joel

"Generally speaking, the errors in religion are dangerous; those in philosophy only ridiculous."
David Hume

Joel is considered to be one of the earliest prophets, as biblical scholars widely believe him to have lived in the time of Elijah (see Book of Kings). The name Joel, in Hebrew, means "Jehovah is my God" and God chose Joel to interpret natural occurrences into God's meaning, so that the Israelites would understand.

He begins with the story of an invasion of locusts that destroy all the crops within the Southern Kingdom of Judah:

"What the locust swarm has left the great locusts have eaten; what the great locusts have left the young locusts have eaten, what the young locusts have left other locusts have eaten." (Joel 1:4 NIV)

I think he could have made the above passage far simpler to understand with the words, "Shit the locusts have eaten everything!" Talk about a word-waster!

Upon waking to see this devastation, which is in a dream of course as it is a prophecy and not a news bulletin, he yells at the village folk to wake up from their wine induced hangovers:

"Wail all you drinkers of wine, for it has been snatched from your lips. A nation has invaded my land, powerful and without number; it has the teeth of lion, the fangs of a lioness. It has laid waste my vines and ruined my fig trees." (Joel 1:5-7 NIV)

This prophecy of using the locusts parable is Joel's unique way of conveying God's message that destruction is on the way because his people are acting like drunkards in their worship of other gods.

Joel demands that the people of Judah repent for their sins and as an immediate call to action he summons an assembly to demand that the declaration of a holy fast in the one true God's honour. The elders and priests refuse to listen to Joel's food abstinence request, thus prompting Joel to forecast pending an immediate doom at God's behest:

"Blow the trumpet in Zion; sound the alarm on my holy hill. Let all who live in the land tremble, for the day of the Lord is coming. It is close at hand – a day of darkness and gloom, a day of clouds and blackness." (Joel 2:1-2 NIV)

A Return to Glory

Like his fellow prophets, Joel foretells that the Israelites will be returned to a state of glory after they have been forced to learn the hard way in captivity.

"In those days and at that time, when I restore the fortunes of Judah and Jerusalem." (Joel 3:1 NIV)

Chapter-Thirty - Book of Amos

"Maybe this world is another planet's hell."
Aldous Huxley

Amos differs from the earlier accounted prophets in the fact that he did not come from a family of wealth or nobility, nor did he have any formal religious training. He was wholly and simply a shepherd of sheep from a town called Tekoa approximately 15 miles from Jerusalem. Now whilst his origins were obviously that of Judah the Southern Kingdom of Israel, his writings concerned mostly the Northern Kingdom of Israel.

Amos begins with a declaration that God will soon cast judgement upon all neighbouring nations including Damascus, Gaza, Edom, Tyre, Ammon and Moab. The following words of God were spoken to Amos whilst Israel and Judah were at the zenith of their powers within the Middle East, in approximately 800 B.C, whilst Jeroboam II was king of Israel and Uzziah king of Judah:

"For three sins of Damascus, even for four, I will not turn back my wrath. Because she has threshed Gilead with sledges having iron teeth, I will send fire upon the house of Hazael that will consume the fortresses of Ben-Hadad. I will break down the gate of Damascus; I will destroy the king who is in the Valley of Aven and the one who holds the sceptre in Beth Eden." (Amos 1:3-5 NIV)

Using somewhat identical words, God promises the destruction to all the neighbouring nations in singularly targeted message. But he doesn't provide his beloved Israelites favourable treatment and promises the following judgment upon the Northern Kingdom:

"Now then, I will crush you as a cart crushes when loaded with grain. The swift will not escape, the strong will not muster their strength and the warrior will not save his life." (Amos 2:13 NIV)

God voices his jealousy once again that Israel refuses to worship him and him only and calls on Amos to demand that the nation repents for its sins, or they will soon know of God's wrath.

"You have lifted up the shrine of your king, the pedestal of your idols, the star of your god – which you made yourselves. Therefore I will send you into exile beyond Damascus." (Amos 5:26 NIV)

Amos prophesizes the destruction of Israel and writes of the vision that God had in store for them. A vision that demonstrates God's murderous intent. As God reveals to Amos that he won't be satisfied until every Israelite idol worshipper is hunted down and destroyed. God tells Amos that he will hunt down every Israelite sinner and kill them by the sword, whether they are hiding in the mountains, in the sea, in the valleys, or underground. No one will be able to hide from God's murderous rampage, no matter how artful they are at the do or die version of the game of hide 'n seek. But the final verse once again makes evident God's schizophrenic nature, as the celestial lord promises to restore Israel to its glory after he has destroyed it.

Chapter Thirty-One - Book of Obadiah

"Everyone wants to go to Heaven but no one wants to die."
Joe Louis

The Book of Obadiah is the shortest of the Old Testament containing only twenty one verses. The theme of the book is that God will not hesitate to destroy any nation that becomes an obstacle for Israel's agenda. The nation made an example of is Edom whose fortified city of Petra was perched high in the mountains, making it impossible for invading armies to conquer due to its rugged vertical cliffs and heavily fortified walls. Edom had been used as an arms depot and rally point for attacks against the Israelites as far back as Abraham's times. A perpetual thorn in the side of Israel, this was the Biblical version of Hitler's 'Eagles Nest' and hence God decreed the destruction of Edom:

> *"Rise and let us go against her for battle... The pride of your heart has deceived you, you who live in the rocks and make your home on the heights, you who can say to yourself, 'Who can bring me down to ground?' Though you soar like an eagle and make your nest among the stars, from there I will bring you down." (Obadiah 1:1 NIV)*

There is no reference to time of writing for this prophecy but we do know that Edom was destroyed the Babylonian army in 150 B.C.

Chapter Thirty-Two - Book of Jonah

"Give a man a fish, and you'll feed him for a day; give him a religion, and he'll starve to death while praying for a fish."
Unknown

The monotony of the prophets passing on the same predictable message from God is briefly interrupted by this marvellous piece of literary fiction. Further, it is one of a select few stories of the Bible that you can tell your children before they fall asleep peacefully at night without inflicting lifelong trauma on their pliable young minds.

God had now selected Jonah, seemingly at random, to add to his growing stable of prophets. God called from the skies commanding that Jonah go to the capital city of Assyria, the nation that would eventually conquer the Northern Kingdom of Israel. The Lord called:

> *"Go to the great city of Nineveh and preach against it, because its wickedness has come before me." (Jonah 1:2 NIV)*

Jonah heard God speak but instead of obeying he fled to hide from God, which seems as profitable as throwing rocks at the sun, considering God is everywhere if you believe him true. Nevertheless Jonah makes it to a town called Joppa to board a fishing boat to Tarshish. Jonah paid his fare, boarded the yacht and hid below deck so that he could dupe God into believing he really wasn't there at all.

Well God did see him and soon after the boat had begun its sea crossing, God whipped up a huge storm that rocked the small vessel so violently that it threatened to rip it apart sending its occupants to an early and watery grave. The men aboard were so terrified that they did what religiously terrified men do, they prayed to their individual and respective gods, seeking protection. They prayed to all types of gods except for '*The*' God and the storm increased its intensity. Jonah was summoned to the deck by the other passengers and asked to join in a panic stricken version of drawing straws to see who was responsible for this storm because it was assumed that that person must have pissed off his god so much that they were all being punished. Jonah drew the short straw and they asked him two questions: what god he worshipped and what had he done wrong to bring this terror upon all of them? Jonah answered:

> *"I am a Hebrew and I worship the Lord, the God of heaven, who made the sea and the land." (Jonah 1:9 NIV)*

Jonah also added that he had heard God speak to him but he failed to acknowledge him and instead this boat trip was his attempt to flee God's calling.

This news made the others even more terrified than before because they could see that this god had powers that they were now pretty sure that their gods didn't. Jonah was wracked with guilt and came to the conclusion that the only way to save his fellow sailor's lives was to throw himself into the sea to appease God for his wrongdoing. This idea seemed ok to the others and they tossed Jonah into the wild ocean and immediately the water became so still that it looked like a sheet of glass. The men felt a little pang of grief that they had to sacrifice Jonah's life to save their own, but after a moments memorial they sailed off on their merry way.

But Jonah was not dead. How could he possibly survive alone without a raft in the middle of the sea, I hear you ask? Well God had that all covered, as written in the book:

"The Lord provided a great fish to swallow Jonah and Jonah was inside the fish three days and three nights." (Jonah 1:17 NIV)

Now not only was he swallowed by a huge fish, presumably a whale, but this is where the Bible becomes a matter of your own interpretation. I don't care much for semantics, fish or whale, he is now living inside a creature for three full days. God damn that would stink! Imagine the odour of decaying sea life and bile? Yuck!

Even more impressive though is the fact that not only did he manage to survive in the fish's belly but he spent that entire time in prayer.

"From inside the fish Jonah prayed to the Lord his God. He said: 'In my distress I called to the Lord and he answered me… Those who cling to worthless idols forfeit the grace that could be theirs. But I, with a song of thanksgiving, will sacrifice to you. What I have vowed I will make good. Salvation comes from the Lord'." (Jonah 2:1-9 NIV)

I would argue that salvation came in a much better form for the other passengers who made it safely back to port without having to spend three days cooped up in a whale's stinky gut. I am sure they were just as thankful to their own respective gods as was Jonah, but without the bullshit story to relay to their friends.

Jonah now convinced of God's glory goes to Nineveh as ordered and tells the Assyrians there:

"Forty more days and Nineveh will be overturned." (Jonah 3:3 NIV)

The Assyrian king believed in God and in trembling fear ordered a nationwide fast as an appeal for clemency:

> *"Let us give up our evil ways and violence. Who knows? God may yet relent and with compassion turn from his fierce anger so that we will not perish." (Jonah 3:8-9 NIV)*

God was mightily impressed with this display of repentance and worship and thus did a little dance of joy before deciding not to bring the destruction he had threatened. But not everyone was happy! Jonah was pissed because he wanted God to carry out his threat to destroy the Assyrians. In his rage against God he asked to be killed and thus put out of his misery. Yes this is all odd to me too. God refused Jonah's request and the young prophet stormed off and sat alone in desolate place outside of the city. Whilst Jonah waited, God made a vine grow overnight so that it would give Jonah shelter from the sun, but in a game of cat and mouse, God made the vine wither away and die the very next morning. And then unleashed a ferociously hot desert wind upon Jonah, who was now suffering sun burn and dehydration. Jonah's anger towards God grew and he asked to be euthanised immediately. But God replied that he had no right to be angry, claiming that he should've attended to the vine whilst he was still alive, adding:

> *"Nineveh has more than a hundred and twenty thousand people who cannot tell their right hand from their left and many cattle as well. Should I not be concerned about that great city?" (Jonah 4:11 NIV)*

The above passage is the final verse of the Book of Jonah and we therefore do not enjoy Jonah's reply to God's question, but I will assume it was removed intentionally to make things sound a little nicer, I believe Jonah's answer to God's question went something along the lines of, "Fuck the Assyrians! Nuke the city so that they don't come and invade us and take us into exile within the next few years."

Chapter Thirty-Three - Book of Micah

"If Triangles had a god, he'd have three sides."
Old Yiddish Proverb

The prophet Micah wrote during the period around 720 B.C during the reigns of King Ahaz and King Hezekiah. Like Amos he was a farmer from the countryside and wrote during the same period as his contemporaries Isaiah and Jeremiah.

His writings are limited to a modest seven chapters and are an echo of the prophets before and after him, that being to denounce the social sins of the day: the primary sin being the worship of other gods; and the forecast of approaching doom for Jerusalem (Judah) and Samaria (Israel); and then finally deliverance from captivity.

His opening verse begins with the familiar cry:

"Therefore I (God) will make Samaria a heap of rubble, a place for planting vineyards. I will pour her stones into the valley and lay bare her foundations. All her idols will be broken into pieces; all her temple gifts will be burned with fire; I will destroy all her images. Since she gathered her gifts from the wages of prostitutes, as the wages of prostitutes they will again be used." (Micah 1:6-7 NIV)

Micah is told by God that he will come to their rescue at a time that he believes that his people have atoned for their sins:

"Do not gloat over me my enemy! Though I have fallen, I will rise. Though I sit in darkness, the Lord will be my light. Because I have sinned against him, I will bear the Lord's wrath, until he pleads my case and establishes my right. He will bring me out into the light; I will see his righteousness. Then my enemy will see it and will be covered with shame." (Micah 7:8-10 NIV)

Chapter Thirty Four - Book of Nahum

"We have just enough religion to make us hate, but not enough to make us love one another."
Jonathan Swift

The Book of Nahum includes just three chapters and tells of a vision given by God to his prophet Nahum of the fall of the Assyrian empire which had taken the Southern Kingdom of the Israelites (Judah) into captivity. Whilst the Israelites are in captivity he writes this book to forewarn them that God will soon avenge the Assyrians for holding his people in slavery, even though ironically it was God who sent them there in the first place.

Nahum opens with a reminder to the Assyrians that God is always up for a fight and will not hesitate to use his celestial powers to protect his chosen people. Nahum also draws an accurate caricature of God when he writes:

"The Lord is a jealous and avenging God; the Lord takes vengeance and is filled with wrath. The Lord takes vengeance on his foes and maintains his wrath against his enemies." (Nahum 1:1-2 NIV)

Maybe realising that he had over steered to the right in making God seem like the utter bastard that he is, Nahum attempts to add some of God's nicer personality traits:

> *"The Lord is good, a refuge in times of trouble. He cares for those who trust in him, but with an overwhelming flood he will make an end of Nineveh; he will pursue his foes into darkness."* (Nahum 1:7-8 NIV)

God promises Nahum that the end of their slavery is near and that he will break the chains of their bondage that he had ordained for them, believing now that the Israelites were truly sorry for their worshipping of other pagan gods prior to their exile. Nahum's vision describes what the battlefield will look like when God comes to their rescue:

> *"'I am against you', declares the Lord Almighty. 'I will burn up your chariots in smoke and the sword will devour your young lions. I will leave you no prey on the earth. The voices of your messengers will no longer be heard.'"* (Nahum 2:13 NIV)

Assyria was eventually conquered more than 150 years after Nahum wrote of this vision, but it did not fall to God, it was acquired, rather than conquered, by the expansion of the Persian Empire.

Chapter Thirty-Five - Book of Habakkuk

"No man ever believes that the Bible means what it says: He is always convinced that it says what he means. "

George Bernard Shaw

There is no biographical information on the prophet Habakkuk; in fact less is known about him than any other writer of the Bible. What is unique about Habakkuk is that he called on God before God called on him. The book is written at the time of Babylonia's growing empire and its threat posed on Jerusalem. The Israelites, God fearing or otherwise, had become anxious that it would not be long before Babylon decided to annex the kingdom of Judah. In a prayer that is a combination of fear and anger Habakkuk lodges a complaint to the man upstairs and asks:

> *"How long, O Lord, must I call for help, but you do not listen? Or cry out to you, 'Violence!' but you do not save?"* (Habakkuk 1:2 NIV)

God happened to be sitting near the phone that day and answered Habakkuk's cry:

> *"I am raising up the Babylonians, that ruthless and impetuous people, who sweep across the whole earth to seize dwelling places not their own." (Habakkuk 1:6 NIV)*

God describes to his self-appointed prophet that he will make the Babylonian army strong to rip apart Israel because of their sins towards him. But in the same breath God denounces the Babylonians for their wickedness, but has yet made them strong. It's all Yiddish logic really!

Habakkuk sends up a second letter of complaint to God:

> *"Your eyes are too pure to look on evil; you cannot tolerate wrong. Why then do you tolerate the treacherous? Why are you silent while the wicked swallow up those more righteous than themselves?" (Habakkuk 1:13 NIV)*

God was now engaged and answering Habakkuk's concerns with prompt retort and to the above complaint he replied that there are five woes that have besieged his people and those that have succumbed to these pursuits will perish, but those that remain righteous will thrive. The five woes include:

- Those that stockpile stolen goods.
- Those that prosper by unjust means.
- Those that build a city by bloodshed.
- Those that get their friends drunk so that they can see their naked bodies.
- Those that worship other gods.

Habakkuk then falls to his knees in prayer and appeals to the better half of God's bipolar personality:

> *"I stand in awe of your deeds, O Lord. Renew them in our day, in our time make them known; in wrath remember mercy." (Habakkuk 3:2 NIV)*

Chapter Thirty-Six - Book of Zephaniah

"The idea that God is an oversized white male with a flowing beard who sits in the sky and tallies the fall of every sparrow is ludicrous."

Carl Sagan

Zephaniah is yet another prophet that we know little or nothing about outside of the Bible, thus his real identity unknown. What is assumed is that the author wrote this at the end of the Babylonian captivity, but backdated it to make it read like a prophecy.

The author opens with a vision in which he conceives a date in the future that God will bring destruction forthwith to all of mankind and only those judged righteous will survive. No doubt using the Book of Genesis for his inspiration, Zephaniah opens with God telling him:

"I will sweep away both men and animals; I will sweep away the birds of the air and fish of the sea. The wicked will have only heaps of rubble when I cut off man from the face of the earth." (Zephaniah 1:2-3 NIV)

The author states that this coming judgement will affect all nations including Zephaniah's home nation of Judah, where he believes God resides. He foretells the destruction and judgment of Philistia, Moab, Ammon, Cush, Assyria but claims that God's wrath will be even more vengeful against evil doing Israelites because they were chosen by him to be the 'light upon the nations'.

God in vitriolic violent fury warns:

"I will bring distress on the people and they will walk like blind men, because they have sinned against the Lord. Their blood will be poured out like dust and their entrails like filth... In the fire of jealousy the whole world will be consumed, for he will made a sudden end of all who live in the earth." (Zephaniah 1:17-18 NIV)

But God shows his softer side once in the final verses of this book and promises a better future for his people that survive judgment:

"Be glad and rejoice with all your heart, O Daughter of Jerusalem. The Lord has taken away your punishment, he has turned back your enemy. The Lord, the King of Israel, is with you; never again will you fear any harm." (Zephaniah 3:14-15 NIV)

This is the promise God has made to the Israelites at the end of their exile, but hello - Holocaust. God must have had his fingers crossed when he committed himself to this pact.

Chapter Thirty-Seven - Book of Haggai

"My atheism, like that of Spinoza, is true piety towards the universe and denies only gods fashioned by men in their own image to be servants of their human interests."

George Santayana

The text of this book claims that Haggai was the son of the governor of Judah and was written in 520 B.C. approximately eighteen years after Babylon had been conquered by Cyrus, thus allowing the captive Jews to return home to Judea. With their exodus and freedom God called on his prophet Haggai to ensure that the Israelites had their priorities in order. The first priority not being to rebuild their homes, or replant their crop fields, number one for God was for his people to rebuild his Temple:

> *"Go up into the mountains and bring down timber and build the house, so that I may take pleasure in it and be honoured." (Haggai 1:8 NIV)*

Haggai passed this word of God onto the governor and the Israelites postponed their own basic survival requirements in order to obey God's command to build his temple for their worship of him. In return for rebuilding his temple, God promises to end the drought that had brought famine in the region.

Chapter Thirty-Eight - Book of Zechariah

"When I told the people of Northern Ireland that I was an atheist, a woman in the audience stood up and said, 'Yes, but is it the God of the Catholics or the God of the Protestants in whom you don't believe?'"
Quentin Crisp

Zechariah prophesized during the same period as Haggai, after the exodus from captivity to the Babylonians. This book is often suitably nicknamed the 'Book of Revelations for the Old Testament' and is certainly from where the New Testament's version plagiarized much of its loony inspiration.

During this period of restoration of the Promised Land, the Israelites were still a shattered nation having spent the better part of seventy years in captivity. It would obviously take them years to rebuild their society and they lived in constant fear that due to their weakness as a developing nation once again their neighbouring nations would attack.

Zechariah's contemporary, Haggai, was constantly nipping at the Israelites heels reminding them that they had spent the past seventy years in exile because they did not worship God enough and that the current drought was a result of not completing the rebuilding of the Temple. God realized that his people would grow tired of one man's voice so he appointed Zechariah to be another vocal whip. Thus Zechariah's first writings are a reminder to all that God had punished them with Babylonian captivity because they worshipped other gods and ignored the most important god of all – God.

The Four Horses

Zechariah then tells of a vision he received from God, a dream that included four horses standing among some myrtle trees, a red horse with a jockey riding it and behind him were another red, a brown and a white horse. Zechariah asked God what the significance of these four horses were. God was busy running a few errands that day and had an angel take care of all incoming calls, to which the appointed angel replied, "I will show you what they are". Then the man riding the red horse stepped forward and said:

> *"They are the ones the Lord has sent to go through the earth." (Zechariah 1:10 NIV)*

Then the angel passed on the message from God that read:

> *"I am very jealous for Jerusalem and Zion, but I am very angry with the nations that feel secure. I was only a little angry, but they added to the calamity." (Zechariah 1:14-15 NIV)*

Doesn't this verse remind you of backyard fights you had with your brother? When in a rage you would say, "You pissed me off a little bit by wrecking my train set, but now I am really mad that you took my bike without asking!"

The Four Horns and The Measuring Line

Zechariah then writes that during this vision he looked upwards and saw four horns. He asked the angel what this meant, to which the winged messenger replied that they represented the four nations that had undone Judah. Next the prophet saw a man with a measuring line in his hand and the angel informed him that this was God measuring the boundary pegs of Jerusalem, because God wanted the rebuilt city to be a city without walls. God said to the angel:

> *"I myself will be a wall of fire around the city and I will be its glory within." (Zechariah 2:5 NIV)*

Zechariah was then shown a gold lampstand, a flying scroll and woman in a basket, all with their own cryptic meanings. Then burst out four chariots from between two mountains. The mountains were not made of rock however, but carved out of bronze. Zechariah asked the angel the meaning of the chariots, to which the angel responded:

> *"These are the four spirits of heaven, going out from standing in the presence of the Lord of the whole world." (Zechariah 6:5 NIV)*

The chariot with the black horse was sent to the north; the one with the white horse to the west and the others to the south.

The Coming of Zion's King

In what Christians believe to be the prophecy of Christ, but the Jews believe to be the prophecy of a messiah that has not yet arrived still to this day, God says to Zechariah:

> *"See your king comes to you, righteous and having salvation, gentle and riding on a donkey." (Zechariah 9:9 NIV)*

Hmm I think I smell a rat, but let's move on.

> *"He will proclaim peace to the nations. His rule will extend from sea to sea and from the River to the ends of the earth." (Zechariah 9:10 NIV)*

Yes I definitely smell a rat!

God further adds to Zechariah's vision that the nation of Israel will mourn for the 'one they pierced':

> *"They will look on me, the one they have pierced and they will mourn for him as one mourns for an only child and grieve bitterly for him as one grieves for a firstborn son. On that day the weeping of Jerusalem will be great." (Zechariah 12:10-11 NIV)*

The Lord Will Come

God then promises he will kill two-thirds of mankind for their sins, with the remaining third to be thrown into the fire but converted into silver to carry forth God's name. Wow my head is spinning!

During these end days before the coming of God to earth, God says:

> *"I will gather all the nations to Jerusalem to fight against it; the city will be captured, the houses ransacked and the women raped. Half of the city will go into exile, but the rest of the people will not be taken from the city." (Zechariah 14:2 NIV)*

Zechariah then writes that on this day that God's feet land on earth, it will be on the Mount of Olives, Jerusalem. The righteous will live in prosperity with God and the evil-doers and non-believers will reap the following fate:

> *"Their flesh will rot while they are still standing on their feet, their eyes will rot in their sockets and their tongues will rot in their mouths. On that day men will be stricken by the Lord with great panic." (Zechariah 14:12-13 NIV)*

Chapter Thirty-Nine - Book of Malachi

"Those of little faith are of little hatred."
Eric Hoffer

The book of Malachi is the final book of the Old Testament and like Zephaniah the identity of the author is unknown, nor is the exact period it was written known.

The author's objective is to steer the Israelites back to following God's laws and commandments after the return from exile in Assyria and Babylon. Regardless of the fact that the prophets had urged the people of the Southern and Northern Kingdoms to follow God's way or suffer another exile-like punishment the Israelites continued to wane in their worship. Thus the prophecy of Malachi to straighten them back on their path of righteousness.

In the very opening verses of Malachi it reveals Israel questioning whether or not God actually does love them:

> *"'I have loved you', says the Lord. But you ask, 'How have you loved us?'" (Malachi 1:2 NIV)*

God then in a fit of jilted lover like rage hammers the Israelites for failing to love him adequately:

> *"A son honors his father and a servant his master. If I am a father, where is the honour due to me? If I am a master, where is the respect due to me?" (Malachi 1:6 NIV)*

In an effort to blurt out the actual punishment for those that fail to worship him in a manner that pleases, God dishes out warning of punishment by defecation:

> *"If you will not give glory unto my name saith the LORD ... I will spread dung upon your faces." (Malachi 2:2-3 NIV).*

Nothing like the threat of shit smeared on your face to maintain your faith in the Almighty!

God via his prophet Malachi also forewarns of judgment day, with typical verve:

> *"Surely the day is coming; it will burn like a furnace. All the arrogant and every evildoer will be stubble and that day that is coming will set them on fire." (Malachi 4:1 NIV)*

The New Testament

This is the juncture of the Bible whereby Christianity continues and Judaism ends and thus the reason the Old Testament is referred to by Jews as the Hebrew Bible.

Whilst Christianity's central tenets are found in the New Testament, its foundations are built on Old Testament lore and prophecy. This is especially obvious when we find a multitude of examples where Christians (after Christ's death) desperately and crudely hacked together scripture in an effort to support Old Testament premonitions with the objective of adding credence to the sparse claims of Christ's divinity.

At the time of the writings of the New Testament the Israelites, or Jews as we will now call them, were living under Roman domination and just like the fictitious times of Moses and Egypt, the Jews were desperate for a saviour. A Messiah to carry them into a new age. A Son of God in human form that would bring the believers and obedient servants to salvation out from under the hardships inflicted on them by the Romans. Although the Jews and Romans coexisted in harmony for the most part.

This national eagerness for a Messiah or deliverer, littered the countryside with opportunistic silver-tongues to proclaim themselves as the new prophet of God. If you can recall Monty Python's *Life of Brian* you get a clear picture of what I am trying to describe. Hundreds of loony eccentric Jews perched atop their 'soapbox' whilst preaching idiotic gibberish and arguing they had a direct line to God. After all, without television or radio, the ancient celebrities were those that could convince others they were on speaking terms with the gods, this ensuring their fame, fortune or both.

Christianity never began as a sweeping movement and for more than three centuries after the alleged date of the crucifixion those that labelled themselves Christians were a modest minority. How modest? Well it is accepted by biblical scholars and ancient historians that in 300 A.D there were less than fifty thousand Christians living under the Roman Empire, a tiny number especially when compared to the more than five million Jews. And in Rome itself, the birthplace of the Church of Christianity, Mr. Lambert author of *Beloved and God,* estimates that in 100 AD less than ten percent of the city's population were Jews and less than ten percent of those Jews were Christians. Thus it is evident that not only did the church of Christianity originate from humble beginnings, but it also highlights that the life of Jesus Christ, if he were actually a real person, was not adequately remarkable to generate a fan base outside of a fringe following with their own motives, fears or desires that we will never truly know.

In fact we know nothing of Jesus outside of his four biographers Matthew, Mark, Luke and John, except for some hardly flattering accounts from the writers of the Gnostic gospels, that were hand-picked as omissions due to their lack of divinical 'spin'. There is absolutely no external independent eye-witness evidence to support or corroborate the stories of the gospels, nor any external historical records, journals or documents that even confirm the existence of Jesus. Mind you this period was not absent of historians. Nor was Jerusalem absent of well publicised historians. Take for instance Philo-Judaeus and Justus of Tiberius, both historians and both living in or near Jerusalem during Jesus' alleged lifetime, but neither utters a single word about this character we know so well today. In comparison consider that similarly proclaimed people of the same era as Jesus Christ, such as Aesop, Plato, Julius Caesar, we have a hundreds and thousands of impartial eye witness accounts. But for Jesus, a man whose pagan mythologically inspired life has undoubtedly caused the needless suffering of tens possibly hundreds of millions of people throughout the centuries, we have no writings outside of this book, albeit for the aforementioned handful of Gnostic gospels that were excluded from the Bible, as a business decision, in 320 AD because they did not support the claim that Jesus was anything more than an average man.

Of the gospels that are written as Jesus' biographies, they were written 70-100 years after his supposed death. Thus not only was nothing written of Jesus whilst he was alive but Jesus himself wrote not a single piece of prose. The claimed Son of God didn't even have it in him to write a book let alone distribute a brochure. These facts must cause you deep concern if you are still holding on to the myth of Christ. Put simply, at the commencement of the second century, an overwhelming majority of citizens of the Roman Empire had never heard of Jesus let alone Christianity. The Romans and Jews believed the tenets of the Christian story, virgin birth, walking on water, crucified as a criminal and resurrection to be so bizarre that instead of hauling this minority sect of wackos to the lunatic asylum they used them for gladiator sports in the Coliseum, where they were pitted, with no protective wear or weapons, against lions and bears.

This invariably leads to defenders of Christianity using the argument that if Jesus were not true, then how did it come about that 2,000 years later his story is still so widely followed and believed? How did the original band of Christian brothers that existed only as a weird fringe group for a three centuries successfully make Christianity the dominant religion of the western world? The answer to that question does not come from the authors of the New Testament, nor from any of Jesus' disciples. You can, however, credit Christianity's success to one man, The Roman Emperor Constantine.

The ancient Romans were pagan worshippers. They had gods for a myriad of elements and things. God of the Sun, God of the Ocean, God of Agriculture, etc. But the turning point for Christianity's fortunes occurred at the Battle of Milvian Bridge in 312 AD. According to legend, it was during the heat of battle, a battle the Emperor's troops were losing, that Constantine had his alleged epiphany. The story has it that Constantine looked skywards and before the sun he saw a cross of light above it with it the Greek words *"Εν Τουτω Νικα"* translated into English meaning "by this, conquer!" Constantine commanded his troops to adorn their shields with the Christian symbol, presumably the cross and thereafter they conquered their enemy. From this point on Constantine became a believer of the obscure religion and the rest as they say is history. Although many believe that his conversion was more a business decision rather than one of religiosity. Seeing an opportunity to rally the people around one god rather than dozens provided an opening to institutionalize religion and he knew if he could achieve that then he could control it and if you can control it you can tax it.

In 313 AD Constantine endorsed the Edict of Milan which declared religious tolerance for Christians, thus putting an end to them being fed to the lions. This edict basically cleared any obstacles for Constantine to profit from his new enterprising venture.

In my conversations with Christians it is apparent, especially amongst the born again 'happy clapper' denominations, that many reject the horrors of the Old Testament and thus stake their claim on the puritanical merits of Jesus. However, if Jesus were a real person, and I'm far from convinced that he was, then he was not the soft and cuddly long-haired, meek and mild evangelist that we have been sold into believing through our church leaders, television and religious propagandists. Jesus introduces us to the wickedness and morally disgusting idea of eternal suffering and torture. Consider that as barbaric as the Old Testament is, at least when you died, your suffering was over. But then Jesus comes along and tells us that we will be burnt perpetually for millions and billions of years in a place called Hell if we don't follow his lead. What a wicked doctrine to scare children with. What an evil concept to motivate people to do what he believes is morally right out of nothing but naked fear alone.

If Jesus were as morally pure as his followers attest, then why did he not denounce the immorality of slavery. Jesus speaks repeatedly about having slaves but never says anything that would suggest he at least questioned the righteousness of it. Furthermore, it always seemed odd to me that Jesus healed a blind man, but didn't cure blindness. What is so super-human of a man who heals only those that he comes in direct contact with in a small patch of the Middle East, but does nothing to heal any suffering of mankind. Additionally he was completely unconcerned by the suffering of non-Jews, this no more evident in the Book of Matthew in which Jesus presents himself as a racist bigot.

As you read the fabricated life of Jesus Christ, bear in mind that the story of his time is not even an original tale. The ancient world is littered with similar fictitious biographies and often with blatant plagiarism on behalf of the Gospels. Thus the story of Jesus is a lazy attempt to offer itself as a unique piece of literature. Consider the following stories of gods that preceded the Jesus era:

- Horus: Sun God of Egypt, born on December 25th of the virgin Isis-Meri. Had 12 disciples he travelled about with, performing miracles such as healing the sick and walking on water. After being betrayed by Typhon, Horus was crucified, buried for 3 days and resurrected.
- Attis of Phyrigia: Born of the virgin Nana on December 25th, crucified, placed in a tomb and after 3 days, was resurrected.
- Krishna of India: Born of the virgin Devaki with a star in the east signalling his coming, performed miracles with his disciples and upon his death was resurrected.
- Dionysus of Greece: Born of a virgin on December 25th, was a travelling teacher who performed miracles such as turning water into wine.
- Mithra of Persia: Born of a virgin on December 25th, he had 12 disciples and performed miracles and upon his death was buried for 3 days and later resurrected.

Important Note

The first four books of the New Testament are the books of Matthew, Mark, Luke and John. Better known as the gospels. As mentioned earlier these are the biographies of Jesus. For a summary of these first four books I will deviate from the path taken to now of dissecting each book separately on its own merit, as these four books appear to tell exactly the same story when read individually, or vertically. However to highlight the contradictions and inconsistencies of the competing biographers I believe it more effective to read them side by side or horizontally. Therefore the next four chapters of the Bible will read as one.

Chapter Forty, Forty-One, Forty-Two & Forty Three - The Gospels

Genealogy of Jesus

Of the four gospels it is only Matthew and Luke that go to the trouble of listing all of Jesus' descendents.

According to Matthew, Jesus is the descendent of Abraham and thus Jesus' lineage travels all the way from Isaac to Jacob. Remember Jacob? The shyster that duped his father and brother to become the father of Israel, in Genesis. Does this not mean that Jesus is the descendent of a fraudulent huckster?

Anyway, the lineage of Jesus carries through the long line of kings of Israel such as David, Solomon, Rehoboam, Ahaz and Hezekiah. This is an obvious attempt by Matthew to show that Jesus is true Israelite blue blood, citing his father Joseph as the son of Jacob in this great Hebrew family tree which includes fourteen generations from Abraham to David, fourteen from David to the exile in Babylon and fourteen from the exile to Jesus. All nice round numbers! However there is only one major flaw to this opening stanza, that being that the family lineage was only documented on the father's side in biblical and Hebrew records. Thus how could Jesus be possibly a descendent of Abraham et al if he were born of a virgin?

Further compounding the coming story of Jesus is that Matthew has already stated that Jesus is the son of Joseph. A transparent attempt by early Christians to convince the Jews that their man was 'the' man, but in doing so they dropped the ball in order to maintain a consistent story.

Luke further compounds the myth by writing that:

"He (Jesus) was the son, so it was thought, of Joseph, the son of Heli." (Luke 3:23 NIV)

So is Heli or Jacob Jesus' grandfather? But more importantly Luke has made the claim in black and white that Jesus is the son of Joseph. Additionally, Luke goes to the effort to show that Jesus' parentage runs right back through to Noah, then to Adam and then God.

The Conception of Jesus Christ

Matthew sets the scene for the immaculate conception in a somewhat idiotic fashion as he claims that at the time of Mary's discovered pregnancy Joseph was only 'pledged' or engaged to be married to her, but before they had ever engaged in sexual congress with one another she informed Joseph that she was carrying a child. Joseph was livid assuming that she must have snuck over the neighbour's fence to get it on with Jesse and in his rage Matthew claims that Joseph wanted to file for divorce. Divorce? But he had said they were only pledged to be married. Time for God to step in and sort this mess out and he does so by sending down one of his angels, who appears to Joseph in a dream:

> *"Joseph son of David, do not be afraid to take Mary home as your wife, because what is conceived in her is from the Holy Spirit. She will give birth to a son and you are to give him the name Jesus, because he will save his people from their sins." (Matthew 1:20-21 NIV)*

One of my favourite all time questions in relation to this ridiculous claim of the virgin birth and a later argument between Mary and Joseph is by author Thomas Paine who asked:

> *"Which do you think it be more likely – that a the law of natural order was suspended, or that a Jewish minx should tell a lie."*

Imagine all of this in a modern setting whereby there is a woman by the name of Sue who had been having an affair with her neighbour Bob, whilst engaged to Harry. Sue is seated in her lounge her eyes bloodshot from sobbing as she holds the home pregnancy test swab in her fingers, which reads 'positive'. Her fiancé Harry, is on his way home but is unaware of the bombshell his soon to be wife is about to drop on him. Conversant of the Bible, Sue knows that stoning to death is warranted. She is riddled with guilt, remorse and panic. With her heart racing at 200mph she suddenly has a moment of clarity. As she lays back on the sofa and ponders her plight, the breeze begins to rustle the curtains and a bright white light shines through the window pane landing directly on her face. "Is that you God?" she asked. The unseen and mysterious voice replied, "Yes my daughter. It is God. Do not alarm yourself, I am here to tell you that neither Harry or Bob is the father of your unborn. It was me that impregnated you whilst you were asleep. The child will be my son and he will rule the world."

When her fiancé returned home later that evening, she told Harry that God had implanted a foetus in her womb. Now ask yourself this, if you were Harry would you believe her?

This immaculate conception story was even impossible to explain to my eight year old daughter. I tried to tell her that God was Jesus' daddy and Mary was his mummy. Her elementary school mind tried to process this before stating in a confused manner, "Oh so God was married to

Mary?" I replied, "No, Mary was married to Joseph." You see this crazy shit ain't easy to explain even to an inquisitive child.

Matthew too ties himself up in double-talk on the conception of Jesus when he writes that the virgin birth occurred as a fulfilment of Isaiah's (7:14) prophecy:

> *"The virgin will be with child and will give birth to a son and they will call him Immanuel – which means, 'God with us'." (Matthew 1:23 NIV)*

An attempt to fabricate the life of Jesus by crafting Old Testament prophecy to his biographical account results in the contradictory absurdity that Jesus now has two names. Jesus and Immanuel! Can you see how ridiculous and sloppy the attempt to create Jesus' story is?

What is further astonishing in the Gospel's biography of Jesus is that of the four, Mark and John don't even mention the virgin birth or anything in relation to the birth of Jesus. Now I ask you to think long, hard and rationally about this question: What journalist or editor that was given the task of writing a story on the life of Jesus Christ would look at all the facts presented before him and then choose to deliberately leave out the bit about him being born of a virgin? It is the equivalent of a CNN journalist piecing together all the facts of September 11, 2001 and opting to leave out of the story the part where two passenger jets slammed into the World Trade Centre buildings.

So Mark and John opt to leave out the virgin birth story, thus you'd assume that at least Matthew and Luke have some kind of consistency on this matter. But wrong. In Luke's account of the pregnancy he makes no mention of any angel visiting Joseph and in fact says the winged messenger appeared to Mary:

> *"Greetings, you who are highly favoured! The lord is with you. Do not be afraid, Mary, you will be with child and give birth to a son and you are to give him the name Jesus. He will be great and will be the son of the Most High." (Luke 1:28 NIV)*

Luke writes that Mary was befuddled by the angel's message as she was not yet married, nor had she done a little of the hokey pokey. To which the angel replied:

> *"The Holy Spirit will come upon you and the power of the Most High will over shadow you. " (Luke 1:35 NIV)*

The Birth of Jesus

The gospels Mark and John include absolutely no mention of the actual birth of Jesus, which is extraordinarily odd as we do know the birth story of so many famous statesmen, kings and philosophers from this time period, but of the central character of the western world's predominant religion we know so little.

It is only via a melding of the respective conflicting stories of Matthew and Luke that we know of the Christmas carol narrative of this alleged son of God. The story that Luke tells us is that Joseph travelled with his pregnant fiancée from the then fictitious town of Nazareth, to Bethlehem to register their 'shot-gun' marriage there. Luke is then very matter of fact when he describes the actual delivery:

> *"While they were there, in Bethlehem, the time came for the baby to be born and she gave birth to her firstborn, a son. She wrapped him in cloths and placed him in a manger, because there was no room for them in the inn." (Luke 2:6-7 NIV)*

Luke then writes that shortly after Jesus had made his first breaths of life in the barnyard, an angel appeared to some shepherds attending to their flocks in a nearby field. The farmers were terrified to see an angel hovering before them, to which the angel said forth:

> *"Do not be afraid. I bring you good news of great joy that will be for all the people. Today in the town of David a Saviour has been born to you; he is the Messiah. This will be a sign to you: You will find a baby wrapped in cloths and lying in a manger." (Luke 2:10-12 NIV)*

The angel fluttered off back to heaven and the shepherds left their flock to go see this new-born Messiah. Luke doesn't mention the shepherds having any difficulty in locating Joseph, Mary and the new born as the very next sentence writes that they found Jesus lying there in the manger. The shepherds soon spread word of their talk with the angel and of seeing baby Jesus.

Matthew's perspective altars somewhat dramatically to Luke's, as he writes that it was not shepherds led by an angel to see the arrival of the new baby Messiah, but that it was three wise men led by a star from the east to the city of Jerusalem where they asked the town folk:

> *"Where is the one who has been born king of the Jews? We saw his star in the east and have come to worship him." (Matthew 2:2 NIV)*

After the three wise men had had a brief introduction and conversation with Roman King Herod, the hovering star led them directly to the place where baby Jesus and Mary were. Matthew makes no reference to this place being a manger, stable, barnyard or otherwise, but regardless the travelling men do find their breast-feeding Messiah directly below the floating star. Which given the size of your average star is akin to giving a friend directions to a local restaurant by telling him that you will find the eatery somewhere under the earth's sun.

The wise men give praise to the newborn and present Mary with a treasure trove of gifts that included gold, incense and myrrh. As you see these are starkly contrasting stories of Jesus' birth between the two of the four Gospels who deemed his birth to have relevance to the biography of Jesus. But this is not where the contrast between Matthew and Luke ends, as Matthew attempting to paint Jesus as a deliverer, just in the way Moses was a deliverer, hacks together a story almost identical to that of Moses. As he writes that King Herod was troubled by news that a Jewish Messiah had arrived and thus became concerned that a celestially sent king would erode what control the Roman Empire had over the Jews and therefore ordered the execution of every baby boy under the age of two years and within the vicinity of Bethlehem.

When the three wise men had ceased kissing the feet of baby Jesus an angel appeared before Joseph and ordered him:

> *"Get up! Take the child and his mother and escape to Egypt. Stay there until I tell you, for Herod is going to search for the child to kill him." (Matthew 1:13 NIV)*

Before you chastise Herod for being God like in his quest to kill babies, there is no record of King Herod or any Roman ruler ever giving such an infanticidal statute. In fact ancient historians such as Josephus, who extensively recorded Herod's crimes, do not mention this baby-murdering which would undoubtedly have been Herod's greatest crime by far. Again just an event of pure fiction in constructing a myth that would appeal to Jewish anti-Roman sentiment.

The story of a 'threatened child becomes a great leader' is commonplace amongst ancient literature and myth. It is a theme of Romulus & Remes, Sargon the Great and Hercules, amongst many others. And now we see it reworked into the story of Jesus by one of the four biographers.

Matthew completes his account of the birth that the young family returned to the fantasy town of Nazareth from Egypt after two years spent in hiding as news was delivered to them, again from an angel, that Herod had passed away.

The Boy Jesus at The Temple

This is an interesting story because of the four biographies this is the only story we have of Jesus between the age of two and thirty. Yes a twenty eight year gap in the story of unarguably the most famous character in history. We know nothing of Jesus as a teenager. Was he a pimply awkward adolescent that refused to do his chores? Was he bad at sports? Did chicks dig him? Did he play 'spin-the-bottle' with the other teenagers in his village? We know none of any of this and the only story we do have of the missing years of Jesus is the one Luke tells of Jesus as a twelve year old.

Luke writes that every year Joseph and Mary would travel from Nazareth to Jerusalem for the Feast of the Passover. A normal family outing for a Jewish holiday it would seem, but this story takes a fast turn for nonsense when he writes:

"After the Feast was over, while his parents were returning home, the boy Jesus stayed behind in Jerusalem, but his parents were unaware of it. Thinking he was in their company, they travelled on for a day. Then they began looking for him among their friends and relatives. When they did not find him they returned to Jerusalem to look for him there." (Luke 2:43-44 NIV)

How drunk or stoned did Joseph and Mary have to be to mistakenly believe that Jesus was right there with them, when he clearly wasn't? Thankfully there was no Department of Child Welfare back then, or this set of parents would be without a child. The story continues that the irresponsible parents return to Jerusalem and at the end of the third day of looking for him, they find the adolescent Jesus preaching to several gathered Jews at the Temple. (For later reference the fact that Luke writes Jesus was found on the third day is no accident). The young Jesus' wisdom astonished those that listened and they were amazed that a youth would have such insight of the world. Joseph and Mary upon finding him here, yell to him:

"Son, why have you treated us like this? Your father and I have been anxiously searching for you." (Luke 2:48 NIV)

If Jesus had any spunk at all, his reply should have been, "Where was I? I am only twelve years of age, you are my father and it was you that fucking left me here you irresponsible git!"

Isn't it interesting that Luke writes that his father, Joseph, had been looking for him? Again the author's oversight in maintaining consistency of truth. Nevertheless Jesus replies to his now concerned parents, who didn't seem all that concerned for his absence for at least the day or two when they thought he was still in the backseat of the car:

"Why were you searching for me? Didn't you know I had to be in my Father's house?" (Luke 2:49 NIV)

God IS his father? Boy am I confused!

Luke finishes off with what I believe to be an amusing line:

> *"But they (Joseph and Mary) did not understand what he was saying to them." (Luke 2:50 NIV)*

If I were a Christian it would trouble me that nothing in the Gospels illustrates Mary being impressed or proud of her prodigy son. This, afterall, is the son that God had put into her womb himself, without the need for her to engage in sweaty, non-airconditioned sex with a pre-deodorant era carpenter fiancé. If she believed Jesus to be the spawn of God, then why does everything that Jesus do, come as some kind of a surprise to her? If we are to draw a charcicature of Jesus through Mary's eyes, based only on the four Gospels, then all we are left with is the illustration of a naughty little boy, and nothing prodigious.

John the Baptist

The story of John the Baptist preparing the way for the now adult Jesus is the first time, the four Gospels write with any matching consensus. In the years before Jesus' arrival on the scene there was John, who baptized Jews in shallows of the Sea of Galilee so that they could repent for their sins. The story of this ordinary man's life is brought to colour so his bio could match the Old Testament messianic prophecy of Isaiah (40:3):

> *"A voice of one calling in the desert, 'Prepare the way for the Lord make straight paths for him'." (Matthew 3:3 NIV)*

Mark describes John the Baptist's appearance as:

> *"John wore clothing made of camel's hair, with a leather belt around his waist and he ate locusts and wild honey." (Mark 1:6 NIV)*

Where Luke takes a flight of fancy from his three contemporaries is that he claims John the Baptist to be a relative of Jesus, claiming his mother Elisabeth to be a relative of Mary and like Mary God played a part in getting her pregnant although doesn't go as far to mention the words 'virgin birth'. Luke writes of the birth of John the Baptist that whilst he was still a baby:

> *"Immediately his mouth was opened and his tongue was loosed and he began to speak, praising God. The neighbours were all filled with awe and throughout the hill country or Judea people were talking about all these things." (Luke 1:64-65 NIV)*

Hmm a talking baby! Maybe this means John Travolta's film 'Look Who's Talking' was actually a documentary. Weird!

The Gospels reunite their testimony in evangelizing the celebrity of this man, claiming that people travelled from the farthest corners of the Mid East region to be dunked under water by this man. Further, judging by scripture, it seems likely that rumours spread throughout the region that John the Baptist was himself the Messiah. Thus causing the Pharisees, the vestiges of Jewish political power at the time, to enquire of this man:

> *"Why then do you baptize if you are not the Messiah, nor Elijah, nor the Prophet?" (John 1:25 NIV)*

To which John replied that he was sent by God to prepare the way for Jesus, before adding modestly:

> *"After me will come one more powerful than I, the thongs of whose sandals I am not worthy to stoop down and untie. I baptize you with water, but he will baptize you with the Holy Spirit." (Mark 1:7-8 NIV)*

Of Christian relevance it is John the Baptist that introduces the Biblical reader to the concept of atonement. A truly wicked concept, in that one can be forgiven for all past moral crimes inflicted upon others, whether that be murder, rape or theft, by merely saying sorry to a mythical sky-God, whilst simultaneously having your head slammed into the water by a pious prick. What of the victims of your crimes? What of personal accountability and the pursuit of social justice? As such the concepts of atonement and redemption are counter-intuitive to establishing a healthy functioning society.

It is also worth noting that John the Baptist also introduces us to the myth of eternal punishment. Till now your suffering ended at the tip of the sword, or by God turning you into a pile of salt at the click of his fingers. You died, game over. However, John implies that continued suffering post-death for the non-baptised and unrepentant awaits. A truly evil idea that Jesus, it will soon be revealed, campaigns on as one of his religiously political platforms. But for now John the Baptist suggests that the following eternal punishment beckons:

> *"The axe is ready at the root of the trees and every tree that does not produce good fruit will be cut down and thrown into eternal fire. I baptise you with water for repentance." (Matthew 3:10-11 NIV)*

The Baptism of Jesus

Matthew's, Mark's and Luke's respective stories concur, in the most part, but their stories of Jesus' baptism conflict with John's who has his own unique account. Matthew and Mark write that Jesus sought John the Baptist to be baptized in the River Jordan. At the moment that Jesus resurfaced whilst held in John's arms both write:

> *"As soon as Jesus was baptized, he went up out of the water. At that moment heaven was opened and he saw the Spirit of God descending like a*

dove and lightening upon him and a voice from heaven said, 'This is my Son, whom I love; with him I am well pleased'." (Matthew 3:16-17 NIV)

Luke's story differs only slightly as he writes that the heavens began to open as soon as Jesus began praying, but the voice from God and the dove and lightening description remain consistent between the two. Whereas John provides the following testimony:

"I saw the Spirit come down from heaven as a dove and remain on him. I would not have known him, except that the one who sent me to baptize with water told me, 'The man on whom you see the Spirit come down and remain is he who will baptize with the Holy Spirit'." (John 1:33 NIV)

Whilst Mathew, Mark and Luke claim that Jesus and John the Baptist were involved in a discussion as to who should baptize who before the actual baptism took place, John claims that he did not recognize him as Jesus until after the baptism.

Temptation of Jesus

Immediately following his baptism, Jesus was led by Satan into the desert. Satan and Jesus are having a chat, but John doesn't believe this astonishing relationship worthy of any mention. And Mark only writes of it as a footnote and in just one sentence:

"At once the Spirit sent him out in the desert and he was in the desert for forty days, being tempted by Satan." (Mark 1:12-13 NIV)

Matthew and Luke add much greater detail to the interaction between Saviour and Slayer, with both writing that Satan appeared to Jesus after he had gone forty days without any food. Satan tempting Jesus with the following test:

"If you are the Son of God, tell these stones to become bread." (Matthew 4:3 NIV)

Jesus answered, with a quote of Isaiah 40:3:

"Man does not live on bread alone but on every word that comes from the mouth of God." (Matthew 4:4 NIV)

Satan then led Jesus to the top of the Temple in Jerusalem and standing high above the paved stones, Satan asked him to jump off to prove that God would save him from being splattered 100feet below where they stood. This time Satan proved he too could reference Old Testament scripture, quoted the following passage from Psalm 91:

"He will command his angels concerning you and they will lift you up in their hands, so that you will not strike you foot against a stone." (Matthew 4:6 NIV)

Jesus threw some Old Testament heat back at Satan and
little verse from Deuteronomy 6:16:

"It says: 'Do not put the Lord your God to the test'." (Luke 4:13 NIV)

For Luke this is the end of the conversation between Jesus and Satan, but Matthew adds that Satan then led Jesus to the top of a very high mountain showing the Son of God all the kingdoms of earth and promising Jesus that all this would be his if he bowed down and worshipped him. Jesus considered the offer for a moment, but replied with another verse from Deuteronomy:

"Worship the Lord your God and serve him only." (Matthew 4:10 NIV)

Whilst I can understand Jesus using this as a counter to Satan's offer it does make worshipping Jesus somewhat problematic now. To whom do I now send my knee-mail?

Jesus Begins To Preach

There is little consistency in regards to the start of Jesus' ministry between the four gospels, with Luke claiming that Jesus first started preaching in the synagogues of Nazareth, where he was threatened to be thrown off a cliff by the people of his own village because he refused to heal a local man suffering from leprosy:

"All the people in the synagogue were furious when they heard this. They got up, drove him out of the town and took him to the brow of the hill on which the town was built, in order to throw him down the cliff. But he walked right through the crowd and went on his way." (Luke 4:28-30 NIV)

Remarkably the other three Gospels mention nothing of Jesus' own tribe wishing to murder the fledgling preacher, and in fact Matthew's account of the commencement of Jesus' preaching career launched after he had learnt of the imprisonment of John the Baptist. It was this news that prompted Jesus to leave Nazareth to reside in a town called Capernaum in the area of Zebulum and Naphtali so that he could fulfill what had been written by the prophet Isaiah (9:1-2)

"Land of Zebulum and land of Naphtali the way of the sea, along the Jordan, Galilee of the Gentiles – the people living in darkness have seen a great light; on those living in the land of the shadow of death a light has dawned." (Matthew 4:15-16 NIV)

Jesus Advocates Violence Not Peace

Surely one of the most controversial passages of the New Testament, as they are words from Jesus' own mouth and as such lay clear that his objective on

.t to bring violence. I guess if we take into .ghtered during the period of Crusades at the Jesus' mission was completed.

ave come to bring peace to the earth, I did not a sword." (Matthew 10:34 NIV)

.y far from an olive branch and just so you can be .t some obscure passage taken out of context:

"Fo. o turn a man against his father, a daughter against her mother, .. er-in-law against her mother-in-law, a man's enemies will be the membe.. of his own household." (Matthew 10:35-36 NIV)

Wow! Am I being a little harsh in labelling these the words of an asshole? If a politician said exactly this he would be chased out of Dodge and rightfully so. Jesus adopts a similar tone of insecure based jealousy as his heavenly father, when he says:

"Anyone who loves his father or mother more than me is not worthy of me; anyone who loves his son or daughter more than me is not worthy of me; and anyone who does not take his cross and follow me is not worthy of me." (Matthew 10:37-38 NIV)

How come Jesus didn't include an exception clause for young children? What chance does a baby or a young child have in obeying this dictum? A child cannot possibly love a Hebrew evangelist more than his or her own parents, therefore this is simply lunacy and ultimately wicked. Furthering the claim that God, in his heart of hearts, indeed hates you.

In my conversations with religious apologists, and non-Christians in particular, it is often asserted something along the lines of, "Oh well maybe he wasn't the Son of God, but he was a great or profound moral teacher!" To this oft made remark, I will allow the late C.S Lewis to do my bidding, from his book *Mere Christianity*:

"That is the one thing we must not say. A man who was merely a man and said the sort of things Jesus said would not be a great moral teacher. He would either be a lunatic – on a level with the man who says he is a poached egg – or else he would be the Devil of Hell. You must make your choice. Either this man was, and is the Son of God: or else a madman and something worse. You can shut him up for a fool, you may spit at him and kill him as a demon; or you can fall at his feet and call him Lord and God. But let us not come with any patronizing nonsense about his being a great human teacher. He has not left that open to us. He did not intend to."

Jesus' First Disciples

To be a bona fide Messiah one of the first things you need in place is a fan base and thus Jesus' initial piece of business was to select some disciples who could help recruit and rally some new supporters. Matthew summarizes this entourage selection process in a neat and tidy two paragraph verse. Writing that whilst Jesus walked along the shoreline of the Sea of Galilee he came across two brothers, Simon and Andrew, who were enjoying a spot of weekend fishing. The only dialogue we have between Jesus and the two brothers is of Jesus:

> *"Come, follow me and I will make you fishers of men." (Matthew 4:19 NIV)*

That's all it took for Jesus to convince the brothers to put down their rods and nets and follow this long-haired guy who claimed to be from a town they had never heard of, Nazareth.

John writes that the brothers were not on the Sea of Galilee but were in fact fishing on the banks of the River Jordan more or less at the exact same spot where Jesus had been baptized by John the Baptist. Whilst Luke has a completely different version of the same event, claiming that Jesus was standing by the Lake of Gennesart with a crowd of people gathered around him to listen to his preaching. Whilst Jesus was philosophizing about the meaning of life he spotted at the water's edge two fishing boats, anchored ashore next to two fishermen who were folding their nets. Jesus, somewhat presumptuously, stepped into one of the boats and demanded that one of the fisherman push him out from shore a few yards or so. The fisherman, his name Simon, agreed to do so and then Jesus took a seat, made himself comfortable and continued preaching from the small vessel to the crowd standing on the shore. Jesus eventually grew tired of jibber-jabbing and demanded that Simon and him go out and catch some fish from the deep water. Simon protested:

> *"Master, we've worked hard and all night and haven't caught anything. But because you say so, I will come and let down some nets." (Luke 5:5 NIV)*

It is odd that Simon, who had no idea who this demanding stranger was, now called him 'Master', but as I have written before, this is not my story. Anyway, Jesus and Simon let down some nets in search for fish and to Simon's amazement they caught so much fish that their boat could not hold their bounty. Simon called for other nearby boats to join in this miraculous fish catch and then threw himself to his knees in praise of Jesus, to which the Messiah replied:

> *"Do not be afraid; from now on you will catch men." (Luke 5:10 NIV)*

I'm not homophobic in the slightest, but if a strange man alone with me on a fishing charter, told me that together we would catch some dudes, then my 'Gay-dar' alert system would be blinking red.

Jesus Begins To Heal

Working through the Messianic checklist: Virgin birth - check; Baptism - check; Fan club administrators - check. Now Jesus would need to bring some wizardry to his shows or the small number of fans that were following him would soon grow tired of his incessant babbling about God and eternity and so forth. Let's face it; it is hard to sell tickets if you don't have an act!

Thus Jesus began to heal those who were demonically possessed. Yes the creator of the universe, God, believed it necessary that his only son would need to exorcise those with a demon inside their bodies. Understandably Jesus was not yet versed on the germ theory of disease, a scientific discovery that would come many centuries later, but nevertheless surely the son of God would be given a little whisper in the ear from his heavenly father, "Psst, Jesus it's me your Dad. The man whose forehead you have your palm on just has a common cold. I will reveal to you all the complexities of bacteria, germs and virus a little down the track, but for now just know that this dude with the high temperature does not have a devil inside of him that needs to be released by you."

This Biblical story whilst seemingly benign on the surface, has led to the torturous deaths of possibly millions of suffering human beings throughout the centuries, all the way through to the Salem Witch Trials in the 18th century in the US. This single narrative led to the belief that people could be intoxicated by Satan and thus we have countless souls burnt at the stake, drawn and quartered, hung, drowned, maimed, all because the claimed Son of God wasn't intellectually advanced enough to denounce this bizarre practice or belief.

Luke claims that the very first miraculous act Jesus performed, before that of healing the sick, was an exorcism:

> *"When the sun was setting, the people brought to Jesus all who had various kinds of sickness and laying his on each one, he healed them. Moreover, demons came out of many people, shouting, 'You are the Son of God!', but he rebuked them and would not allow them to speak, because they knew he was the Christ'." (Luke 4:40-41 NIV)*

Mark tells more or less the same story, but John introduces us to a problematic theme that Jesus and early followers had to deal with, that being the healing of the sick on the Sabbath. An act forbidden by God when he gave his laws directly to Moses, but laws that Jesus often saw himself above, whilst simultaneously endorsing Mosaic law on a number of occasions, as we will review later. In this particular story John writes that Jesus visited a swimming pool like complex which in Aramaic was called a Bethesda. This particular pool was frequented daily by a vast number of people suffering all kinds of disabilities and illnesses. On this day Jesus chose to visit and approached an invalid man who had not walked in thirty-eight years. Jesus laid his hand on him and said:

"Get up! Pick up your mat and walk." (John 5:8 NIV)

The man was cured and ran around like a teenage kid without his Ritalin. However, the Jewish elders in attendance were surprisingly underwhelmed by this miracle and instead of praising Jesus, they opted to denounce the former invalid for being healed on the Sabbath. The elders approached him and asked who it was that healed him and he replied that he did not know. Whilst this discussion was taking place, Jesus had slipped out through the back door.

The Gospels all have different stories of Jesus healing people suffering from leprosy to blindness, from paraplegia to male pattern baldness. Well maybe I made the last ailment up, but he did heal many. Oddly though Jesus, with the powers of God, only chose to heal those that came in his direct path and thus it would have been far nobler for the Holy Ghost, Holy Father, or Holy Son to have cured blindness or leprosy in total, rather than just the odd believer here and there.

This miraculous claim to healing presents a conundrum for Christians; of all the tens of thousands, possibly millions of believers who have claimed to be healed by prayer thus ultimately through Jesus, never once has an amputee been afforded this benevolence. Thus the question we must ask is why does the 'big guy upstairs' bear such a grudge against amputees? A question that one atheist website recently posted a US$100,000 reward for any proof to demonstrate that God has restored the limb of an amputee via prayer. Interestingly in the more than twelve months this challenge has stood, not one religious believer has taken up the offer and considering there are more than 50,000 new amputees courtesy of returning US soldiers from Iraq or Afghanistan, an overwhelming majority of which are Christians, there should be no shortage of takers for an easy few extra bucks. At least that's what one would think.

This question truly holds a microscope to the fundamental aspect of prayer and thus exposes it for critical observation. The result of applying this blowtorch is we are left with two clouds of uncertainty; ambiguity and coincidence.

A clever hypothetical put forward by the website 'Why Won't God Help Amputees' (*www.whywontgodhealamputees.com*) illustrates this brilliantly. Let's imagine that your doctor has diagnosed you with an aggressive form of bowel cancer. You opt to take the chemotherapy that your doctor is recommending and as this god awful remedy of radiation exposure begins you are naturally terrified at the prospect that the number of your days on earth are dramatically falling. Assuming you are a Christian you begin to pray to God or Jesus for some divine intervention and thus you pray morning and night, before, during and after surgery that your heavenly father will spare you an early visit to the grave.

A few months after the chemo your doctor is delighted to tell you that you have survived the tumour and all signs of the life threatening disease have now vanished. Naturally you give thanks to God for heeding your prayers and your conviction and faith in Jesus is stronger than ever before. Praise the Lord!

But how do we objectively rationalize the above scenario? What saved you from seemingly imminent doom? Well there are several possibilities. Was it the surgery, radiation therapy, your body's natural defence, or was it God's interference? On the surface the answer to this question seems ambiguous. God may have miraculously cured your disease, as many Christians would believe. But if God is fiction then it had to be either the chemotherapy, surgery and/or your natural immune system that cured you.

There is only one way to remove coincidence of prayer from this scenario and that is to eliminate ambiguity. In a non-ambiguous situation, there is no potential for coincidence. Because there is no ambiguity, we can actually *know* whether God is answering the prayer or not. The examination of amputees allows us to completely remove all ambiguity, and by doing creating an unambiguous situation we can see for our own eyes that prayer never ever works. Therefore we can be sure that whenever a believer has proclaimed instances of miraculous healing through prayer we can be certain that the possibility of coincidence was present.

What we find is that whenever we create an unambiguous situation like this and look at the results of prayer, prayer never works. God never answers prayers if there is no possibility of coincidence.

Water Into Wine

Interestingly John's first account for the miraculous powers of Jesus are not of healing the sick, but of performing a magic trick that would ensure the Holy One to be the first man invited to any Sigma Chi Frat party.

John tells of a wedding that Jesus attended in Galilee accompanying his mother, Mary and his disciples. The wedding hosts are drunk dry by their wine-swilling guests and it is left to Mary to point this out to all in attendance, which suggests to me that she too was a little bit of boozer. With her glass empty she turns to her son Jesus and gives him a little nudge so as her Holy son could do something about it, Which more than suggests she had no ethical issues in utilizing her son's super-hero powers for less than noble purposes. Jesus turns angrily to his mother and says:

> *"Dear woman, why do you involve me. My time has not yet come."*
> *(John 2:4 NIV)*

I thought this would have constituted a stoning under the terms of the commandments for disrespecting ones parents. Mary is now upset that her son has been so abrupt towards her and she verbally lashes out on a nearby slave and demands that he do whatever her son commands. Jesus then ordered this servant to fill six stone jars with water, each holding approximately thirty gallons. He then demanded that a cup of this water be brought to the master of the wedding banquet so that he can taste its contents. Drawing the cup to his lips, the master is astonished that the cup is filled with wine and says to Jesus:

> *"Everyone brings out the choice wine first and then the cheaper wine after the guests have had too much to drink; but you have saved the best till now."*
> *(John 2:10 NIV)*

Having several Jewish friends myself this party trick seems such a Jewish thing to do, that being to do anything to avoid having to pay for a round of drinks. And really I guess this miracle wasn't so miraculous when you consider that I once turned an entire personal bank loan into vodka in one summer whilst in my early 20s.

John closes this narrative with a footnote that reads that this was indeed the first miraculous sign Jesus performed in front of his two disciples and thus they were now true believers. Comical isn't it? I am sure I too could find more than two disciples if I could convert tap water into Moet.

Jesus Clears the Temple

A story unique to John is one in which it shows meek and mild Jesus to actually have somewhat of a fiery temper, a personality trait that has been well hidden by modern day evangelists of this mythical character. The narrative includes Jesus making a visit to Jerusalem for the Jewish Passover holiday and no Passover would be complete without a visit to the Temple. In the grounds of the temple, Jesus discovered all kinds of commerce taking place such as money changing, livestock sales and ornament markets. Jesus became furious that the temple resembled that of a neighbourhood swap-meet and to vent his rage he grabbed a nearby whip and started lashing the sellers, overthrowing money-changing tables and chasing all and sundry out of the court with his bull-whip in hand, whilst shouting:

> *"Get these out of here! How dare you turn my Father's house into a market?" (John 2:16 NIV)*

As he stood there exhausted, his face reddened from yelling and whipping, some Jewish elders approached the hot-tempered Jesus and asked him:

> *"What miraculous sign can you show us to prove your authority to do all this?" (John 2:18 NIV)*

In reply Jesus demanded that they destroy the temple and if they did so he would raise it in three days. The Jews mocked him and informed him that it took forty-six years to build and it would therefore be impossible for one man to rebuild from scratch in just seventy-two hours. This is the end of the dialogue between Jesus and the two Jewish elders, but John writes that this was Jesus' cryptic way in forecasting his resurrection on the third day after his future death.

Recognition of Old Testament Law

In my own personal debates with Christians more often than not they will retreat to defending the Bible in such manner, "Oh yes sure the Old Testament has some bad things in it, but all that changes when Jesus comes along with his teachings of peace and love." Or words to that effect. Well here is the problem for that evasive tack, as John quotes Jesus' endorsement of not just Mosaic Law but *all* Old Testament laws commanded by God:

> *"Anyone who breaks one of these commandments and teaches others to do the same will be called least in the kingdom of heaven, but whoever practices and teaches these commands will be called great in the kingdom of heaven. For I tell you that unless your righteousness surpasses that of*

the Pharisees and the teachers of the law, you will certainly not enter the kingdom of heaven." (John 5:1 NIV)

Well there we have it, yet another smoking gun! What Jesus in effect has said is this: any genuine moral crusader or civil rights activist who stands up and denounces God's decree for stoning a child to death because she disrespected her parents, has no place in heaven. Helen H. Gardner said it right when she commented on Jesus' endorsement of the Old Testament:

"It teaches us that a father may sell his daughter (Exodus 21:7), that he may sacrifice her purity to a mob (Judges 19:24) and that me may murder her and still be a good father and a holy man. It teaches that a man may have any number of wives; that he may sell them, give them away, or change them around and still be a perfect gentleman, a good husband, a righteous man and one of God's intimate friends."

Whilst this may seem a squandered opportunity for Jesus to distance himself from the wickedness of God, you have to remember the target audience for these books. The motivation for writing all of the New Testament was to recruit fellow Jews to their fledgling religion and by denouncing the law of the time, that being Mosaic law, would have meant that the Jesus following Jews would have been bashed to death for blasphemy. And if you defend Jesus' endorsement of Old Testament barbarism as merely a strategic or life preserving tactic then you are not only calling Jesus a liar, but also a coward for failing to make a principled stance for morality, peace and harmony. What a beautiful conundrum!

John writes one of the most well known pieces of the Bible in an attempt to show that the Jewish elders and Pharisees were a cunning bunch but no match for quick-witted Jesus. But in doing so he further illustrates the conundrum that Christians today have in divorcing themselves from the wickedness of the Old Testament. John exemplifies this in the tale of a young lady caught in the act of adultery. The Pharisees dragged this woman by the hair and threw her onto the ground in front of Jesus, demanding to know if he agreed that the female perpetrator be stoned to death as per Mosaic Law. This, the Pharisees thought would place Jesus in a catch-22. If he did not agree with her being stoned to death, then he was in violation of the law. If he did agree then he contradicted his teachings of forgiveness for sin. Jesus sensed the trap that had been set. Knowing this he stooped onto his haunches and began writing something unintelligible with his finger in the dirt and in a calm soft voice replied:

"If any of you is without sin, let him be the first to throw a stone at her." (John 8:7 NIV)

John writes that the crowd promptly dispersed one by one until only he and the adulteress remained. To which Jesus said to her, "I forgive you. Go forth and sin no more". A couple of issues this raises, that being if it was only her and Jesus that remained how do we know this is what he said to her? And where was the husband she had committed adultery with, as the law would demand his execution too?

Further, on what authority did Jesus have to forgive her? And as God's law of adultery applies only to women, what of her aggrieved husband? Did he forgive her? On this issue, C.S Lewis, in *Mere Christianity*, makes the following stinging point:

> *"Now, unless the speaker is God, this is really so preposterous as to be comic. We can all understand how a man forgives his offenses against himself. You tread on my toes and I forgive you, you steal my money and I forgive you. But what should we make of a man, himself unrobed and untrodden-on, who announced that he forgave you for treading on other men's toes and stealing other men's money? Asinine fatuity is the kindest description we should give his conduct. Yet this is what Jesus did. He told people that their sins were forgiven, and never waited to consult all the other people whom their sins had undoubtedly injured. He unhesitatingly behaved as if He was the the party chiefly concerned, the person chiefly offended in all the offenses. This makes no sense only if he really was the God whose laws are broken and whose love is wounded in every sin. In the mouth of of any speaker who is not God, these words would imply what I can only regard as silliness and conceit unrivalled by any other character in history."*

Walking On Water

Three of the four gospels believe it interesting enough to write of Jesus' ability to walk on water, but Luke must have thought that miracle was so 500 B.C. The narrative has it that Jesus sent his disciples on ahead of him in a separate boat to cross over to the other side of a sea. Jesus wanted to remain behind by himself so that he could pray. Matthew writes that Jesus then walked to the top of a nearby mountain to spend the next four days praying in solitude before performing his aqua miracle, but Mark and John claim that he walked on water the same day he had sent his followers forth.

The stories collaborate in the most part from here, with the three Gospels writing that the boat carrying his disciples was not only at least three miles from shore but was also being buffeted by huge waves and a storm. The disciples feared for their lives, but in the middle of the night one of the oarsman spotted what he thought was a ghost off in the distance walking across the waves towards them, before another yelled out, "Holy shit it is

Jesus!" The relieved disciples welcomed their teacher onto the boat and for Mark and John that it is the end of this story. For Matthew his wild imagination leads him to further indulge this piece of fanciful fiction, as he adds that rather than being merely helped into the boat by his disciples, it was Peter who first spotted Jesus and he stepped out of the boat and across the surface of an angry sea to greet Jesus, with both men shaking hands whilst the water lapped below their sandals. The reality, however, of what was happening quickly dawned on Peter and he became concerned that he would sink beneath the waves because whilst he was managing to walk on water without difficulty he could not swim. Jesus seeing Peter's fear and trepidation grabbed him by one arm and said famously:

"You of little faith, why do you doubt?" (Matthew 14:31 NIV)

Both men returned safely to the boat and the other disciples fell to their feet in praise.

Whilst I enjoy this Biblical story from an entertainment perspective, I do prefer an old Russian proverb from a perspective of wisdom, that says:

"Pray for help. Fine. But whilst are you doing that don't forget to row like hell."

Was Jesus a Racist?

I bet this headline shocked you, even if you aren't a believer. But believe me the passage I am about to refer to is one that equally shocked me when I stumbled upon it. Without question this narrative lays the charge that Jesus was indeed a racist and contemptuous of non-Jews.

The story is told in Matthew, whereby Jesus and his disciples leave for the region of Tyre and Sidon. Once parked there for the night, a Caanite woman, non-Jew, approached Jesus pleading that he heal her daughter who was suffering from demonic possession:

"Lord, Son of David, have mercy on me! My daughter is suffering terribly." (Matthew 21:22 NIV)

Demonstrating that whilst she may not have been of Hebrew origin, she at least had faith in Jesus. Evidently this is not adequate as Jesus responds:

"I was sent only to the lost sheep of Israel." (Matthew 21:24 NIV)

Advising the woman that his mission from God was to heal Jews only, she falls to her knees crying, and kissing Jesus' feet, pleading that whilst she is not a Jew, she believes that he is the Son of God. Jesus growing exasperated replies callously:

> *"It is not right to take the children's bread and toss it to their dogs." (Matthew 21:26 NIV)*

Thus implying that the Caanites are only Hebrew slaves and not worthy of God's love or care. The woman grows increasingly desperate, and in victim language consistent with anyone who has been oppressed says:

> *"Yes Lord, but even the dogs eat the crumbs that fall from their master's table." (Matthew 21:27 NIV)*

Jesus rises from his chair, looks down upon this grief-stricken woman, and says to her that she is of great faith and therefore he will make an exception in her case.

What a guy!

Jesus Disses His Mother

We have already witnessed the surly and ill-tempered Jesus disrespect his mother Mary at the wedding where Jesus turned water into great tasting vino, and according to Matthew and Luke he is guilty once more of treating his dear mum with contempt during a moment when Jesus is preaching to a small crowd milling around him. One of the audience members, called out, "Hey Jesus your mother and brothers are standing outside, wanting to speak to you." Jesus in an act of impetuous teenage-like rebellion replies:

> *"'Who is my mother and who are my brothers?' Pointing at his disciples he said, 'Here are my mother and my brothers'." (Matthew 12:48-49 NIV)*

Luke writes that Jesus replies:

> *"My mother and brothers are those who hear God's words and put it into practice." (Luke 8:21 NIV)*

Regardless whether it is Matthew's words, or that of Luke's that is correct, if this event were to have taken place it does provide an insightful perspective into Jesus' character. An insight that reveals that he'd rather play guru with his handful of fans than show his mother a little piece of son-mother acknowledgement and another example showing Jesus' lack of parental respect, as per Mosaic laws. Matthew even has Jesus endorsing this command when he tells of a verbal exchange between Jesus and some Jewish priests. Jesus chastises the priests for failing to execute their own children for disrespect, claiming that they have turned a blind eye to this law so they may continue to use their children as workers:

"And why do you break the command of God fo. For God said, 'Honour your father and mother a, father or mother must be put to death'." (Matthew

I am sure your Christian friends have no idea murder of children, but there it is.

The Twelve Disciples

Jesus quickly grew his disciple base from the initial ive as the small legion of fans had increased from a few dozen to more than a couple hundred and like any growing fan club the greater number of administrative tasks required additional volunteers. Jesus then called on the following twelve, giving them the authority to:

> *"Drive out evil spirits and to heal every disease and sickness." (Matthew 10:1 NIV)*

The following men became the twelve: Simon and his brother Andrew; James and his brother John; Philip and Bartholomew; Thomas and Matthew the tax collector; James; Thaddaeus; Simon the Zealot and Judas Iscariot.

Jesus set forth strict instructions that they were to pass on his teachings to Jews only and forbidden to speak to those uncircumcised men of the Gentiles (non-Jews). Echoing his racist overture within the earlier story of him refusing to heal a Caanite woman's daughter.

Jesus asked them to preach the following message:

> *"The kingdom of heaven is near. Heal the sick, raise the dead, cleanse those who have leprosy, drive out demons. Freely you have received, freely give. Do not take along any gold or silver or copper in your belts; take no bag for this journey, or extra tunic, or sandals or a staff; for the worker is worth his keep." (Matthew 10:6-10 NIV)*

Sending them off, he bid them farewell with the words, "I am sending you out like sheep among the wolves".

John only provides names for the first four disciples and Luke writes that the tenth of the twelve disciples is Judas son of James, whereas Matthew had included Thaddaeus.

In regards to Simon the Zealot, he is arguably the only one of the twelve to be of some moral courage, as the term zealot in those times was a label given to those that conspired to overthrow the Roman occupation. The zealots were the Jewish freedom fighters of the day.

parable of the narrow and wide gate is his next piece of worldly wisdom:

> *"Enter through the narrow gate. For wide is the gate and broad is the road that leads to destruction and many enter through it. But small is the gate and narrow the road that leads to life and only a few find it." (Matthew 7:13-14 NIV)*

I have always had difficulty in fathoming this message, as it implies that a large proportion of mankind (us) are doomed for failure and doomed for eternal hell. This is not really a message inspiring hope and pitiful in comparison to the soaring rhetoric of Martin Luther King, the kind that leads ordinary people to do extraordinary things. Jesus is demonstrating his low expectations of his fellow man, his pessimism and doubt. Which poses somewhat of a logistical nightmare of sorts, for example, there are almost six billion of us currently inhabiting the earth, excluding anyone born after yesterday, all six billion of us will die within the next 110 years. Applying Pareto's 80/20 law, which seems to work for everything else in nature, business and sport, only 1.2 billion of us are going to heaven, whilst 4.8 billion of us heathens are going to hell. Add in the eighty percent of every single person that has ever inhabited the earth in the past 2,000 years and we are talking about a severe shortage of real estate in Satan's Inn. Certainly an opportunity to build some long-term condominium developments by the shores of Sulphur Lake.

Jesus shows shades of his father's wrath, fury and jealousy in his parable of the 'tree and its fruit', when he warned:

> *"Watch out for false prophets. They come to you in sheep's clothing, but inwardly they are ferocious wolves. By their fruit you will recognize them... A good tree cannot bear bad fruit and a bad tree cannot bear good fruit. Every tree that does not bear good fruit is cut down and thrown into the fire." (Matthew 7:15-19 NIV)*

Jesus apologists will defend this statement as purely a metaphor for the choice of wisdom, but don't be fooled. This is soft-spoken Jesus calling for non-believers to be, "cut down and thrown into the fire" and for the death of those that try to sway you away from his side. How many pagans, Jews, heretics and witches were cruelly burnt at the stake during the Inquisitions because of this quote? The human suffering that has been inflicted by one religious denomination or sect on another because of this careless and wicked edict is incalculable. You cannot defend this as just something that man has taken out of context and thus misinterpreted

Jesus' meaning because Jesus doesn't talk to us anymore and naturally it is left to man to decipher. But again further evidence that shows a lack of measurable foresight that one might hope for in a loving human-god, with super-human intellect.

> *"The knowledge of the secrets of the kingdom of heaven has been given to you, but not to them. Whoever has will be given more and he will have an abundance. Whoever does not have, even what he has will be taken from him. This is why I speak to them in parables: Through seeing, they do not see; through hearing, they do not understand." (Matthew 13:11-13 NIV)*

That's a pretty fucking ordinary explanation given the fact that people are struggling to understand you the first time around and now you are making it more difficult by speaking in riddles. But before I admonish the anointed one for speaking in a manner so ridiculous, this is once again another effort of the author to match Old Testament prophecy to Jesus biography:

> *"So was fulfilled what was spoken through the prophet (in Psalm 78:2): 'I will open my mouth in parables, I will utter things hidden since the creation of the world'." (Matthew 13:35 NIV)*

But if you are looking for a little more Jesus-fueled fire and brimstone, then you might like this one:

> *"The field is the world and the good seed stands for the sons of the kingdom. The weeds are the sons of the evil one and the enemy who sows them is the devil. The harvest is the end of the age and the harvesters are angels. As the weeds are pulled up and burned in the fire, so it will be at the end of the age. The Son of Man will send out his kingdom everything that causes sin and all who do evil. They will throw them into the fiery furnace, where there will be weeping and gnashing of teeth." (Matthew 13:38-42 NIV)*

Now there's some wholesome bedtime reading for the kiddies. And what is with the 'gnashing of teeth'? Is that some kind of homo-erotic Freudian slip on behalf of the author? Buddha or Socrates, who preceded Jesus time, never said anything as remotely vindictive and indignant as this. What are we to make of a man that speaks in such a manner to those that dare challenge his preachings?:

> *"You snakes! You brood of vipers! How will you escape being condemned to Hell?" (Matthew 23:33 NIV)*

It is doubtful that we would anoint such a person with the honour of 'enlightened'.

Looking beyond the parable psycho-babble of Jesus, a stand out piece of narrative in this chapter is one which entails the people of Jesus' hometown to question his Messianic legitimacy. Although his fellow locals were undoubtedly impressed by tales of his travelling magic show, they still harboured doubts in regards to claims that he was anything more than an ordinary man:

"Isn't this the carpenter's son? Isn't his mother's name Mary and aren't his brothers James, Joseph, Simon and Judas? Aren't all his sisters with us? Where then did this man get all these things? And they took offence of him." (Matthew 13:55-57 NIV)

How did Jesus react to this rejection by his own town folk? Well he gave the school yard equivalent of, "I am so the Messiah and you aren't, so there!" then trudged off, as it is written:

"And he (Jesus) did not do many miracles there because of their lack of faith." (Matthew 13:58 NIV)

Not only a form of 'you will see when you believe it' but also an ass-backwards strategy to convert as many Jews as possible to the holy path. It would make logical sense that if God wanted all of mankind to be saved and thus remove the possibility of man murdering each other in religious conflict, it would be more sensible for the Son of God, or God himself to come before *all* of us and put the record straight once and for all. Why leave it to the oratory and argumentative skills of a few Middle Eastern farmers and one guy named Jesus to do all the convincing on his behalf? Therefore we have one more charge to add to the growing litany of character flaws that God doth have – Idiot!

The parable of the prodigal son is told in chapter fifteen, in which Jesus tells the story of a father who has two sons. The youngest son demands that his father pay him his share of his inheritance whilst his father is still alive and kicking. His father agrees to the request and divides his net worth between the youngest and eldest son. The youngest son takes his share and heads off to foreign lands, parties like a rockstar, squandering his money on booze and prostitutes until all the money is eventually spent. Out of cash he has to work as a pig farmer to survive, but decides to travel home to throw himself at the mercy of his father. His father welcomes him home with open arms and says:

"Let's have a feast and celebrate. For this son of mine was dead and is alive again; he was lost and is found." (Luke 15:24 NIV)

The eldest son who stayed devoted to his father, working tirelessly for him and asking of nothing gets the shits for this favoured treatment bestowed on his younger, party animal brother and lets his displeasure be known:

"Look! All these years I've been slaving for you and never disobe
Yet you never gave me a young goat so I could celebrate with r
when this son of yours who has squandered your property u
comes home, you kill the fattened calf for him!" (Luke 15:29-30 NI

To which the father replies,

"My son, you are always with me and everything I have is yours. But we had to celebrate and be glad, because this brother of yours was dead and is alive again; he was lost and is now found." (Luke 15:31-32 NIV)

Is this not another mindless message couresty of ole Jesus? Effectively it says do what you want, but as long as you say you're sorry then all is forgiven. People should be held accountable for their actions in life, a principle this parable is not in synch with. This is an implication that we are free to hurt others, hurt ourselves, squander all, but as long as we repent when we have had our fun then all is good. Certainly there is nothing wrong with forgiveness, but punishment must follow crimes that involve a victim. In this parable the victim was the father and the bad son had to pay no penalty for his wrong-doing because 'sorry' redeemed his actions. Having read this why on earth would you want to be the good son? The bad son got to spend all the money on drugs and hookers and was rewarded for it, whilst the good son got no such reward for living a righteous life.

Jesus Wanted To Kill His Enemies

Certainly one of the most well known lovey kumbaiah messages attributed to Jesus is the 'Love thy neighbour' philosophy:

"Love your neighbour and love your enemies." (Matthew 5:43-44 NIV)

What a majority of Christians are unaware of is the fact that this is a passage taken directly from the mundane and barbaric book of Leviticus:

"...but thou shalt love thy neighbor as thyself: I am the Lord."
(Leviticus 19:17-18)

Still this is unarguably Jesus' most quoted remark and one that is often promoted by Christian evangelicals on bumper stickers. But I am sure an overwhelming majority of believers are acutely unaware that Jesus makes a mockery of this teaching, when he says, according to Luke:

"But those enemies of mine who did not want me to be a king over them – bring them here and kill them in front of me." (Luke 19:27 NIV)

Whilst this passage further shatters the myth of mild, peace-loving Jesus, it may offer some comfort to believers as it does at the very least show hat he shared the same genetic predisposition for blood lust as his Biblically alleged father – God.

Other Teachings

Most of us are already familiar with the more virtuous teachings of Jesus, including 'love thy neighbour'; 'turn the other cheek'; 'do unto others'; 'blessed are the meek'; 'return good for evil'. These are what I call the Christian sound-bites that appeal to those seeking some sort of external guidance. These are the equivalent of the World War One recruitment posters that played heavy on emotion such as, 'What did your daddy do during the Great War?', or 'Uncle Sam needs YOU'. Sound-bites sell because most people don't have time to drill deep into the heart of the issues. But Christians will have you believe that Jesus has some sort of trademark ownership on these moral or ethical principles when as a matter of fact they were written many hundreds of years before Jesus' time and by non-Jews too. It was Buddha that said the following almost seven hundred years before Jesus' time:

> *"Do unto others as ye would that they should do unto you."*

Likewise others had said similar earlier:

> *"One who is injured ought not to return the injury, for on no account can it be right to do an injustice; and it is not right to return an injury, or to do evil to any man, however much we have suffered from him" – Socrates*

> *"Let us not listen to those who think we ought to be angry with our enemies and who believe this to be great and manly. Nothing is so praiseworthy, nothing so clearly shows a great and noble soul, as clemency and readiness to forgive." – Cicero*

Further, the Gospels contradict one another wildly on a number of occasions in instances where they are allegedly quoting Jesus. A standout contradiction that utterly makes a confusion of who Jesus really was, is recorded in the gospel of John whereby he writes Jesus saying:

> *"If I testify about myself, my testimony is NOT valid." (John 5:31 NIV)*

This declaration by Jesus, according to John, is not contradicted by Matthew, Mark or Luke, but by John himself. What hope have we of uncovering the truth of Jesus' life if not only do the biographers of him contradict one another, but they also contradict their own writings? A mere three chapters later John walks into his own trap of fiction, when he has Jesus declaring:

> *"Even if I testify on my own behalf, my testimony IS valid." (John 8:14 NIV)*

Other then self-contradictions there are a number of irresponsible and unwise teachings of Jesus that include recommendations for fasting, love for enemies, choice between God and money and the stupendously ridiculous advice to his followers that they should not worry about anything during their earthly existence as Jesus says:

"Do not worry about your life, what you will eat or drink; or about your body, what you will wear." (Matthew 6:25 NIV)

If ever was a teaching to discourage human endeavour and individual achievement then this may be the one. In effect Jesus has told me that I can just sit on my arse, do nothing and all will be provided for by the heavenly father. Life is good for the believer!

In Matthew's repeated attempts to create the fictitious life of Jesus with alignment to prophecy he makes the error of stretching the 21st century readers intolerance for bullshit, in confirming the story of the Prophet Jonah, in which Jesus is written to have said:

"For as Jonah was three days in the belly of a huge fish, so the Son of Man will be three days and three nights in the heart of the earth." (Matthew 12:40 NIV)

The son of God has verified the ludicrous writings of a rambling 5th Century B.C. prophet that indeed a man can survive inside the belly of a fish for three days. Even if Jesus was ever a real man and claimed to be the son of the universal creator, this quote here would be adequate enough for me to dismiss him as mentally unsound. To then believe that it is only through him that I can enter the kingdom of heaven makes that a giant leap of faith.

Obviously Matthew's eagerness to place this particular passage onto the lips of Jesus is a transparent effort to continue the three day theme throughout Jesus' biography.

Jesus' Triumphal Return Into Jerusalem Riding a Donkey

This narrative provides us with a further example where Matthew removes any doubt of his aims to fabricate events in Jesus' life to fulfill what was written in the Old Testament, even if it meant creating an absurd depiction. In this story, Jesus was to make a supposed triumphal return to Jerusalem after travelling the regions preaching his wisdom. This story is created to fulfil the prophecy of Zechariah. Unfortunately for Matthew his fellow gospels, Mark, Luke and John were far better skilled in interpreting Hebrew text and understood that in Hebrew the word 'and' was used to give emphasis to a narrative and not used as an added. Thus Mark, Luke and John tell of Jesus riding into Jerusalem upon a donkey. However, Matthew has him riding simultaneously upon a donkey and a horse. Not only is this amusing but it is also a highly impressive piece of equestrian stunt riding. Matthew cites the passage Zechariah 9:9, further highlighting his folly:

> *"Say to your Daughter of Zion, 'See your king comes to you, gentle and riding on a donkey, on a colt, the foal of a donkey'." (Matthew 21:5 NIV)*

This is one of the most damning pieces of evidences that unequivocally demonstrates the fabrication of Jesus' biography. Matthew writes that his disciples covered both the donkey and the colt in cloaks and he rode both of them simultaneously into the city to be greeted by a few fans who threw robes onto the ground before him in praise, but others looked on flummoxed as to the identity of this ass riding Jew. Thus plenty in the crowd booed and jeered Jesus, to which Jesus reacted spitefully:

> *"The days will come upon you when your enemies will build an embankment against you and encircle you and hem you in on every side. They will dash you to the ground, you and the children within your walls." (Luke 19:43-44 NIV)*

Jesus proving that, like his spiritual father God, he too seems ok with the idea of baby killing.

The Pharisees

The gospels repeatedly go to great pains to vilify the Pharisees, by painting them as the perpetual enemy of Jesus. The repeated references suggest that this internal enemy is the threat to Jesus' growing fan base. Matthew even suggests that the Pharisees were in the midst of hatching a conspiracy to assassinate Jesus:

> *"The Pharisees went out and plotted how they might kill Jesus."*
> *(Matthew 12:14 NIV)*

So who were the Pharisees? The New Testament doesn't make it clear, but scholars of the Jewish faith likened them to a Jewish political party, or social movement of sorts. There seems to be consensus that the Pharisees were primarily motivated by the desire to re-establish Mosaic law and to resist Roman rule. I presume this is why the gospels present Jesus as an objector to the Pharisees because these were the Jews he or his disciples could not sway. Further Jesus believed in abiding by Roman rule so that peaceful coexistence could continue, this is evident in one scene whereby the Pharisees devise a scheme to catch Jesus publicly denouncing the

Roman Empire so that they could facilitate his arrest. Luke writes that the Pharisees sent Roman spies to ask Jesus:

"Teacher, we know that you speak and teach what is right and that you do not show partiality but teach the way of God in accordance with the truth. It is right for us to pay taxes to Caesar or not?" (Luke 20:21-22 NIV)

Jesus asked for a small silver coin called a denarius, inscribed with the image of the Roman Emperor Caesar on one side. Jesus thumbing the coin between his forefingers replied:

"Then give to Caesar what is Caesar's and to God what is God's"
(Luke 20:35 NIV)

Certainly Jesus had cleverly dodged the word-trap set by the Pharisees but he now paints himself as a moral coward because the Jews despised the Roman occupation and thus Jesus shows us that he is not a man of courage in the way Martin Luther King was when he stood up against white oppression. So is this really a man to be admired? Aren't great moral crusaders of history those that put their agenda ahead of their own well self-interests?

The Pharisees then bring Jesus a demon-possessed man that was also blind and mute. Jesus wasted no time in performing his 'abracadabra' trick and the man was healed. Gathering witnesses were astonished, but the Pharisees amongst them cried out accusatory that Jesus was no more than Satan incarnate. They yelled:

"It is only Beelzebub, the prince of demons, that this fellow drives out demons."
(Matthew 12:24 NIV)

Jesus defended himself against this claim, with a speech that has been reshaped by politicians throughout the ages:

"Every kingdom divided against itself will be ruined and every city or household divided against itself will not stand. If he who is not with me is against me. You brood of vipers, how can you who are evil say anything good? For out of the overflow of the heart the mouth speaks."
(Matthew 12:25-34 NIV)

The Pharisees continued to taunt poor old Jesus. Tempting him to impress them with more miracles as evidence that he is who he claims to be. Jesus replied to their taunts:

"A wicked generation asks for a miraculous sign! But none will be given it except the sign of the prophet Jonah." (Matthew 12:39 NIV)

Thus Jesus' own defence against performing miracles to prove his divinity is to retell the miracle of a man living in a fish story. The Pharisees were dummies though and they continued to call Jesus on his lunatic-like ramblings, tempting Jesus to blaspheme so that they could stone him to death on the spot. Jesus was standing amongst a group of Pharisees who asked him point blank, "Are you the Son of God?"" Jesus answered that he and the Father are one, which is a definitive self-claim that Jesus is God, which makes him the son of himself doesn't it? Weird! The Pharisees had heard enough and were ready to stone him on the spot, but Jesus rushing to his own defence asked:

> *"I have shown you many great miracles from the Father. For which of these do you stone me?" (John 10:32 NIV)*

The above statement contradicts Jesus' own claim that the performing of miracles should not be a prerequisite in believing in him and thus the Pharisees replied:

> *"We are not stoning you for any of these (miracles), but for blasphemy, because you, a mere man, claim to be God." (John 10:33 NIV)*

Jesus then provides a nonsensical response in which he claims not to be God, but that his miracles are evidence that he shares the same powers as God and therefore must be God. If you can make sense of that you are doing better than me. This story ends, like all pieces of fiction, where the hero always makes a miraculous escape, with Jesus fleeing to the other side of the River Jordan.

The False Prophecy of Jesus

This is a remarkable chapter and one that I cannot believe has not been taken hold of by non-believers more tightly as another jig-saw piece compilation of evidence that everything in this book is a result of shoddy workmanship. Starting at the end first, Jesus promises his disciples that the end of the world will come before the then current generation had passed. A bold prediction no less, but one made by someone claiming to have a direct line to God, the creator and master of the universe. A prediction that has proven to be 2000 years wrong and counting! We are still here and no prophet has descended from heaven to greet us with rapture whilst riding a white horse.

Jesus was sitting on the Mount of Olives with his disciples when he foretold of the signs of the end of times. He warned that nation will rise against nation; wars would ravage the earth; famine would inflict the earth; and false prophets would appear. Jesus then quoted a passage from Isaiah 13:10:

"The sun will be darkened and the moon will not give its ligh will fall from the sky and the heavenly bodies will be shaken."

Jesus told them that they would not be forewarned of the actua the end of the world, but he promised them this:

"I tell you the truth, this generation will certainly not pass away until all these things have happened." (Luke 21:32 NIV)

This is not just an isolated narrative by Luke, as this promise of return before the current generation, those alive in 1AD, is made 37 times in the New Testament. This belief or promise is consistent with Jesus' teaching:

"Therefore I tell you, do not worry about your life, what you will eat or drink; or about your body, what you will wear." (Matthew 6:25 NIV)

In fact Jesus tells his followers three times during his sermon on the Mount that they should not be concerned or anxious about the future, because the end of days is near, and they will lifted into Heaven before their generation has passed. His early followers believed him so that they didn't even bother to sow their fields. Let this be a financial warning to those living under the pretense that Jesus will return anytime soon.

Consider for a moment what Jesus' doctrine of not worrying about tomorrow actually implies. It means to disregard financial, parental, physical, and social responsibilities. What sort of moral teaching is this? It's absolutely immoral. CS Lewis quite rightfully said that either Jesus was a madman, or he really did believe the world was soon coming to an end. And if he is truly the Son of God then to have not returned within the time frame he promised is irrefutably, in itself, a wicked act.

Ultimately, the false prophet proved to be Jesus! If you are a Christian you really need to consider a conversion to Judaism because the Jews were correct in calling Jesus a phoney, based on this prophecy alone. And if this were a Mosaic trial case, the jury would have no choice but to find Jesus guilty of blasphemy.

The Last Supper

The Pharisees, chief priests and the elders of the Jewish people were becoming increasingly anxious to take Jesus down and thus they schemed a plan that would instigate the arrest of Jesus. This plan would be put into action after the festivities of the Passover, as the conspirators worried that the people would riot in the streets if his followers got wind of this subpoena during the feasts.

The chief priests successfully recruited an 'inside man', one of the twelve disciples, to be the point for the sting operation. His name: Judas

Iscariot. The priests agreed to pay Judas a sum of thirty silver coins for his part. His role was to identify an opportunity that would present the most opportunistic moment to befall his mentor.

Although Jesus did not know of the details of this plot he did confide in his disciples with the following prediction:

"As you know, the Passover is two days away – and the Son of Man will be handed over to be crucified." (Matthew 26:2 NIV)

Whereas John tells of Jesus calling to God, and God answering in the presence of his disciples, who threw themselves to the floor upon hearing the invisible voice from Heaven, with Jesus comforting them with forecast of his resurrection:

"The voice was for your benefit, not mine. Now is the time for judgment on this world; now the prince of this world will be driven out. But I, when I am lifted up from the earth, will draw all men to myself." (John 12:30-32 NIV)

On the first day of the Passover celebrations, Jesus' disciples came to him and asked how he would like them to prepare for him the Passover, to which Jesus answered:

"Go into the city to a certain man and tell him, 'The Teacher says: My appointed time is near. I am going to celebrate the Passover with my disciples at your house'." (Matthew 26:17-18 NIV)

The twelve disciples prepared a huge banquet of some of the best cuisine available at the time. As they dined, Jesus stood in the centre position of the long dining table and proclaimed:

"I tell you the truth, one of you will betray me." (Matthew 26:21 NIV)

His disciples were shocked that a 'rat' could possibly be amongst them and they replied in unison, "Surely not our Lord?" As such Jesus replied somewhat cryptically:

"It is the one to whom I will give this piece of bread when I have dipped it in the dish." (John 13:26 NIV)

Whereas Matthew says Jesus outed his would-be nemesis disciple:

"The one who has dipped his hand into the bowl with me will betray me." (Matthew 26:23 NIV)

Whilst Mark's narrative doesn't single out anyone in particular:

"One of you will betray me – one who is eating with me." (Mark 14:18 NIV)

However, Judas Iscariot knew that Jesus was implicating him as the would-be traitor and in a declaration of his innocence he rose to his feet and pleaded:

"'Surely not I, Rabbi?' Jesus looked directly into the would-be traitor's eyes and replied, 'Yes it is you.'" (Matthew 26:25 NIV)

Oddly the narrative doesn't include any further dialogue demonstrating allegation and denial between Judas and Jesus, as the passage continues to show that all thirteen men continued to enjoy the food and wine. Jesus rose to his feet once again though and gave a toast to his disciples offering his gratitude for their support and service, before breaking a loaf of bread with a strange cannibalistic metaphor:

"Take it and eat; this is my body. Drink from this cup; this is my blood." (Matthew 26:26-27 NIV)

It is from this incredibly odd passage that us rationalists often bear witness to seemingly intelligent friends who function as rational human beings Monday through Saturday, but come Sunday these same friends will step towards an altar and passionately believe they are eating the body of Christ in the form of a cracker, whilst washing it down with a cup of wine they believe is his blood. Ignoring the grotesque nature of this ritual, this is just stupid and we should no longer remain timid in our ridicule of these foolish friends of ours. I am sure though that many just do this out of tradition and observation without thinking how daft it is, but I believe you can change that with a solid slap to the side of their head. Try it!

As the wine flowed, Jesus became increasingly accusatory as many drunks do and this time he turned towards Peter, with a recitation of the prophecy of Zechariah 13:7:

"I will strike the shepherd and the sheep of the flock will be scattered." (Matthew 26:31 NIV)

Jesus using this Old Testament prophecy to predict that as a result of tough times ahead, his weakest followers will disperse into the night so as to save themselves. Naturally, Peter firmly denied this could ever be true and replied:

"Even if all fall away, I will not!" (Mark 14:29 NIV)

Jesus kept on the attack however and countered Peter's defence testimony:

"I tell you the truth, this very night, before the cock crows, you will disown me three times." (Matthew 26:34 NIV)

This is a glaring contradiction to Mark's account:

"Before the cock crows twice, you will deny me three times." (Mark 14:30 NIV)

Naturally the dinner ended on a very sombre note and Jesus led his disciples later that same night to a town called Gethsemane. Once there he displayed his concern that the end was near for him:

> *"My soul is overwhelmed with sorrow to the point of death. Stay here and keep watch with me." (Matthew 26:36 NIV)*

However his disciples were tired and were unable to stay awake in order to stay on guard against the enemies that Jesus believed were assembling against him. And as dawn approached, his disciples remained asleep, only to be awoken by Jesus' sudden declaration:

> *"Look the hour is near and the Son of Man is betrayed into the hands of sinners. Rise, let us go! Here comes my betrayer." (Matthew 26:45-46 NIV)*

As Jesus continued speaking, the doors flung open and a large number of armed Roman soldiers and mercenaries sent from the chief priests stormed the house where Jesus and eleven of his disciples had taken refuge for the evening. The armed assailants were led, as predicted, by Judas Iscariot. Judas had pre-arranged a signal with the would-be captors and foretold them:

> *"The one I kiss is the man: arrest him." (Matthew 26:48 NIV)*

Judas stepped towards where Jesus was seated and pronounced, "Greetings Rabbi!" before kissing his teacher on the cheek. The infamous Judas kiss. But this is only according to Matthew. With far less dramatic effect John, however, makes no mention of a kiss, as he writes that Judas led the arresting officials to the house and only stood amongst them.

It is very unclear as why the Gospels needed to include the story of a betrayal other than so that a few more prophecies could be fulfilled. The Pharisees, Jewish elders and Romans did not need such a betrayal as Jesus could have been arrested any number of times and his identity, according to the Gospels themselves, was hardly a secret amongst the religious authorities of the time. The whole episode is pure fiction and, as expected, it is riddled with contradictions and inconsistencies.

The armed men subsequently stepped forward and placed Jesus in handcuffs. As this was taking place, several of his disciples lunged at the captors with their swords with the aim to protect Jesus till the death. Jesus put a stop to his servant's intended retaliation:

> *"Put your sword back in its place. For all who draw the sword will die by the sword." (Matthew 26:52 NIV)*

John writes that Jesus shouted at Peter, who was the only one of the disciples to wield a sword:

"Put your sword away! Shall I not drink the cup the Father has given me?" (John 18:11 NIV)

Jesus then turned to his armed assailants in an effort to convince them that he had no intention of resisting arrest and that in fact he was indeed pleased that things were all going to God's plan, which makes no sense of the fact that Jesus chose to hide from the arresting authorities:

"Am I leading a rebellion, that you have come out with swords and clubs to capture me? Every day I sat in the temple courts teaching and you did not arrest me. But this has all taken place that the writings of the prophets might be fulfilled." (Matthew 26:53-56 NIV)

According to Matthew, Judas, now riddled with guilt and remorse for fingering Jesus, decided to return the thirty silver coins paid to him by the Priests for his part in Jesus' arrest. Matthew then once again makes a major historical blunder and writes that this event fulfilled the prophecy of Jeremiah:

"They took the thirty silver coins, the price set on him by the people of Israel and they used them to buy the potter's field, as the Lord commanded." (Matthew 27:9-10)

Only one *big* problem, silver coins as currency had gone out of circulation at least three hundred years before the time of Jesus. In fact, minted coins bearing the insignia of the Roman Emperor of the time were used and weighted currency such as silver were used at the time of Jeremiah, but Matthew's lack of investigative journalist skills demonstrates the fiction of this story yet again.

The final act of Judas was him throwing a piece of rope over a tree and hanging himself. We will return to the death of Judas in the Book of Acts, as this story is one of the largest blunders of the New Testament.

The Trial of Jesus

Jesus was then taken away to be placed in front of Calaphas, the high priest and his disciples deserted and fled. Although Peter followed safely from a distance to stand amongst the crowd awaiting the official charges to be laid against Jesus. The hearing was nothing more than a legalized dog and pony show, as the priests and high priest were looking for any false testimony they could pin on Jesus so they could sentence him to death. One of two false testimonies was quickly thrown out for lack of 'credible' evidence and the fact that Jesus refused to answer their questions. The high priest growing frustrated rose to his feet and demanded Jesus answer the following question:

"I charge you under oath by the living God: Tell us if you are Christ, the Son of God." (Matthew 26:63 NIV)

Jesus did not hesitate to answer the question:

"Yes, it is as you say. But I say to all of you: In the future you will see the Son of Man sitting at the right hand of the Mighty One and coming on the clouds of heaven." (Matthew 26:64 NIV)

The high priest seizing the opportunity declared at the top of his voice:

"He has spoken blasphemy! Why do we need any more witnesses? Look, now you have heard the blasphemy. He is worthy of death." (Matthew 26:65-66 NIV)

The assembled gallery of onlookers then proceeded to spit in the face of Jesus, whilst others kicked and punched him. The lesson here is, do not represent yourself in court, better to hire a good lawyer in an expensive suit.

As this was all taking place Peter fled the scene of the court and found refuge outside under a nearby tree. A passer-by recognized him as one of Jesus' disciples and said to him. "You also were with Jesus of Galilee." But Peter denied that he had ever known such a man, before quickly setting off to the other side of the city. But once there, another person approached him and said, "You were with Jesus of Nazareth weren't you?" Peter again denied knowing him, nor having had any relationship with him. Again he promptly walked away to avoid detection. Sure enough he is recognized for a third time and this time in frustration and desperation he yells, "I don't know the man!" But just as the last word was leaving his mouth, a rooster crowed loudly a few yards away and Peter remembered what Jesus had said to him at the Last Supper:

"Before the cock crows, you will disown me three times."

Peter dropped to the ground and began to sob uncontrollably for he, as Jesus forecasted, denounced his teacher. Interestingly this means John's prediction didn't come true, as the cock had crowed before he had completed his third denial and Mark's account proven false also as the cock crowed only once.

Jesus was then brought before the Roman Governor of Jerusalem, Pontius Pilate. Pilate asked the members of the Jewish high court what charges had they laid against the man standing before him, Jesus. The Jews claimed that Jesus was indeed a criminal, otherwise they would not have bothered the Governor in such matter. But upon hearing the case against Jesus, Pilate continued to believe this was purely a case to be tried in the Jewish religious courts. The Jewish elders protested claiming that as

Roman Citizens they did not have the authority to execute those convicted within their courts. Pilate then summoned Jesus and asked him if he was the king of the Jews, because any Jew that claimed kingship status within the Roman Empire could be tried for treason. Jesus replied:

> *"My kingdom is not of this world. It if were, my servants would fight to prevent my arrest by the Jews. But now my kingdom is from another place." (John 18:36 NIV)*

Pilate, somewhat confused by this answer, then asked seeking clarification, "So you are a king then right?" To which Jesus replied:

> *"You are right in saying I am a king. In fact, for this reason I was born and for I came into the world, to testify to the truth. Everyone on the side of truth listens to me." (John 18:37 NIV)*

According to the remainder of John's version of events, Pilate stated that he found no basis for a charge against Jesus, but ordered Jesus to be flogged and a twisted crown of thorns placed around his head, this being adequate punishment. This version of events contrasts, however, to Luke who writes that Jesus was not only brought before Pilate but also Herod. The same former Roman Governor Herod who wanted baby Jesus dead, forcing him and his parents to flee to Egypt. This is problematic for Luke because Matthew wrote that Herod had long passed away, enabling Jesus to return to Nazareth from Egypt.

Pilate then brought Jesus and a murderer named Barabbas before the Jews, as the Bible claim's that it was customary for the Roman Governor to offer clemency to a Jewish prisoner as part of the annual feast of celebrations. This is again a matter of total fabrication, as the only authority given by Rome to a Roman governor in situations like this was postponement of execution until after the religious festival. Release was always out of the question. The motive of the Gospels to include such a passage is to remove the responsibility of Jesus' death from Pilate or the Romans in general and thus place responsibility on the Jews.

As a matter of fact the four Gospels go to extraordinary lengths to absolve the Romans of Jesus' crucifixion in order to blame it on the Jews. The reasoning behind this was two-fold. Firstly the church of Christianity was going to have to exist under Roman rule, which is the reason why the New Testament contains nothing critical of the Romans, even though they were truly despised by the Jews for their prejudiced taxation laws.

Anyway the Gospels write that Pilate repeated his findings that he believed Jesus to have done nothing that deserved death but the crowd called out, "Release Barabbas!" Pilate again stated that he didn't believe

Jesus' crime befit any further punishment, but the crowd yelled, "Crucify Jesus". But who was this the Barabbas character? Mark and Luke claim that he was guilty of murder, whereas John writes that he was a thief.

This entire piece of Biblical fiction is just as comedic as that portrayed by the movie *'Life of Brian'*, where Michael Palin portrays Pilate with a speech impediment lisp that makes it difficult for him to pronounce the letter 'R'. Standing on a balcony above the crowd below Palin asks which prisoner they would like to see set free. The crowd mocking their ruler's speech impediment demand that Roderick be released. Palin replies, "Ok as you will. Welease Wodderick," which only caused the mob to break out into further hysterics.

As in the movie and as in the scripture Pilate the populist caved to their demands and Jesus' fate was sealed.

The Crucifixion

Jesus was then flogged to near death and handed over to Roman centurions to be nailed to the cross. The Bible's portrayal of this grotesque blood lustful execution is no less graphic than that depicted in Mel Gibson's grotesque and self-indulgent movie, *'Passion of the Christ'*.

Once in the hands of the Roman centurions, they continued to beat him, spit on him and in mockery of his king of the Jews self-acclaimed title they twisted together a crown of thorns and set in on his head. The barbs piercing his skin of his face, head and neck. Then they led him away to be crucified.

In Roman times, crucifixion was reserved only for the most heinous of villains due to its inhumane prolonged period of suffering prior to inevitable death. Jesus was laid down on the wooden cross, 6 inch nails hammered through his palms and feet into the timber beneath. The cross raised vertically with the force of gravity slowly tearing at the flesh. Above Jesus' head was a placard that read:

THIS IS JESUS, THE KING OF THE JEWS.

Matthew and Mark claim that Jesus was crucified with two robbers, on either side of him. This a historical flaw too, as the Romans did not crucify robbers. This execution method was reserved only for insurgents against the Roman state and rebellious slaves.

Passers-by hurled abuse at Jesus, spat at him and mocked him with taunts such as, "If you really are the Son of God, come down from the cross and save yourself." Much in the same way the chief priests shouted at him:

"He saved others but he can't save himself! He's the King of Israel! Let him come down now from the cross and we will believe in him. He trusts in God. Let God rescue him now if he wants him." (Matthew 27:42-43 NIV)

John writes that standing near the cross were the 'three Marys'. Mary his mother, Mary his aunt and Mary Magdalene. Jesus seeing his mother there cried:

"Dear Mother, here is your son." (John 19:26 NIV)

Again this is a fallacy that defies historical fact, that being that the Roman Centurions did not allow anyone near the crucifixion fields, certainly not family and friends who might facilitate an escape for the condemned.

It is then written that between the morning hours of 6am to 9am an eerie darkness fell over the land. Day had become night. At approximately nine am, Jesus cried out in a loud voice:

"My God, my God, why have you forsaken me?" (Mark 15:34 NIV)

Hey, far be it for me to ridicule Jesus for this obvious last minute crisis of faith at a time of immense agony and suffering. I think I would have shouted, "Fuck you God, thirty two years of total subservient obedience and this is what I get?" But that's me! Nevertheless this was Jesus throwing a huge cloud of doubt regarding his belief in his mythical father. Which seems hard to comprehend given that the Gospels repeatedly claim that Jesus had predicted his death on a number of occasions and that this was all part of God's divine plan. "Why have you forsaken me?" suggests to me at least, that not all were reading from the same script. But then again a reread of Psalm 22 of the Old Testament suggests indeed the Gospels were on the same page with the plagiarism of identical wording:

"My God, my God, why have you forsaken me?" (Psalm 22 NIV)

Jesus cried out once more damning his God, the final effort exhausting his fight to live and there on the cross he passed away. His final words according to Luke were:

"Father, into your hands I commit my spirit." (Luke 23:46 NIV)

Whereas John writes Jesus' final words to be:

"It is finished!" (John 19:30 NIV)

What the scripture says next is one of complete bullshit, but I will recite it anyway:

"At that moment the curtain of the Temple was torn in two from top to bottom. The earth shook and the rocks split. The tombs broke open and the bodies of many holy people who had died were raised to life." (Matthew 27:51-52 NIV)

Matthew taking another flight of fancy with the claim that dead people rose to life. Not only is this incredible claim not corroborated by the other Gospels, but there is nothing recorded anywhere outside of this passage in any document to claim such a nature defying event took place

Later that evening Jesus' body was removed from the cross, his corpse covered in a clean linen cloth and placed in a tomb that had been cut out of rock. A large stone was rolled in front of the tomb's entrance. The following day the Pharisees approached Pilate to express their concern that Jesus' followers will attempt to remove his body from the tomb so as to deceptively prove that he had risen from the dead and thus fulfilling his prophecy:

> *"We remember that whilst he was still alive that deceived said, 'After three days I will rise again'." (Matthew 27:63 NIV)*

Pilate acknowledged their concern and appointed two centurions to guard the entrance.

Resurrection

This is the critical component of the Christian faith. No resurrection after death, then no Messiah. Whilst one may try and wriggle out of believing in the virgin birth whilst still maintaining faith in Christianity, it is impossible to do so with the resurrection. But like the stories of the virgin birth, the story of the resurrection is one of complete contradiction and conflicting narratives. Before we take a look at what the Bible has to say about this, I want to include the narrative from a cartoon I found on the internet at *www.russellsteapot.com*:

Priest: *Thanks everyone for participating in this year's Easter Pageant. Alright kids we need to rehearse the part where it's Easter morning and the first visitors arrive at Jesus' tomb. Now who's in this scene?*

Child 1: *I am! Matthew 28:2-5 says an angel came down from heaven to greet them.*

Child 2: *No, it wasn't an angel! It was a 'Young man', Just look at Mark 16:5!*

Child 3: *Hello! Luke 24:4 says very clearly it was 'Two men'.*

Child 4: Well according to John 20:1-2 nobody was there.

Priest: *Children the contradictions don't matter! What matters is that we unquestioningly accept the magic of the resurrection even within the face of such glaring contradictions within the story.*

Child 4: *Father that was the most wonderfully concise summary of Christianity I have ever heard.*

Priest: *Thank you child. It is blind submission to authority that got me where I am today.*

Back to the Bible - here is the preamble by Matthew that leads us to the conflicting narratives:

> *"At dawn on the first day of the week, Mary Magdalene and the other Mary went to look at the tomb. There was a violent earthquake, for an angel of the Lord came down from the tomb, rolled back the stone and sat on it." (Matthew 28:1-2 NIV)*

An angel pushes back the stone guarding the tomb's entrance, whilst an earthquake is taking place and then casually takes a seat on top of the stone in view of the two women. Matthew then describes the stone wielding angel and the guard's reaction to seeing such a sight in candid detail:

> *"His (the angel) appearance was like lightening and his clothes were white as snow. The guards were so afraid of him that they shook and became like dead men." (Matthew 28:3-4 NIV)*

Why would an angel wear clothes and where would he buy them? Is there a GAP outlet store in heaven?

The angel then said to the women:

> *"Do not be afraid, for I know that you are looking for Jesus, who was crucified. He is not here; he has risen just as he said. Come and see the place where he lay. Then go quickly and tell his disciples." (Matthew 28:5-7 NIV)*

This contrasts with Mark who makes no mention of an angel, or the guards at the tomb but only that of a young man dressed in a white robe, who said to the women:

> *"Don't be alarmed. You are looking for Jesus the Nazarene, who was crucified. He has risen! He is not here. See they place where they laid him. But go, tell his disciples and Peter, 'He is going ahead of you into Galilee. There you will see him, just as he told you'."*

Luke contradicts both Matthew and Mark by writing of the women's visit to the tomb:

> *"While they were wondering about this, suddenly two men in clothes that gleamed like lightning rods stood beside them." (Luke 24:4 NIV)*

Luke adds that the women were frightened by the sight of these two men, to which the men in lightening rod robes said:

> *"Why do you look for the living among the dead? He is not here; he has risen!" (Luke 24:6 NIV)*

Matthew then continues his account of the angel's conversation with the women, summarizing the following instructions:

"Do not be afraid. Go and tell my brothers to go to Galilee; there they will see me." (Matthew 28:10 NIV)

Alright then so who did the women tell of the fact that Jesus' body had been removed. Agaib conflicting accounts between the Gospels:

"They said nothing to anyone." (Mark 16:8 NIV)

"They ran to report it to his disciples." (Matthew 28:8 NIV)

"They reported these things to the eleven and the rest." (Luke 24:9 NIV)

"Mary Magdalene announces to the disciples that she has seen the Lord." (John 20:18 NIV)

We will stick with Matthew's course of events as he writes with more flavour than the others. Matthew writes that whilst all this was happening, the Guards who had been put on duty to guard the entrance of the tomb, rushed to the chief priests to inform them that Jesus' body was no longer there. A public relations plan was quickly hatched and the guards were paid a large sum of money to keep their mouths shut and if asked they were to say that Jesus' disciples had come during the middle of the night and stole his corpse away whilst they (guards) were sleeping. Matthew concludes this narrative with a pithy little Jewish jab:

"And this story has been widely circulated among the Jews to this very day." (Matthew 28:15 NIV)

Meanwhile the two Mary's successfully located all eleven disciples and told them of their encounters with the angel and Jesus, remembering that Mark claimed the women told no one. As such the band of eleven trekked to the top of a mountain outside of Galilee which is where Jesus had advised them to go. Once there Jesus appeared to them and said:

"All authority in heaven and on earth has been given to me. Therefore go and make disciples of all nations, baptizing them in the name of the Father and of the Son and of the Holy Spirit and teaching them to obey everything I have commanded you. And surely I am with you always, to the very end of the age." (Matthew 28:18-20 NIV)

Thus ending the alleged life and times of Jesus Christ on earth.

Summary of The Gospels

So, in summary, the man (or myth) that more than a billion people believe is the gatekeeper to the kingdom of heaven and who believe he died for our sins and is the son of God, is based on what we have reviewed in the Gospels. So what was so astounding about this character? What did the son of God really accomplish during his thirty odd year mission? Sure he allegedly healed a few people here and there that he came in direct contact with who were afflicted by demonic possession and then there was the walking on water trick, but how did he benefit mankind, or at the very least how did he benefit the people of his time?

Jesus talked about slavery but never denounced it as morally abhorrent. He healed a blind person but didn't cure blindness. He healed a leper but didn't cure leprosy and he proved himself less of an equal to moral courageous leaders such as Ghandi, Martin Luther King and Nelson Mandela in his political manoeuvring in avoiding denouncing any of the barbaric Old Testament laws. And he never stood up for the Jewish people whilst they begroaned under Roman oppression. Most significantly he failed to impress all but a handful of Jews that he was in fact the descendent of the Almighty. If there were a God and this was his son, then shouldn't we all feel a sense of profound disappointment at his lack of achievement?

Chapter Forty-Four - Book of Acts

"Man cannot make a worm, yet he will make gods by the dozen."
Michel Eyquem de Montaigne

It is widely accepted by biblical scholars that the Book of Acts, or Acts of the Gospels as it was previously known as, is written by the same author of the Gospel of Luke at least 70-100 years after the death of Jesus.

The author begins with a prologue addressed to a character named Theophilus, in addition to a reference to 'my earlier book', which we know to the Luke.

Acts provides somewhat of a historical account of the early days of Christianity and its struggle to establish itself as a bona-fide religion amongst Roman-led Jews. The author begins with a narrative proclaiming Jesus as the saviour and that the end of time draws near:

> *"In my former book, Theophilus I wrote about all that Jesus began to do and to teach until the day he was taken up to heaven, after giving instructions through the Holy Spirit to the apostles he had chosen. After his suffering he showed himself to these men and gave many convincing proofs that he was alive… He (Jesus) said to them: 'It is not for you to know the end times or dates the Father has set by own his authority. But you will receive power when the Holy Spirit comes on you; and you will be my witnesses in Jerusalem and in all Judea and Samaria and to the ends of earth'."* (Acts 1:1-8 NIV)

Not content to leave the opening passage with some sense of realism, the author indulges a little magical, mystery imagery:

"After he (Jesus) said this, he was taken up before their very eyes and a cloud him from their sight." (Acts 1:9 NIV)

Doesn't it seem at least a tiny bit obvious that 1st century man would use descending and ascending clouds as a depiction of the mode of transport to heaven? I would think it more creative if Jesus were to transform into an albatross before their eyes, mutter a few words, steal a chip, then flap off into the sunset. Or did I once dream that whilst experimenting with hallucinogenic fungi a few years ago? I can never tell!

At the end of the first chapter the process to nominate a replacement for the treacherous Judas is named, as is a roll-call for the twelve disciples who now carry the responsibility to spread the Christian message. This first roll call included the disciples Peter, John, James, Bartholomew and Matthew; James son of Alphaeus and Simon the Zealot and Judas son of James. This coming together also included Mary the mother of Jesus and his brothers. With all present eligible to vote, they elected Matthias to be the replacement for the now deceased Judas.

The Mystery of Judas

The Gospel Matthew had told the story that a guilt ridden Judas, remorseful and tormented by his own treachery, paid guilt money to the priests at the temple before throwing a rope over a tree and hanging himself. Certainly a tragic ending to a tragic figure. But the book of Acts completely contradicts this story, and shows God once again to be an unforgiving murderous thug. The passage reads:

"With the reward he (Judas) got for his wickedness, Judas bought a field; there he fell headlong, his body burst open and all his intestines spilled out." (Acts 1:18 NIV)

For me the question is not so much whether Judas hung himself or his intestines exploded, but why, if he was remorseful for his actions, as Matthew had illustrated, did God end his life in such a grotesquely violent manner? The early Christians were eager to caricaturize God as a more loving, forgiving father figure in the New Testament but they really do a number on themselves in this conflicting narrative. A narrative that only strengthens our case against God.

The Holy Spirit Comes At Pentecost

In these early days the disciples were continually met with stiff resistance from their fellow Jews, who by and large were not swayed by the messianic claims of Jesus during his life or after death. Thus the disciples and therefore Luke had to continue to increase the bullshit rhetoric in hope that this would sway some easily duped fools. Luke tells of a moment whereby all twelve disciples were gathered in the same place observing the day of the Pentecost, when:

> *"Suddenly a sound like the blowing of a violent wind came from heaven and filled the whole house where they were sitting. They saw what seemed to be tongues of fire that separated and came to rest on each of them. All of them were filled with the Holy Spirit and began to speak in other tongues as the Spirit enabled them." (Acts 2:2-4 NIV)*

Tongues of fire! Hence the reason Pentecostal and born-again loonies practice the utterly ridiculous, self-humiliating act of speaking in nonsensical gibberish on Sundays. I do enjoy Luke's final remark though to the speaking of tongues episode:

> *"Some however, made fun of them and said, 'They have had too much wine!'" (Acts 2:13 NIV)*

I love that. 'Some made fun of them'. Of course they did. That is fucking hilarious. Better, is that this single sentence also suggests that the twelve disciples were closet winos! Getting drunk and talking shit. No different to what happens on weekends around my house during midnight poker games.

Even more comedic is Peter's defence of the non-believer's accusations of their inebriation:

> *"Fellow Jews and all of you who live in Jerusalem, let me explain this to you; listen carefully to what I say. These men are not drunk, as you suppose. It's only nine in the morning!" (Acts 2:14-15 NIV)*

It's only nine in the fucking morning? Well there's a defence I could never use with my wife, as I have been known to crack open a lager for breakfast, or more often imbibe the medicinal properties of a Bloody Mary as a cure for a Sunday morning hangover.

Peter then launches into a tirade against the Jews that laid the foundation for the atrocities of the Crusades in the 11th Century, and continues to fuel Christian anti-Semitism even today:

> *"Men of Israel, listen to this: Jesus of Nazareth was a man accredited by God to you by miracles, wonders and signs, which God did among you through him, as you yourselves know. This man was handed over to you*

by God's set purpose and foreknowledge; and you, with the help of wicked men, put him to death by nailing him to the cross. But God raised him from the dead, freeing him from the agony of death, because it was impossible for death to keep its hold on him." (Acts 2:22-24 NIV)

Based on this I think the author needs a reread of his former book as it didn't seem that God spared Jesus any agony. So much so that Jesus' final words were: "Father why have you forsaken me?" Not the words of a man enjoying his journey to God's right hand. But more importantly, it is a direct accusation against the Jews for the responsibility of Jesus' death.

The Believers Begin To Grow In Numbers

The Jewish non-believers continued to persecute the apostles, seizing Peter and John to put them before the chief priests, elders and teachers of the law in Jerusalem. These Jewish statesmen were displeased that this rag-tag bunch of followers of an charismatic preacher were running around proclaiming the deceased Jesus to be the son of God and his alleged resurrection as evidence of this. Furthermore, Peter's healing of the crippled man was called into question and the Jewish council requested they stop all healing of lepers, cripples and the vision impaired, out of concern that these miracles would convince Jews to convert to the small but growing army of Jesus worshipers. To this demand, Peter replied defiantly:

"Rulers and elders of the people! If we are being called to account today for an act of kindness shown to a cripple and are asked how he was healed, then know this, you are all the people of Israel: it is by the name of Jesus Christ of Nazareth, whom you crucified but whom God raised from the dead, that this man stands before you healed." (Acts 4:8-10 NIV)

Without finding proper charges to lay against their alleged crimes, Peter and John were released and allowed to return to their people. Safely back amongst their flock of fellow Jesus worshippers, Paul led the posse in prayer:

"Now, Lord, consider their threats and enable your servants to speak your word with great boldness. Stretch out your hand to heal and perform miraculous wonders and signs through the name of your holy servant Jesus." (Acts 4:29-30 NIV)

This is problematic for my money. The basis for 'selling' Jesus to the non-believers is the wonder of his 'alleged' miracles. But it is apparently obvious that for all the supposed miracles Jesus reportedly performed within these Jewish towns he fell well short of impressing more than a small band of followers. If he really was so special whilst he was alive, then why did his people dismiss him as little more than a raving lunatic?

Christians today will argue that the Jews rejected him because they wanted to see miracles, well he did perform them and now his followers were performing them in the same manner as Jesus did. Why didn't Jesus give the 'smoking-gun' evidence so that we would not have this Abrahamic, monotheistic shit fight we have today between the Muslims, Christians and Jews? Why was it left up to his travelling salesmen such as Peter and the rest of the apostles to promote the Jesus brand?

At this stage in the Christian recruitment drive the number of followers is said to have grown to a very modest 5000. And upon witnessing the success the perpetual performing of miracles was having on growing their flock the Apostles continued from town to town. As following crowds began to bring their demonically possessed and crippled loved ones into the streets so they would be restored to full health by the tap on the head from Peter. But the Jewish high priests and elders became envious of the Apostles' growing star power and celebrity and subsequently issued an arrest warrant for all twelve of them. Once in jail, an angel of the Lord came to visit them and opened the doors to the cells, freeing the inmates in the middle of the night. The angel gave instructions that they should return to the temple courts to continue to preach the word of Jesus. As dawn broke the priests were made aware that the Apostles had escaped and soon thereafter found them preaching again at the temple courts. The chief priest addressed his fugitives:

> *"We gave you strict orders not to teach in this name. Yet you have filled Jerusalem with your teaching and are determined to make us guilty of this man's blood." (Acts 5:28 NIV)*

To which Peter replied:

> *"We must obey God rather than men! The God of our fathers raised Jesus from the dead – whom you had killed by hanging him on a tree." (Acts 5:29-30 NIV)*

What? Although the respective gospels' account of Jesus' death wildly contradict they were at least unanimous that he was crucified, but now Peter states quite clearly that it was death by hanging. Oh Peter what have you done?

When the chief priests and elders heard this blasphemy they flew into a rage and demanded that the Apostles be put to death immediately. But after some deliberation they opted not to execute them and instead elected for the softer option of a good public flogging. They were also given strict instructions to never speak of Jesus in public again, or a crucifixion would await their disobedience. But in defiance the Apostles continued to preach the merits of Jesus from house to house throughout Jerusalem.

The Execution of Stephen

With the continued growing number of converts, albeit modest numbers, to this fledgling religion of Christianity, the twelve Apostles became bogged down in the day to day operations of feeding and caring for their flock of followers. Thus, by committee they decided to elect seven of their Greek believers to the role of stewards, to prepare the meals, hand out bread to the hungry and to perform some miracles on the side. They chose:

> *"Stephen, a man full of faith and of the Holy Spirit; also Philip, Procorus, Nicanor, Timon, Parmenas and Nicolas from Antioch, a convert to Judaism. These men were presented to the Apostles who prayed and laid hands on them."* (Acts 6:5-6 NIV)

Of the seven it was Stephen who stood out from the other six, as he took straight to his new found role with much vigour and enthusiasm, performing great wonders and miraculous signs amongst the believers. Word of this Stephen character travelled quickly to the high priests and they accused him of blaspheming against the word of Moses and God. Brought before the Hebrew court, the elders allegedly brought false witnesses against Stephen to ensure a speedy trial and quick conviction. In his own defence he delivered a long speech that retraced the history of the Jewish people, providing a summary of their escape from Egypt; the birth of Moses; the rise of Joshua; and to the kingdom of David. All things that would please the listening ears of his Jewish accusers. Unfortunately for Stephen, he did not stop his rant there and finished with a verbal lambasting that all but ensured his doom:

> *"You stiff-necked people, with uncircumcised hearts and ears! You are just like your fathers: You always resist the Holy Spirit! Was there ever a prophet your fathers did not persecute? They even killed those who predicted the coming of the Righteous One. And now you have betrayed and murdered him – you who have received the law that was put into effect through angels but have not obeyed it."* (Acts 7:51-53 NIV)

When the court heard this blasphemous blast, they wasted no time in ordering his execution. There was no death row waiting time in those days and he was dragged by the scruff of his collar to be stoned to death in the dirt outside.

The Church Persecuted and Scattered

On the day of Stephen's execution a great tidal wave of public animosity was raised up against the Apostles and the Church in Jerusalem was annihilated and the Apostles and their followers forced to flee to scattered villages throughout the Judean countryside. We are introduced to a character called Saul of Tauras, who is described as the 'Jewiest' of Jews and a man determined to destroy all remnants of this fledgling anti-establishment religion. Saul went from house to house, hunting out all followers of the deceased Jesus, throwing them into prison for heresy.

Whilst it was certainly a case of two steps forward, three steps back, the Apostles continued to preach in the small towns and with a little more discreet vigour.

Saul Converts to Paul

For an unspecified, but assumedly significant period of time Saul continued to hound down anyone that had ties to the blasphemous Apostles, or those that made public declarations of attachment to the Christian belief. This all changed one day, however, when Saul was on a donkey journey from Jerusalem to Damascus, and the ghost of Jesus appeared before him:

> *"Suddenly a light from heaven flashed around him. (Saul) He fell to the ground and heard a voice say to him, 'Saul, Saul, why do you persecute me?'*
>
> *"'Who are you?' replied a terrified and shaking Saul.*
>
> *"'I am Jesus, whom you are persecuting. Now get up and go into the city and you will be told what you must do.' Jesus replied." (Acts 9:3-6 NIV)*

The men travelling with Saul did not see anyone but heard the voice from the sky. Saul picked himself up off the dirt and as he regained his footing he realized that he was now blinded and could not see one foot in front of him. Thus his servants led him by hand into the city of Damascus. Now safely in a friend's house within the city, Saul sat there in shock and did not sleep or eat for three days, with his sight still lost. Like he had seen a ghost. But isn't that a contradiction in terms? How does one see something invisible? God I love the Bible.

Meanwhile a disciple by the name of Ananias was called by God in a vision, with specific instructions, "Go to the house of Judas on Straight Street and ask for a man named Saul from Tarsus, for he is praying. Once there lay your hands on him and his sight will be restored." Ananias tried to argue with God, that he did not want to lay hands on a man who had persecuted Christian Jews so viciously and joyfully as Paul had done so in Jerusalem. I am not sure why these disciples continue to argue directly with God? I love a debate as much as the next man, but if a voice from the clouds spoke to me I would be, "Yes sir, on my way sir, you won't hear a peep of a problem out of me sir, just keep those lightning bolts away from my ass is all I ask Sir!" As usual God wins the argument with this stubborn fool by reassuring him with the words:

"This man is my chosen instrument to carry my name before the Gentiles and their kings and before the people of Israel. I will show him how much he must suffer for my name." (Acts 9:15-16 NIV)

Ananias carried out God's orders as instructed, laying his hands on Saul. As he did this, fish-scales covering Saul's eyes fell to the ground and he could see again.

Obviously grateful for his new set of eyes, Saul began to preach the word that Jesus was the son of God in synagogues throughout Jerusalem and Damascus. The chief priests were mortified upon learning of his conversion and immediately set out a plan to capture and kill him. Saul stumbled onto their plot and fled, in the process changing his name to Paul. (St. Paul) And thus begins his journey as the most important man in the marketing of brand Jesus.

Peter's Journeys

Back to Peter for moment. After visiting the house of a sympathetic Roman centurion's house, Peter had become so hungry that he would have eaten from a street side cart in a dusty Mumbai alleyway. His hunger pangs allowing him to fall into some kind of trance. During his hallucinogenic state he saw heaven open up, with a large white sheet falling from the sky to earth that contained a menu listing of all animals forbidden as food under Jewish law. Then God's voice boomed from the clouds telling him to hunt everything on this list, and that he could now eat anything and everything, despited what he had told Moses all those years ago. I mean c'mon if you were Peter caught with a pork chop in your mouth, you'd too tell those approaching that God said it was ok. In feigned protest, Peter replies:

"Surely not Lord! I have never eaten anything impure or unclean." (Acts 10:14 NIV)

God assured Peter that everything he had created was officially now 'clean, and that he could go forth and hunt and eat pigs for example. We are now at loggerheads with what God had earlier commanded in the painfully long diatribe of Leviticus that included and precluded just about every species of animal, reptile, bird or fish, when he said to Moses:

"I am the Lord your God. Do not defile yourselves by any of these creatures." (Leviticus 11:43 NIV)

Whilst feasting on these once God forbidden foods, Peter travelled throughout the lands of the Gentiles (non-Jewish Christian believers) teaching the word of Jesus to any who would listen. But upon returning to Jerusalem his fellow Jewish disciples became annoyed that Peter had eaten with uncircumcised men during his travels. Peter answered his colleagues with the same words given to him by God:

> *"Fear not my brothers, all men are created by God and he does not play favourites and thus no man including those men uncircumcised are impure if they believe the words of God."*

This set Peter and his disciples off on a journey to farer lands of the Gentiles, such as Greece, Italy and Turkey, to spread the word of God. A decision that would pave the way for a dramatic upswing in recruitment effort now that they were no longer confined to just converting circumcised Jews.

The first official Christian church was established in the Greek town of Antioch, where Peter taught. And it is from this point in history, according to the Bible, that the disciples were first called Christians.

Peter Imprisoned

King Herod continued to persecute Christians in Jerusalem and he had James, the brother of John, put to death. His execution pleased the Jews and Herod wasted no time in summoning for Peter. Shackled by leg irons and imprisoned in a cell for hardened criminals, Peter awaited his court trial. On the eve of his hearing, an angel of the Lord appeared shining a light into his cell. Peter was asleep and had to be tapped on the shoulder by the angel to be awoken, which I find comical. Nevertheless the angel told Peter to get up and as soon as he did the chains miraculously fell off him to the floor. Being a bossy little upstart of an angel, the ghost with wings commanded Peter to throw on his sandals and cloak and to follow him out of prison. Once outside the perimeter walls Peter ran to the house of Mary, the mother of John.

Herod was furious with his guards that Peter had escaped and promptly ordered their execution. Shortly thereafter Herod passed away for failing to thank God in a speech he delivered in Caesarea. For his ungrateful of the holy he was struck down by the invisible hand of the Lord, and his body immediately consumed by worms.

Paul's Travels

Meanwhile, in the background, Paul travelled throughout the Mediterranean preaching the words of Jesus, in places such as Cyprus, Macedonia and Syria.

The Council at Jerusalem

The teachers and church leaders of Antioch (Greece) were becoming pissed off that travelling preachers from Jerusalem were telling Gentile believers that unless a man is circumcised he cannot be saved. This God to Moses command was causing restlessness and concern amongst the uncircumcised Greeks, Syrians and Macedonians. So Paul took off for Jerusalem to speak with the Council, to urge them to drop this law of God so they could continue to make conversion of the Gentiles to Christianity with the tip their penises intact. Paul making the case:

> *"It is my judgment, therefore, that we should not make it difficult for the Gentiles who are turning to God. Instead (of circumcision) we should write to them to abstain from food polluted by idols, from sexual immorality, from the meat of strangled animals and from blood." (Acts 15:19-20 NIV)*

The Council voted and made the decision on behalf of God that circumcision was no longer a prerequisite to entering the kingdom of heaven, a decision overturning God's covenant with Abraham and without God's consul. Does not this prove that the entire fundamental belief of the New Testament is absolutely man-constructed? The Christians, with so much of their faith based on the Old Testament, are now overturning God-commanded laws by committee.

A letter was then drafted by the apostles and elders, addressed to the Gentiles in Greece, Syria and Cilicia that read:

> *"Greetings.*
>
> *"We have heard that some went out from us without our authorization and disturbed you, troubling your minds by what they said. So we all agreed to choose some men and send them to you with our dear friends Banabas and Paul - men who have risked their lives for the name of our Lord Jesus Christ. Therefore we are sending Judas and Silas to confirm by word of mouth what we are writing. It seemed good to the Holy Spirit and to us not to burden you with anything beyond the following requirements: You are to abstain from food sacrificed to idols, from the meat of strangled animals and from sexual immorality. You will do well to avoid these things.*
>
> *"Farewell" (Acts 15:23-29 NIV)*

The Gentiles with their uncircumcised penises were obviously delighted to learn of this new decree, so up ya bum Abraham and God, no need to destroy the male member anymore. Paul, the world's first great marketing CEO, had repackaged and rebranded Christianity and now this fledgling religion was on its way.

Paul In Prison

Whilst travelling through Macedonia, Paul and Silas were met by a young girl, a child of slaves. She earned a reasonable amount of cash practicing as a fortune teller and her ability to foretell the future was well revered in the area. As Paul and Silas walked through the town that she happened to be reading palms in, she cried out, "These men are servants of the most high God, they are going to tell you the way to be saved." She kept this up for a number of days, before Paul eventually tired of her incessant ranting. Turning towards the girl, he placed his hand on her head and shouted:

> *"In the name of Jesus Christ I command you to come out of her!"*
> *(Acts 16:17 NIV)*

At that moment the 'spirit' that enabled her to predict the future left her. When her parents learned of this they were furious that this revenue stream had been cut off by Paul's 'spiritual healing' and quickly rounded up a mob to lynch Paul and Silas. Bringing them before the proper authorities, her parents accused:

> *"These men are Jews and are throwing our city into uproar by advocating customs unlawful for us to Romans to accept or practice." (Acts 16:20-21 NIV)*

Paul and Silas were then duly flogged and thrown into prison, with a guard appointed to ensure their captivity. At a minute past midnight, the two prophet prisoners began singing hymns in praise of God. As other prisoners listened to these soulful ballads, a great earthquake struck the city and the foundations of the prison were shaken and moved. At this moment the doors to the prison flew open and every prisoner's foot and handcuffs became loose. As other prisoners ran for their freedom, Paul and Silas sat unmoved in their cell to the disbelief and surprise of their guard who was visibly nervous after witnessing the preceding events. Paul told the guard that he need not worry, as the pair had no intentions of plotting an escape. The guard fell to his knees and begged to be baptized with the spirit of God for what he had seen. At the break of dawn the head magistrate came to the jail and ordered that Paul and Silas be set free so that no further trouble would beset their city.

Paul Travels All Through Greece and Macedonia

Spreading the word of Jesus from Thessalonia to Berea; from Athens to Corinth, Paul continued to perform a countless array of miracles for converting Greeks. Paul was well received everywhere he travelled within the country because Greeks loved to discuss and debate philosophy and theology and were therefore always open to new perspectives. The only trouble he encountered was in Corinth, when some Jews abused him for talking rubbish. As he lay in bed one night in fear of a Jewish reprisal against him, God appeared to Paul in a vision:

> *"Do not be afraid; keep on speaking, do not be silent. For I am with you and no one is going to attack and harm you, because I have many people in this city." (Acts 18:9-10 NIV)*

God doing his best to sound like a Mafia boss. "Don't worry my friend, the family will look after you. We take care of our own."

With God's protection racket in place, Paul decided to stay in Corinth for eighteen months to spread the word.

Paul Heads Back To Jerusalem

Paul's journey by sailing boat from Corinth to Jerusalem took him to a number of stops throughout the Mediterranean including Rhodes, Tyre and Cyprus. In Caesarea a prophet approached Paul and warned him that he would be arrested and most probably executed if he returned to Jerusalem, in reprisal for converting the Gentiles away from Moses and telling them not to circumcise their children or live their lives according to the customs of the Old Testament. Paul told the prophet that he was not concerned and would deal with whatever he came his way.

> *"As soon as Paul approached the temple in Jerusalem some Jewish passers-by shouted, "Men of Israel, help us! This is the man who teaches all men everywhere against our people and our law and this place. And besides, he has brought Greeks into the temple area and defiled the holy place'." (Acts 21:28 NIV)*

The entire city instantaneously broke into riots, as mobs converged to demand the death of Paul for his blasphemy. An entire Roman regiment had to be brought into the city to calm the crowd and several centurions were required to carry Paul away to the sanctuary of the nearest prison, in part to protect him from being lynched and also to appease the rioters by formally arresting him. Once at the barracks, Paul made a request to the prison commander if he could address the crowd, to which he was given permission. During his speech to the angry mob, he gave an account as to the reasons why he chose to convert from Judaism, as Saul, to Christianity as Paul. Pointing out that Jesus had spoken to him in a vision whilst travelling to Damascus years earlier and thus he now felt responsible to carry forth the word of Christ. Then he said:

"The God of our fathers has chosen you to know his will and to see the Righteous One and to hear the words from his mouth. You will be his witness to all men of what you have seen and heard. And now what are you waiting for? Get up, be baptized and wash your sins away, calling on his (Jesus) name." (Acts 22:14-16 NIV)

The crowd listened attentively to his speech, but his continual endorsement of Jesus as son of God, left the Jewish crowd with no alternative but to demand his execution. "Rid the earth of him," they shouted.

The Romans agreed to carry out a public flogging of him and he was taken to the flogging station for a good ole hometown whipping. Tied to the post and with the centurion's whip cocked and ready to inflict its devastating pain, Paul yelled out, "Is it legal for you to whip a Roman citizen who hasn't even been found guilty?" When the commander heard this, he called for an immediate end to the punishment. A Roman would not be flogged under his watch under any circumstances unless proven guilty in a Roman court. Subsequently the commander handed Paul over to the Jewish high priests to determine what this prisoner had been found guilty of doing. As Paul stood before the high priest, Paul went on the verbal offensive:

"God will strike you, you whitewashed wall! You sit there to judge me according to the law, yet you yourself violate the law by commanding that I be struck!" (Acts 23:3 NIV)

The priests and elders rose in uproar that he would dare speak to the high priest with such contempt. Paul then softened his rhetoric a touch and offered:

"My brothers, I am a Pharisee, the son of a Pharisee. I stand on trial because of my hope in the resurrection of the dead." (Acts 23:6 NIV)

The key word there 'hope'. The wish for death after life. With these words a fight broke out amongst the Pharisees against the Sadducees (another political group), as the Sadducees believe that there are no such things as angels or spirits and that it is impossible for one to be risen from the dead. Well, they were dead right on that account! With the infighting and no resolution as to what do with Paul, the Romans took him back to the barracks for the evening. Later that night, Jesus, appearing as a ghost, stood before Paul in his cell and said:

"Take courage! As you have testified about me in Jerusalem, so you must also testify in Rome." (Acts 23:11 NIV)

But the Jews were plotting to kill Paul for his treason. Forty men were assembling to storm the prison to hack him to pieces, but fortunately Paul's sister learned of the plot. Which, based on numerous Biblical stories to now, makes me believe the Jews are possibly the worst people in the world for keeping a secret. How many times has a similar story been told in the Bible to this point? A plot to assassinate is foiled because of a leak, surely a dozen instances we have already uncovered. Anyway, Paul's sister informs the prison commander and convinces him to relocate her brother to Caesarea with an armed escort of two hundred soldiers and seventy horsemen. The commander penned a letter to Governor Felix of Caesarea, ahead of Paul's arrival, that read:

> *"Greetings.*
>
> *"This man was seized by the Jews and they were about to kill him, but I came with my troops and rescued him, for I had learned that he is a Roman citizen. I wanted to know why they were accusing him, so I brought him to their council. I found that the accusations had to do with questions about their (Jewish) law, but there was no charge against him that deserved death or imprisonment. When I was informed of a plot to be carried out against the man, I sent him to you at once. I also ordered his accusers to present to you their case against him." (Acts 23:27-30 NIV)*

The Trial Before Felix

Five days later Paul was brought before Governor Felix to be trialled. His accusers had travelled from Ananias to outline their accusations against Paul, which read:

> *"We have found this man to be a troublemaker, stirring up riots among the Jews all over the world. He is a ringleader of the Nazarene sect and even tried to desecrate the temple; so we seized him. By examining him yourself you will be able to learn the truth about all these charges we are bringing against him." (Acts 24:5-8 NIV)*

Paul made his defence on the basis that he was not a trouble-maker and that he followed the same God as the Jews, but with his added belief that Jesus was the son of God, was resurrected after death and will one day return to save all believers. At the conclusion of the trial, Governor Felix was unable to determine a verdict and had Paul returned to prison, where he sat for the following two years. In this time Governor Felix was replaced by Governor Festus.

The Trial Before Festus

Once Festus was in power, the Jews petitioned the Governor to have Paul transferred back to Jerusalem, so that they could carry out their plot to kill him. Festus listened to both sides and then sought the consul of King Agrippa. Festus provided the King with an overview of the case, informing the Greek King that it was not the Roman custom to hand over any man before he had had an opportunity to face his accusers and to defend himself against their charges. The King asked Festus what exactly was the nature of the dispute, to which Festus replied:

> *"They have some points of dispute with him about their own religion and about a dead man named Jesus whom Paul claimed was alive, but is physically dead. I was at a loss how to investigate such matters." (Acts 25:19-20 NIV)*

The King then told Festus that he would like to hear from Paul himself and the next day he was summoned before the King amongst great pomp and ceremony. Paul made his appeal to the King:

> *"Why should any of you consider it incredible that God raises the dead? I too was convinced that I ought to do all that was possible to oppose the name of Jesus of Nazareth. And that is just what I did in Jerusalem." (Acts 26:8-10 NIV)*

Paul continued to provide the history of his conversion from Judaism to Christianity based on his vision of Jesus on the road to Damascus, to which Festus interrupted with:

> *"You are out of your mind, Paul! Your great learning is driving you insane." (Acts 26:24 NIV)*

Thank you Festus! You summed it up perfectly. I couldn't have put it better myself. When people tell me of visions and conversations they have with ghosts, I am with you Festus. But King Agrippa, obviously a nutter, saw it differently and told Paul that he will be sent to Rome to have his case heard before Caesar.

Paul Shipped off to Rome

Paul was assigned to a sail boat alongside a number of fellow prisoners, under guard from centurions of the Imperial Regiment. The total number of passengers aboard the vessel was two hundred and seventy six. An unimaginably slow journey that would take a total of three months. The journey took them through a number of Greek Island ports including Crete, where they encountered a storm that threatened to sink the boat.

The men were saved by God according to Paul, who reassured the other passengers that The Almighty was on their side and that he'd ensure them safe passage to Rome. A few days later, however, the ship ran aground off the coast of Malta and many opted to swim to shore. The centurions fearing that the prisoners would make a run for freedom, elected to kill all prisoners there on the spot, but Paul convinced them against this. The locals of Malta welcomed the marooned prisoners and guards and after a few days assisted in helping them to a cargo ship headed to Rome.

Upon arriving in Rome, Paul was allowed to reside in a home under house arrest by a single guard. A few days later he called an assembly of the city's Jewish elders to come visit him so that he may discuss his case. He told them what he had said in earlier trials, that he denounced Jesus like the majority of Jews, until he met with the ghost of Jesus on the road to Damascus. A large proportion of the elders called him a fool, but a handful stayed to listen to his teachings of his messiah. And from this point and for the next two years Paul taught the principles of Christianity from his house without hindrance.

The Letters of Paul

The Letters of Paul, whilst incarcerated in Rome, are presented in the next ten books of the New Testament. Each book a different letter authored by Paul to a slightly different audience. The ten books of Paul include: Romans; Corinthians; Galathians; Ephesians; Philippians; Colossians; Thessalonians; Timothy; Titus; Philemon.

It is important to note that in his letters Paul makes numerous statements regarding the Christian faith that none of the gospels had Jesus saying. One might conclude this quite a daring feat in citing conversations with a dead man he had never met. The key element here, to keep in mind, is audience. The gospels were writing to a Jewish audience and thus they could not have the character of Jesus denouncing Old Testament laws because this would have warranted the death penalty for heresy. But Paul's audience were the Gentiles, the non-Jewish citizens of Rome, Greece and Persia, thus Paul could position Christianity as a more appealing product for non-Jews. This making Paul the founder of Christianity, although 'Paulanity' is a more logical naming of the religion but doesn't quite have the same ring to it.

Chapter Forty-Five - The Book of Romans

"When someone tells me that 'the Almighty told me to do this', I want to see the transcript."
Fred Reed

The Book of Romans is arguably the most valued book of the Holy Scriptures for the Christian faithful and as such has been appropriately coined the Cathedral of Christianity. It is the first of Paul's letters and as the name suggests this is Paul's letter to the church in Rome. A letter that is brilliantly written and certainly the most literarily profound of all books of the Bible. In lay terms it reads as a 'How to Guide for Christian worship'.

As a matter of fact Paul contributes far more insight and teachings to the way of Christianity than Jesus ever did. As we will discover there are a number of phrases, words, observances wrongly attributed to Jesus by practicing Christians today, depriving the rightful creator his due credit.

Paul's opening declaration of his letter to Romans is:

"Paul, a servant of Christ Jesus, called to be an apostle and set apart for the gospel of God – the gospel he promised beforehand through his prophets in the Holy Scriptures regarding his Son, as to his human nature was a descendent of David and who through his spirit of holiness was declared with power to be the Son of God, by his resurrection from the dead." (Romans 1:14 NIV)

As proven in the contradictions of Jesus' genealogy, which renders his blood-line meaningless, Paul now has created a further problem for the fledgling Church by writing that Jesus is the descendent of David. In the New King James version of the Bible, the passage actually states that Jesus, "was born of the seed of David". This, again, is impossible if he was born to a virgin. Thus either way the church is unable to prove Jesus' fulfilment of messianic prophecy because if he was born of a virgin then he is not a descendent of David. And if born of the seed of Joseph, thus a descendent of David, then he is not born of a virgin. Paul just fucked up the whole story in his first letter. This is important because not only do two of the four gospels make no mention of the virgin birth of Jesus, neither does the founder of the faith. Leaving a 3-2 jury verdict in favour of the natural laws of the universe in the case versus supernatural phenomenon.

The second stanza of the opening of Romans indicates that the church in Rome had been established for a number of years as Paul writes that he had planned many times to visit his Christian brothers in Rome, but had been prevented so for reasons not disclosed. However, whatever difficulties he had faced in his efforts in returning to Rome had been dealt with, and this letter forewarns his planned visit.

"I long to see you so that I may impart to you some spiritual gift to make you strong – that is, that you and I may be mutually encouraged by each other's faith. I do not want you to be unaware, brothers, that I planned many times to come to you but have been prevented from doing so until now, in order that I may harvest among you, just as I have had among the other Gentiles." (Romans 11-13 NIV)

Paulanity

A clever marketer was Paul. Unlike the Gospels whose audiences were the Jews, Paul was writing mostly to a Gentile audience and in his first piece of religious remodelling he 'chops' the circumcision covenant by edifying that heaven is not just a destination for Jews but also for the uncircumcised. But straight off the bat Paul has over ruled what Jesus had said in in Matthew regarding non-Jews, as he made it perfectly clear to his twelve disciples that the word of God is to be preached only to the circumcised crew. Jesus said:

> *"Do not go among the Gentiles or enter any town of the Samaritans. Go only among the lost tribe of Israel." (Matthew 10:5 NIV)*

His explanation and denouncement of this Old Testament belief, is somewhat 'wishy-washy' and a blatant attempt to make the rules up as he goes. Paul fumbles to explain why it was that Abraham was directed by God to mutilate his and his family's genitals, so as to seal the covenant between the two, whilst Gentile believers need not do same and that the promise of eternal life comes now from faith and obedience alone.

> *"Circumcision has value if you observe the law, but if you break the law, you have become as though you had not been circumcised. If those who are not circumcised keep the law's requirements, will they not be regarded as though they were circumcised?" (Romans 2:25-26 NIV)*

Circumcision and the law are not mutually exclusive. If one isn't circumcised he is in violation of God's laws, so what does it matter if he breaks another? He is already a law-breaker. Thus this attempt to divorce circumcision from God's law is nothing more than a populous penis gimmick to promote Christianity to a wider audience.

Aware that he will be cornered into providing an explanation of all Mosaic laws, laws that the philosophy loving Greeks found repugnant, especially animal sacrifice and the Romans found archaic, Paul made a daring but tactically brilliant move to declare all of God's laws irrelevant in the pursuit of righteousness on the sole proviso that one believed Jesus Christ to be the son of God:

> *"Therefore no-one will be declared righteous in his sight by observing the law; rather, through the law we become conscious of sin... This righteousness from God comes through faith in Jesus Christ to all who believe." (Romans 3:20-22 NIV)*

Paul wastes no time in turning on the flames of fear in his letter in an effort to embolden the believers and recruit the naysayers, as he launches straight in with a list of actions that will ensure God's wrath:

> *"The wrath of God is being revealed from heaven against all the godless and wickedness of men who suppress the truth by their wickedness." (Romans 1:18 NIV)*

Homosexuality

Interestingly, whilst Jesus made no reference or mention of homosexuality in any of the passages of the Gospels, Paul sees it fit to single out their immorality on numerous occasions, making him arguably the world's first human-form homophobe!

> *"Even their women exchanged natural relations for unnatural ones. In the same way the men also abandoned natural relations with women and were inflamed with lust for one another. Men committed indecent acts with other men and received in themselves the due penalty for their perversion." (Romans 1:26-27 NIV)*

Once again the ignorance of 1st century man is evident in this passage. An ignorance we can forgive the writer, Paul. But why should we forgive those intolerant and hostile towards homosexuality in the 21st century because of their belief in this scientifically flawed and ancient text? We shouldn't! Quite clearly homosexuality is prevalent throughout the animal kingdom. In fact in a 1999 review by researcher Bruce Baghemihl, it was proven that nearly 1500 species, ranging from primates to gut worms, engage in homosexual behaviour. According to Baghemihl:

> *"The animal kingdom does it with much greater sexual diversity – including homosexual, bisexual and non-reproductive sex – than the scientific community at large have previously been willing to accept."*

Religious fundamentalist groups across the world will continue to cover their eyes and shut their ears to these facts because they fundamentally contradict and then call into question the validity or relevancy of their texts. Thus providing the religious with another segment of mankind to direct its God-inspired, hateful wrath towards.

Paul continues to denounce all non-believers in a vengeful tone:

> *"They (non-believers) have become filled with every kind of wickedness, evil, greed and depravity. They are full of envy, murder, strife, deceit and malice. They are gossips, slanderers, God haters, insolent, arrogant and boastful; they invent ways of doing evil; they disobey their parents; they are senseless, faithless, heartless, ruthless. Although they know God's righteous decree that those who do such things deserve death, they not only continue to do these very things but also approve of those who practice them." (Romans 1:29-32 NIV)*

Not only is this passage full of vim and verve but confirmation that the ideals of Christianity are no less barbaric or more enlightened than its Judeo foundations. Note, also, the twisted irony of what Paul says immediately following this virtual proclamation of war against non-believers, when he writes in the next chapter:

> *"For whatever point you judge others, you are condemning yourself." (Romans 2:1 NIV)*

In one breath he has judged the non-followers of his faith for a litany of alleged sins, then in the next he tells us not to judge others. If this is a little piece of ironic wit on Paul's behalf then I applaud him, but if he wrote this with 'straight-talk' intent then it is even funnier.

Paul then moves forward with a little 'carrot and stick' motivational prose, warning death and destruction to those that fail to obey the laws of God, whilst offering the promise of eternal life to the obedient.

> *"Because of your stubbornness and your unrepentant heart you are storing up wrath against yourself for the day of God's wrath... To those who by persisting to in doing good seek glory, honour and immortality, he will give eternal life." (Romans 2:5-7 NIV)*

And so that we are all crystal clear on our innate wickedness, Paul reminds us that we, humans, are born in sin, filth and wretchedness and only belief in Jesus as the son of God can wash away our figuratively slime-covered bodies:

> *"I know that nothing good lives in me, that is, in my sinful nature. For I have the desire to do what is good, but I cannot carry it out." (Romans 7:18 NIV)*

Thankfully, according to Paul, we can wash away our loathing for ourselves by accepting that:

> *"Righteousness from God comes through faith in Jesus Christ to all who believe." (Romans 3:22 NIV)*

Death for Our Sins

It is Paul who introduces us to the concept of vicarious redemption through Jesus Christ. The repugnant concept that our sins against others can be atoned by saying "sorry" to an unhurt or unaffected third-party. A dead one at that! Bearing in mind that this concept doesn't even receive the credit for being original. It's merely an adaptation of the old theme of human sacrifice, practised by countless civilizations at one time or another to redeem their respective and collective sins or errs. It's from whence the term 'scapegoating' derives from. Tribes would saddle a goat with its wrong doings before sending the goat out into the wilderness to inevitably die of thirst or starvation, so that the tribe would be cleansed or purified of its sins.

Paul writes that God loved his one and only son so much that he carefully laid out a plan to have his beloved offspring butchered on a stake before a ridiculing mob. Some love isn't it? It's this act of 'love' that Paul writes absolves believers of their mortal sins. Paul asserts that we are all sinners but if we believe in Jesus then at the point of our deaths, we will journey to him in the afterlife.

It is the sadomasochistic writings of Paul that contend that God incarnated himself in human form as Jesus Christ, his torture and death an atonement for all of our sins. Not only the sins that we may or may not have personally committed in the past but also the sins we may execute in the future. This is a rather ass-backwards mandate, don't you think? This is God we are talking about so why not just forgive all our sins and rationalize them as human nature? Why does God deem it appropriate to ensure the brutal crucifixion of his son to prove this point?

> *"We were therefore buried with him through baptism into death in order that, just as Christ was raised from the dead through the glory of the Father, we too may live a new life. If we have been united with him in his death, we will certainly be united with him in his resurrection. For we know that our old self was crucified with him so that the body of sin might be done away with, that we should no longer be slaves to sin – because anyone who has died has been freed from sin."* (Romans 6:4-7 NIV)

To reinforce this point, or more like ram it home, Paul drenches this teaching with a large dose of guilt. Leading his readers to believe that we are indeed wretched beings and only redemption in the afterlife through believing the resurrection true will atone for our earthly sins. The mental trauma of guilt that has been inflicted on billions of people throughout the last two millennia begins in these passages:

> *"It is sin living in me. I know that nothing good lives in me, that is, in my sinful nature. For I have the desire to do what is good, but I cannot carry it out. For what I do is not the good I want to do; no, the evil I do not want to do – this I keep on doing. Now if I do what I do not want to do, it is no longer I who do it, but it is the sin living in me that does it… What a wretched man I am! Who will rescue me from this body of death? Thanks be to God – through Jesus Christ our Lord."* (Romans 7:17-25 NIV)

So not only does God have a bizarre way of displaying his love and affection but he wants you to always bear in mind what low worthless scum you truly are. I guess so that you will keep turning up to Church on Sunday to show your appreciation.

This really is a vile premise and an immoral teac believers to believe they are nothing but depraved anima animalistic urges only, unless they bow down to the memory eccentric preacher. This is how all cults form and sustain their men through convincing you that you are nothing but scum, and a ticke a waiting spacecraft awards those that submit to the power of the unseen and unproven. This is mental disintegration and far from teaching humans to love themselves which is irrefutably a mentally healthy state of mind.

God Created Evil

I personally rate the passages that relate to the concept of pre-destination to be in my top five - "Wow, are Christians going to be pissed when they learn this" - list. This argument on its own *proves god to be the creator of evil.*

More often than not Church leaders claim that evil exists because God gave man free will. The assertion being that God gave us free will because he didn't want us to behave like robots, but with free will comes both good and evil. Evil the root of those who suffer from weak faith resulting in an inevitable fall into temptation thus submitting to Satan's devilish plan with the execution of evil deeds. We are led to believe that through faith and in obedience to God we can overcome the dark forces lurking beneath that wrestle for control of our soul. This is a *bogus* claim! I cannot find any passage that directly states such anywhere in the Bible, whereas I can point to several passages that say the complete opposite in irrefutable black and white, such as:

> *"It does not, therefore, depend on man's desire or effort, but on God's mercy. For the scripture says: 'I raised you up for this very purpose, that I might display my power in you and that my name might be proclaimed in all of the earth. Therefore God has mercy on whom he wants to have mercy and he hardens whom he wants to harden.'" (Romans 9:16-18 NIV)*

Paul then extends this proclamation with the metaphor of a clay potter:

> *"Does not the potter have the right to make out of the same lump of clay some pottery for noble purposes and some for common use?" (Romans 9:21 NIV)*

This is not some vague implication that Paul is making here, this is a statement of fact. This states that God created us as he chose and therefore he makes the arbitrary decision to reward whom he made good and punish those he made evil. *Therefore god created evil!* Which means God is evil. Gotcha!

Contempt of Jews

Much of the final passages of Romans refers to Paul's contempt for the non-believing Jews of Israel. The overwhelming majority of Jews continue to reject Christian belief and still believe Jesus to be little more than a dead, eccentric preacher. Paul prays that Israel will one day join the gradually growing ranks of Christians:

"Brothers, my heart's desire and prayer to God for the Israelites is that they may be saved. For I can testify about them that they are zealous for God, but their zeal is not based on knowledge." (Romans 10:1 NIV)

Attempting to lure them from away their Abrahamic worship of God to that of Christ, he offers the carrot of eternal life:

"That if you confess with your mouth, 'Jesus is Lord,' and believe in your heart that God raised him from the dead, you will be saved." (Romans 10:9 NIV)

The Israelites for the most were not swayed by Paul's promises or godly threats, but not disheartened by their rejection of him and Jesus, he predicted that Israel will one day eventually end its stubbornness and turn to Jesus as a result of continued recruiting and conversion of non-Jews to the Christian faith:

"Israel has experienced a hardening in part until the full number of the Gentiles has come in. And so all Israel will be saved, as it is written." (Romans 11:25-26 NIV)

Well he got that part wrong didn't he? 2000 years later and Israel is not a Christian nation!

It is Paul that urges the utterly absurd idea to love your enemies and to feed them when they are hungry. Are we to love the purveyors of Islam that fly planes into our offices? Are we to love fundamentalist Christian activists that bomb abortion clinics killing innocent doctors and their staff? I know these kinds of teachings seem nice and rosy on the surface, but they are not practical; they are not rational; and therefore they are ridiculous. If you consider that somewhere in the Muslim world there is a nineteen year old would-be suicide bomber just itching to splatter your brains and intestines across a cafeteria wall, I believe the only thing we should be feeding this guy is lead. As rationalists it should be our aim to continue to take the fight to the enemies of reason armed with education and knowledge to lower the number of nutbags willing to kill themselves in order to harm us or our children. But when education is too late, then intervention is required and that does not mean helping your enemy with food and shelter. Richard Dawkins said in his documentary, *The Root of Evil,*

"On the surface religion looks charming, peaceful and appealing (candle light, music, ceremonies that bring certain parts of a community together) – but it is

the start of that slippery slope that leads to men strapping rucksacks to themselves and blowing themselves up and scores of innocent bystanders."

Reasoning with men who are not only prepared to die for their religious belief, but wish for death is futile. Sometimes war is a necessity of the human condition, in ensuring our own genetic survival. By choosing to insert flowers down the barrel of a jihadist's rifle will certainly ensure the death of your genetic code. Just trust me on this.

Paul finishes his letter to the Romans with the words:

"I have been longing for many years to see you, I plan to do so when I go to Spain. I hope to visit you while passing through and to have you assist me on my journey there, after I have enjoyed your company for a while. Now, however, I am on my way to Jerusalem in the service of the saint there. Pray that I may be rescued from the unbelievers in Judea and that my service in Jerusalem may be acceptable to the saints there, so that by God's will I may come to you with joy and together with you be refreshed. The God of peace be with you all. Amen." (Romans 15:23-32 NIV)

Philosophical Trap

A philosophical delink that Paul, via the early church of Christianity, has trapped itself in is that Paul preaches that the only way to the kingdom of heaven is for one to believe that Jesus is not only the son of God, but he also died for our sins on the cross. Those that don't believe are sent for torture for the duration of eternity. The question that this begets is what happens to babies or young children that die before they have the chance to know who Jesus was? Where do these dead babies go to in the afterlife? Are babies and young children tortured 24/7 in the bowels of Hell? This is preposterously evil, if so. But Christians today choose to speak on God's behalf by presuming that babies do go to heaven because they haven't had the opportunity to sin yet.

Well this positioning only creates a further dilemma as a lack of evidence for the existence of God, the choice of a thousand religions a growing child or adult is faced with and the temptation to commit any number of seemingly minor infractions which would cause a trip to Hell. It would appear that it is in your baby's best interest to kill them whilst they are still young, thus ensuring them an eternity in heaven. Thus if Christianity is to be believed and rationalized then God has inspired us to become baby killers just like he was in Egypt and throughout other conquests in the Old Testament period.

Chapter Forty-Six - Book of Corinthians 1

"The religion that is afraid of science, dishonours God and commits suicide."
Ralph Waldo Emerson

The book of Corinthians 1 is Paul's first of two letters to the Church in the Greek town of Corinth. The city of Corinth was one of the most vibrant cities of Greece during the lifetime of Paul. A cultural centre that welcomed foreign travellers, for the Greeks were fond of learning and debating new ideas. Pick up any book on first century Corinth and it will concur this metropolis to be one of the most cosmopolitan and tolerant of religious freedom or expression. Although I did find one prominent Christian author who described the city differently. Dr. Henrietta Mears wrote in her book *What the Bible is All About*:

> *"As in most cities, there was a large colony of Jews who had kept a strong moral standard and held to their religious beliefs. But the city itself was the centre of a debased form of the worship of Venus."*

Mears implies that only believers in the God of Abraham or Jesus can be capable of morality. This being a worrying example of how religious belief causes division, elitism and exclusion. Mears further writes that the 'immoral' pagan practices of the freedom and tolerant Corinthians were penetrating the Christian church there:

> *"Practices common to this wicked city soon crept into the Church. There were divisions among them; Christians were going to law with Christians before heathen judges; behaviour at the communion table was disgraceful; the women of the church no longer observed standards of modesty."*

Isn't it lovely that Christians label anyone that doesn't share their belief a 'heathen'? How quickly the 'love thy neighbour' creed gets lost in the wash.

Remembering that these letters were written approximately 70 - 100 years after the death of Jesus, there were still no churches as we know churches to be today. The churches that Paul refers to are small congregations of men that met in secret so as to avoid Roman or Jewish persecution. The first church, in the way that we understand a church to be, did not appear until a further 200 years after the final book of the New Testament in 337 A.D, after Emperor Constantine had made the persecution of this fledgling minority religion illegal.

Whilst Mears' summary of Corinth is misguided she is correct in asserting that Paul's concerns were that the early Christians were being led astray by non-believers and were therefore backsliding in their faith. Paul also expresses angst in relation to rumours he had heard, that there has been quarrelling and division within the Church. As a number of the church members argued amongst themselves who it was that they should be following, as the Christian doctrine was not yet defined. Some of the church-goers were choosing to follow Paul, whilst others were still worshipping Greek gods such as Apollo and Venus. But few were actually praising the headline act, Jesus Christ. Paul, in his letter, attempts to set the record straight and advises them that it is foolish to follow him as he is but a messenger and that they should save their worship for Jesus only.

> *"So far as I can remember, there is not one word in the Gospels in praise of intelligence." - Bertrand Russell*

Paul then draws his attention to making derogatory remarks against scholars, the wise within Corinth, as the educated elite dismissed the evangelism of Jesus' followers. A demographic statistic that continues to run 2000 years later, where the correlation of increased education equates to reduced religiosity. But as the smarty-pants of the day posed a threat to the conversion of the masses to the way of Christ, Paul launches a scathing attack against the intellectuals:

> *"Where is the wise man? Where is the scholar? Where is the philosopher of this age? Has God not made foolish the wisdom of the world? For since the wisdom of God the world through its wisdom did not know him." (1 Corinthians 1:20-21 NIV)*

Paul adds that 'true' wisdom can only be sought through the spirit of Jesus Christ, as he writes:

> *"But God has revealed it (knowledge) to us by his Spirit. The Spirit teaches all things, even the deep things of God."*

Paul also writes an articulate warning against those that indulge in processed foods, simple carbohydrates and/or smoking cigarettes:

> *"Don't you know that you are God's temple and that God's Spirit lives in you? If anyone destroys God's temple, God will destroy him; for God's temple is sacred and you are that temple." (1 Corinthians 3:16-17 NIV)_*

Whilst managing to 'stay on point' with his anti-homosexuality rhetoric:

> *"Do not be deceived: Neither the sexually immoral nor idolaters nor adulterers nor male prostitutes nor homosexual offenders nor thieves nor*

> *the greedy nor drunkards nor slanderers nor swindlers will inherit the kingdom of God." (1 Corinthians 6:9-10 NIV)*

Paul's stance on sexuality is somewhat humorous. He claims that our bodies are not our own, that sins outside of the body such as stealing or murder are in fact less of a crime because those are not sins against God's property, you!

> *"You are not your own; you were bought at a price. Therefore honour God with your body." (1 Corinthians 6:19-20 NIV)*

He rams this point home with a reminder of God's track record in smiting those that have deviated from Christian or Jewish sexual norms:

> *"We should not commit sexual immorality, as some of them did – and in one day twenty three thousand of them died. We should not test the Lord." (1 Corinthians 10:8 NIV)*

Paul's Thoughts on Women

If to this point you had any doubt that Paul was frustrated with his lack of sexual charisma, then his attitude towards the fairer sex in general should put that doubt to rest. Here he opines what involvement women should have in the Church:

> *"Now I want you realize that the head of every man is Christ and the head of every woman is man and the head of Christ is God." (1 Corinthians 11:3 NIV)*

If the above passage isn't enough to convince women that little accommodation is made for them in the church of Christianity, then let this writing from Paul put your mind at ease:

> *"As in all the congregations of the saints, women should remain silent in the churches. They are not allowed to speak, but must be in submission, as the Law says. If they want to enquire about something, they should ask their own husbands at home; for it is disgraceful for a woman to speak in the Church." (1 Corinthians 14:33-35 NIV)*

Allow me to paraphrase the above passage in plain speak: Women are disgraceful and should be subjugated by their husbands so that they remain silent. Of all the Gods and religions that man has created, it baffles me that any rational woman with a shred of feministic pride would touch any of the three monotheistic religions with a ten-foot barge pole. Christianity should have as much appeal to women as does the Ku Klux Klan for Blacks. Little wonder that the Eastern religions, such as Buddhism, have Western women trending to them in great numbers.

If I had a little more spunk, and a lot more cheek, I would visit the nearest church on Sunday handing out 'speaking violation' tickets to any woman that even uttered "hello" – just to bring attention to the misogyny of the Bible.

False Prophecy

But without doubt the single greatest blunder of Paul's letters, including Corinthians, is his perpetual endorsement of the false second coming of Jesus prophecy included in the Gospels. Paul like Mathew, Mark, Luke and John was of the belief that time was running out for Jews to convert to Christianity. Kind of a 'only for a limited time' advertising campaign. Paul urging believers to change their ways and non-believers to convert, writes:

> *"What I mean, brothers, is that the time is short. From now on those who have wives should live as if they had none; those who mourn, as if they did not; those who are happy, as if they were not; those who buy something, as if it were not theirs to keep; those who use the things of the world, as if not engrossed in them. For this world in its present form is passing away." (1 Corinthians 7:29-31 NIV)*

Chapter Forty-Seven - Book of Corinthians 2

"When people are fanatically dedicated to political or religious faiths or any other kinds of dogmas or goals, it's always because these dogmas or goals are in doubt."
Robert M. Pirsig

The second letter of Paul to the Church in Corinth begins again with Paul's claim that he is the apostle of Jesus Christ and begins this correspondence by giving thanks to God for sacrificing his only son and thus through God's barbaric actions the believers can find comfort to ease the sufferings in their own lives. Well that maybe a slight paraphrasing of sorts, but a fairly accurate summary of the opening verses.

Paul makes an outlandish and obscene claim that we should all feel guilty for the execution of Jesus, even though we weren't present for it, witness to it, or knowledgeable of it. Christopher Hitchens in his book *God is Not Great* puts it far more eloquently than I:

> *"Ask yourself the question: how moral is the following? I am told of a human sacrifice that took place two thousand years ago, without my wishing in and in circumstances so ghastly that, had I been present and in*

possession of influence, I would have been duty-bound to try and stop it. In consequence of this murder, my own manifold sins are forgiven me and I may hope to enjoy everlasting life."

This persistent tactic of fear, guilt, punishment and reward model for Christian recruitment is certainly something I find somewhat repulsive. Even if I did believe that this God was real and that his son did in fact die for our sins, why should I be subjected to psychological scaring by being saddled with the gruesome execution of a man that died 2000 years before I had in inhabited the earth?

The rest of this letter is a reminder to the church members that he and his fellow apostles have endured much persecution in preaching the message of Christ and that they should be grateful for their efforts. And also mindful of not falling into the trap of being led away by the non-believers to alternative Gods, a fear he repeats several times.

"I fear that there may be quarrelling, jealousy, outbursts of anger, factions, slander, gossip, arrogance and disorder. I am afraid that when I come before you again my God will humble me before you and I will grieved over many who have sinned earlier and have not repented of the impurity, sexual sin and debauchery in which they have indulged." (2 Corinthians 12:20-21 NIV)

Chapter Forty-Eight - Book of Galatians

"If two philosophers agree, one is not a philosopher.
If two saints disagree, one is not a saint."
Tibetan Proverb

This is a letter from Paul to a number of early Christian communities within the Roman province of Galatia. The central objective of the letter is to express his concern that Jewish majority, i.e. non-believers of Christ, had been orchestrating successful marketing campaigns to scare the Gentiles from following the fledgling Christian faith. Jewish elders had succeeded in convincing the small sect of Christian followers in this region into believing that all of Moses' laws need to be obeyed because not only had Jesus said so himself, but that Jesus was a Jew and therefore Christianity rightly or wrongly was based on Judaist principles. This made the Galatians nervous as they were in no great hurry to circumcise themselves. Paul's concern is articulated in the very opening of his letter, which reads:

"I am astonished that you are so quickly deserting the one who called you by the grace of Christ and are turning to a different gospel – which is really no

gospel at all. Evidently some people are throwing you into confusion and are trying to pervert the gospel of Christ. If anybody is preaching to you a gospel other than what you accepted, let him be eternally condemned!" (Galatians 1:6-9 NIV)

So in your face Moses! Your laws are no gospel at all according to Paul.

Paul then attempts to claim that he is not a liar, as some had charged, and that none of his words are just the words of a mere mortal man. Claiming that Jesus speaks through him and all truth has been revealed to him alone. With this in mind I do hope God and or Jesus have learnt a valuable lesson in the last 2,000 years, that being that the next time either one wants to get a message to us humans, then how about a nice 'fireside' chat, FDR style, on live TV so that we can all *fucking get it*! No arguments about interpretation, or intended meanings, and then ultimately we would have one God and one denomination of faith rather than the 38,000 denominations of Christianity that we currently have today.

In an effort to get his message across to the doubting Gentile followers, he portrays himself as the poster-boy for conversion. Telling his readers that he was a practicing Jew, that persecuted Christians until that point on the road to Damascus that Jesus spoke to him. Obviously an effort to reach across the aisle to the Gentiles that believed the tedious, perplexing and often brutish laws of Judaism to be unnatural fits to their cultural roots and traditions.

According to Christian fundamentalist and author Dr. Henrietta C. Mears:

"This Epistle (letter) has done more than any other book in the New Testament to free our Christian faith from Judaism and from the burden of salvation by works, taught by so many false cults, which has threatened the simple gospel of the Lord Jesus Christ."

This further demonstrates that the roots of the church of Christianity are made more on Paul's whims and decisions rather than that of Jesus himself. As Jesus made it quite clear that *all* Mosaic Law are to be adhered to, as written in the Gospels:

"Anyone who breaks one of these commandments and teaches others to do the same will be called least in the kingdom of heaven, but whoever practices and teaches these commands will be called great in the kingdom of heaven. For I tell you that unless your righteousness surpasses that of the Pharisees and the teachers of the law, you will certainly not enter the kingdom of heaven." (John 5:1 NIV)

But Paul sticks to his guns and ridicules the Galatians for being fooled into thinking that Old Testament law matters. He makes the point that faith in a man crucified for their sins is more righteous than following the 613 commandments as given to Moses in the first five books of the Bible:

> *"You foolish Galatians! Who has bewitched you? Before your very eyes Jesus Christ was clearly portrayed as crucified. I would like to learn just one thing from you: Did you receive the Spirit by observing the law, or by believing what you heard?" (Galatians 3:1-2 NIV)*

It is through this book, Galatians, that I can see why Christianity appeals as it does to Americans, because if ever there was a religion that you can follow from the comfort of your own sofa then this is it and you can thank Paul for that. No laws, no commands, just believe that Jesus died for your sins and you are in. Presto!

The balance of this letter reads as a rally cry to stand strong against doubters and naysayers, as he reinforces the mantra that freedom can only be found through Christ and that zealous opponents will continue to attempt to drag them from their faith.

Chapter Forty-Nine - Book of Ephesians

"But who prays for Satan? Who, in eighteen centuries, has had the common humanity to pray for the one sinner that needed it most?"
Mark Twain

The central theme of Paul's letter to the Church in Ephesius appears to be a message to newly converted Jews who viewed their Christianity to be more righteous than that of their Gentile brethren. Paul's letter is an attempt to bring unity to the church, demonstrated by his reminding the followers that all believers of Christ are made equal and alive by Christ, whether they be Jewish converts or Gentile newbie's.

> *"Remember that formerly you who are Gentiles by birth and called 'uncircumcised' by those who call themselves 'the circumcised', but now in Jesus Christ you who were once far away have been brought near through the blood of Christ." (Ephesians 2:11-14 NIV)*

And to reinforce this principal of church unity he finishes his second part of the letter with:

> *"And in him you too are being built together to become a dwelling in which God lives by his spirit." (Ephesians 2:22 NIV)*

Paul reminds the Gentiles that in acceptance of Christ as the son of God, they are now pure and saved and that they are no longer the wretched filth they once were as uncircumcised non-believers:

> *"You were taught with regard to your former way of life, to put off your old self, which is being corrupted by its deceitful desires; to be made in new in the attitude of your minds; and to put on the new self, created to be like God in true righteousness and holiness." (Ephesians 3:22-24 NIV)*

And just in case you were still fooled by self-righteous Christian fundamentalists that the New Testament is far more enlightening than its Old Testament predecessor, herewith are a couple of passages to challenge that falsehood.

Paul on Marriage

> *"Wives, submit to your husbands as to the Lord. For the husband is the head of the wife as Christ is the head of the church, his body, of which is the Saviour. Now as the church submits to Christ, so also wives should submit to their husbands in everything." (Ephesians 5:22-24 NIV)*

Everything? Wow 'everything' leaves the door wide open for a wife to submit to doesn't it? Too bad then if my wife isn't up for anal sex because I own her and if that's what I want, then that's what she gets! "Says so in the Bible honey!"

Paul on Slavery

> *"Slaves, obey your earthly masters with respect and fear and with sincerity in your heart, just as you would obey Christ." (Ephesians 6:5 NIV)*

If you are a Christian, then you are to believe that Jesus is speaking through Paul, therefore Jesus, in effect, is endorsing slavery just as his father did so through Moses and Abraham. At a stretch one could argue that the writers of the Old Testament and therefore God were, were 'unenlightened' on the issue of bondage and human trafficking. But the writers of the New Testament, including Paul, had the benefit of writing an extra one or two thousand years after their Biblical predecessors, thus we should hold Christians accountable for these immoral attitudes of their Gods.

Chapter Fifty - Book of Philippians

"If God doesn't like the way I live, let him tell me, not you."
Unknown

This is a letter from Paul to the Church in Philippi, Macedonia, the first Christian Church established in Europe. Paul writes this letter whilst bound in chains in prison and reads as encouragement that pain is good, pain is what Jesus went through and we should all rejoice in the pains of life together. Whilst there doesn't seem to be a clear objective to this letter it does include all the usual messages such as praise Jesus only; salvation comes through Jesus alone; don't perform sexual acts of immorality; and all believers are equal in the eyes of Jesus.

Another of his main thrusts in this letter is that the founding followers of Christ need to modify their behaviours so as to be walking billboards or advertisements for the new religion so that others will be drawn to it like shining stars:

> *"Do everything without complaining or arguing, so that you may become blameless and pure, children of God without fault in a crooked and depraved generation in which you shine like stars in the universe as you hold out the word of life." (Philippians 2:14-16 NIV)*

Paul finishes this letter with the promise that Jesus' return to earth from heaven is near, which is always a great method for securing your fellowship:

> *"Rejoice! Let your gentleness be evident to all. The Lord is near." (Philippians 4:4-5 NIV)*

Chapter Fifty-One - Book of Colossians

"With or without religion, you would have good people doing good things and evil people doing evil things. But for good people to do evil things, that takes religion."
Steven Weinberg

Written at around the same time as his letter to the church in Philippi whilst imprisoned in Rome, Paul writes this letter to the congregation of the church in Colossae, to express his concern that the followers there have incorporated pagan rituals into their worship of Jesus.

Paul expresses his concern that the congregation have been fooled by wise sounding men to observe and worship sun and moon gods and that this is all part of the Devil's plan to lead them away from the 'truth' of God. Paul says of these pagan worship practices:

> *"These are all destined to perish with use, because they are based on human commands and teachings. Such regulations indeed have an appearance of wisdom, with their self-imposed worship, their false humility and their harsh treatment of the body, but they lack any value in restraining sexual indulgence." (Colossians 2:22-23 NIV)*

I believe Paul could have saved himself a dozen or more words by just writing, "Their gods are bullshit and ours is the one true religion. They are bad, we are good!"

Paul's Preoccupation With Sex

Paul continues to express his frustration for not getting any tail, with his continued damnation of sexual immorality. He includes warnings against taking part in orgies, and other acts he deems depraved, even doggy-style. Ok I just made that last part up, but one can see from this letter, amongst his others, whereby Christians attain their unhealthy guilt as a result of natural sexual urges. I find this passage interesting:

> *"Put to death, therefore, whatever belongs to your earthly nature: sexual immorality, impurity, lust, evil desires and greed, which is idolatry." (Colossians 3:5 NIV)*

Paul admits here that sexual immorality, as determined by the Bible, is in our human nature. It's natural! And if God made us, who are we to suppress the natural impulses that He instilled in us. This passage further diminishes the role of the Devil in creating evil. How can the Devil be held responsible for God's design?

Treating Your Slaves

Paul advises that Christians should treat their slaves fairly because they too have their own 'Master' in heaven. How sweet! But he also has a word of advice for slaves, writing that they should obey their masters for everything and not just to win favour but because it is the right thing for a slave to do. Who said the Bible was anti-egalitarian?

Chapter Fifty-Two - Book of Thessalonians 1

"It is wonderful how much time good people spend fighting the devil. If they would only expend the same amount of energy loving their fellow men, the devil would die in his own tracks of ennui."
Helen Keller

This book is a letter Paul writes to the church in Thessalonia. Like others, this letter encourages the fellowship there to maintain their faith and continue to practice the correct worship of Jesus.

The primary objective of this letter is to set the record straight as to what happens to Christians in the afterlife, as there appears to be a great level of confusion amongst the believers as to what happens to a Christian after death. It is evident that many believe that an afterlife would only be available to those who live long enough to see the second coming of Jesus.

Using a simple bullet point format to summarize Paul's explanation for transportation to heaven, it is simply this:

- Christ will descend from the heaven riding a cloud.
- The dead, Christians only, will be risen from their graves to meet Jesus in the sky.
- Then those living will be judged prior to being given entry passes.

Sometimes comedy just writes itself and with that in mind here is the passage to make any rational mind giggle like a pervert at a Benny Hill show:

> *"After that, we who are still alive and are left will be caught up together with them in the clouds to meet the Lord in the air." (1 Thessalonians 4:17 NIV)*

With this 3-point plan Paul reassures his fellowship that they need not concern themselves with grieving for their dead beloveds, as all believers in Christ, dead or alive, will be granted access to the heavenly show.

Heaven Is Still Empty In 2009

What I find alarming about the whole entry into heaven thing is the fact that this is not the story many believers are led to believe. Naturally I can only speak anecdotally but it is my experience that a majority of Christians believe that the deceased are taken from their bodies to heaven at the point of death. In fact every funeral I have ever attended the Priest has said words to the effect of, "We can all take comfort that Daisy is now in heaven with her husband Frank." But this is an outright fallacy. There is no one in heaven today. Heaven is an empty house. No one goes to heaven until Jesus returns for a second time and since we are more than 1900 years beyond his promised return, then it seems the dead will remain in the dirt for a long time to come.

How terribly depressing for those who spend their lives in certitude and hope that there is something better beyond the ether. I am certainly not a believer but I just made myself depressed learning this.

Signs of His Coming

Repeatedly throughout the Gospels and Paul's letters we are told that Jesus' return will come like a thief in the night. We will not know the exact date, but believers will recognize the 'signs'. In Matthew 24:3 we read the story of Jesus sitting amongst his disciples on the Mount of Olives, who asked him, "What will be the sign of your coming and the end of the age?"

Jesus answered:

> *"Nation will rise against nation and kingdom against kingdom. There will be famines and earthquakes in various places. All these are the beginning of the birth pains." (Matthew 24:7 NIV)*

Cynically this is the reason why the Christian Right in the United States are so willing to support a President to go to war, or are so unconcerned about environmental issues and global warming. If you strongly believe these texts then you welcome terrible events and is that not a wicked thing to wish for?

Chapter Fifty-Three - Book of Thessalonians 2

"Fear of things invisible is the natural seed of that which everyone in himself calleth religion."

Thomas Hobbes

In Paul's second letter to the congregation in Thessalonia, he warns of Satan's trickery and that the devil will attempt to dupe Christians into believing that the second coming of Christ has already occurred by presenting a prophet that can perform all kinds of miracles, signs and wonders. And that those who are led by this forger will perish, but if you remain strong in defiance of Satan then you will be rewarded with even greater treasures in heaven.

The second coming of Jesus was so vitally important to the early founding fathers of the Church because it gave Christianity its own unique marketing brand over other religions at the time, namely an afterlife. As a matter of fact the second coming is mentioned 318 times in the 260 chapters of the New Testament, thus you can see how important this promise was for Paul in his efforts to not only maintain membership numbers but also bring newbies into the fold.

Although the wicked promise of violence and destruction is still sprayed venomously towards all non-Christians:

> *"This will happen when the Lord Jesus is revealed from heaven in blazing fire with his powerful angels. He will punish those who do not know God and do not obey the gospel of our Lord Jesus. They will be punished with everlasting destruction and shut out from the presence of the Lord and from the majesty of his power." (2 Thessalonians 1:7-9 NIV)*

It seems part of Paul's objective in this second letter to Thessalonia is to ensure his congregation don't get too carried away in their excitement of anticipating Jesus' promised second coming. He writes that they should continue to carry on their normal daily lives and therefore not to stand around staring at the sky all day in search of a descending cloud carrying the ghost of Jesus:

> *"We hear that some among you are idle. They are not busy. Such people we command and urge in the Lord Jesus Christ to settle down and earn the bread they eat."(Thessalonians 3:11-12 NIV)*

Thankfully the church members got back to work because they would've eventually died of starvation waiting for the second coming, a long time ago.

Chapter Fifty-Four - Book of Timothy 1

"I am convinced that I am acting as the agent of our Almighty Creator. By fighting the Jews, I am doing the Lord's work."

Adolf Hitler, Mein Kampf, p. 65

The Book of Timothy is a letter written by Paul to his sidekick Timothy and reads like an Assistant Manager's handbook, as it outlines for Timothy the rules for worship and the qualification standards for church leaders.

In regards to the instructions for worship, the stand out ordinance is:

> *"A woman should learn in quietness and full submission. I do not permit a woman to teach or to have authority over a man; she must be silent. For Adam was not the one deceived; it was the woman who was deceived and became a sinner. But women will be saved through childbearing – if they continue in faith, love and holiness with propriety."* (1 Timothy 2:11-15 NIV)

There's the saddle of the original sin again, as a sanction for treating women as second-class citizens. But women will be saved if they continue to lie on their backs and submit for whenever their husband's urges require and only if they continue in faith. Further, the fairer of our species also have a *but* and an *if* in their contract of salvation, but not so for righteous man.

The qualifications for holding office within a church include:

- Must be a male.
- Must not be a drunk.
- Must not be violent.
- Must not be argumentative.
- Must be married with at least one child.
- Must be sincere.
- Must have a clear conscience.

Unfortunately for hundreds of thousands, possibly millions, of children sexually abused by the church at one time or another, Paul unfortunately omitted:

- Must not put your perverted grubby hands down a little boy's shorts.

It is in the final few verses of Paul's letter to Timothy, that he writes the famous:

> *"For the love of money, is the root of all kinds of evil."* (1 Timothy 6:10 NIV)

Before leaving his final charge to his young protégé:

> *"Timothy, guard what has been entrusted to your care. Turn away from godless chatter and the opposing ideas of what is falsely called knowledge, which some have professed and in so doing have waned from the faith."* (1 Timothy 6:20-21 NIV)

The above being the same warning that all cults use to keep their flock from going astray, that the thirst for knowledge outside of the sect or cult is dangerous, as the procurement of knowledge leads men to reason and away from irrational beliefs.

Chapter Fifty-Five - Book of Timothy 2

"Life in Lubbock, Texas, taught me two things: One is that God loves you and you're going to burn in hell. The other is that sex is the most awful, filthy thing on earth and you should save it for someone you love."
Butch Hancock

In his second letter to Timothy, Paul urges his young disciple to take the good fight to the non-believers, 'onwards Christian soldiers,' and not to shy away from those that ridicule their fellow brethren. Paul forewarns Timothy that there will be testing times ahead, all manipulated by Satan and that he must lead the church as an example of righteous lifestyle. One such example is to avoid falling for 'weak-willed women' who will tempt him with their unholy, lustful desires. He is to stay strong in the face of such human desires and preach the word of Jesus.

Paul, still imprisoned in Rome, predicts the coming of his death, which ultimately results in a beheading at the order of the Roman Emperor Nero and thus the importance that Timothy understand that the success of the Church is now in his hands, as Paul writes:

> *"For I am already being poured out like a drink offering and the time has come for my departure. I have fought the good fight, I have finished the race, I have kept the faith. Now there is in store for me the crown of righteousness, which the Lord, the righteous Judge, will award to me on that day – and not only to me, but also to all who have longed for his appearing." (2 Timothy 4:6-8 NIV)*

Paul also advises Timothy to prepare for the final days before Jesus' second coming, suggesting again that Paul was convinced that Christ would return at least during the lifetime of his new charge:

> *"But mark this: There will be terrible times in the last days. People will be lovers of themselves, lovers of money, boastful, proud, abusive, disobedient to their parents, unforgiving, slanderous, without self-control, brutal, not lovers of the good, treacherous, rash, conceited, lovers of pleasure rather than lovers of God." (2 Timothy 3:1-4 NIV)*

Chapter Fifty-Six - Book of Titus

"Christians must disregard [scientific hypotheses or theories] that contradict the Bible."
Biology for Christian Schools

This is a letter from Paul to Titus. Titus heads the church in Crete and the letter is just a reminder that Titus should carefully appoint righteous elders and head of all churches in the region, whilst also remaining vigilant against rebellious or questioning followers and to act promptly to suppress those that may cause division from within. Paul writes:

> *"For there are many rebellious people, mere talkers and deceivers, especially those of the circumcision group. They must be silenced, because they are ruining whole households by teaching things they ought not to teach." (Titus 1:10-11 NIV)*

Silencing opposition, the hallmark of all oppressive regimes from Fascism to Totalitarianism.

Chapter Fifty-Seven - Book of Philemon

"I don't know that atheists should be considered as citizens, nor should they be considered patriots. This is one nation under God."
President George H.W. Bush

In terms of number of words, this is the shortest of all books of the Bible consisting of only 335 words. It is letter written by Paul, whilst imprisoned, to Philemon, a leader in the Colossian church.

The letter reveals nothing as to the reason Paul finds himself in prison, nor for what duration is his sentence. It reads simply as a plea to some guy called Philemon, that a fellow prisoner may be released because he has converted to Christianity.

This is the final letter of Paul before his execution.

Chapter Fifty-Eight - Book of Hebrews

"A man's ethical behavior should be based effectually on sympathy, education, and social ties; no religious basis is necessary. Man would indeed be in a poor way if he had to be restrained by fear of punishment and hope of reward after death."
Albert Einstein

The Book of Hebrews is written by an unknown author, but whilst his identity may remain a mystery, the target audience is obvious, the Jews. The book urges Jews to cease their worship of what the author claims are now secondary prophets such as Abraham, Moses, Joshua and David, and to put their complete faith in the one and only Jesus who now supersedes all that came before him. For this reason many scholars regard this book as the fifth Gospel.

> *"In the past God spoke to our forefathers through the prophets at many times and in various ways, but in these last days he has spoken to us by his son, whom he appointed heir of all things and through whom he made the universe. The Son is the radiance of God's glory and the exact representation of his being, sustaining all things by his wonderful word." (Hebrews 1:1-3 NIV)*

If there is a single more offensive passage to Jews then you will do well to find better than this, as the author shows no timidity and thus pulls no punches when he claims that Jesus is far greater than Moses:

> *"Jesus has been found worthy of greater honour than Moses, just as the builder of a house has greater honour than the house itself. For every house is built by someone, but God is the builder of everything. Moses was faithful as a servant in all God's house, testifying to what could be said in the future. But Christ is faithful as a son over God's house." (Hebrews 3:3-4 NIV)*

Sorry Moses but the Christians want a new star.

The book of Hebrews offers the all too familiar warnings to non-believers of Christianity, such as death and destruction in fiery pits of sulphur, But it does advise them that it is not too late to convert because the final days have not come yet. Using a jab of mockery he belittles the Jews for their non-belief as a matter of poor intellect:

> *"We have much to say about this, but it is hard to explain because you are slow to learn. You need milk, not solid food! Anyone who lives on milk, being*

still an infant, is not acquainted with the teaching about righteousness." (Hebrews 5:11-13 NIV)

The above derogatory statement the equivalent of, "Hey, we Christians understand you don't get the stuff about virgin births and resurrection after death, because your brains are not as evolved as us vastly superior Christians, so in your face!"

The New 'Christian' Covenant

If this book hadn't upset Jews by now then the most controversial of all passages in this book relates to the denunciation of the old covenant between the Jewish people and God, and it's replacement with the one made via Jesus.

> *"The ministry of Jesus has received is as superior to theirs (Jews) as the covenant of which he is mediator is superior to the old one and it is founded on better promises. For if there had been nothing wrong with that first covenant, no place would have been sought for another. But God found fault with the people and said, 'The time is coming when I make a new covenant with the house of Israel and with the house of Judah." (Hebrews 8:6-8 NIV)*

The last sentence of the above passage is taken by the author from Psalm 110, i.e. from the Old Testament. Henceforth God never said during or after Jesus' lifetime that the death of his son was to be the new covenant. Just another example of early Christian writers cutting and pasting verses from the Hebrew Bible to justify the Christian faith and credibility.

Nothing sacred of Jewish belief is left unscarred in Hebrews, even the sanctimony of what Jews regard as the holy of holy, the Tabernacle. The author derides the Tabernacle and all its inclusions as nothing more than man-constructed ceremonial nick-nacks as offerings to God, but the blood spilled by Jesus on the cross is now the new covenant and to honour his sacrifice is far holier than worshiping some fine curtains, candles and golden altars.

> *"For this reason Christ is the mediator of the new covenant, that those who are called may receive the promised eternal inheritance – now that he has died as a ransom to set them free from the sins committed under the first covenant." (Hebrews 9:15 NIV)*

The author includes a relatively long passage on the importance and virtue of faith. And that God will reward those who put their faith in him and his son Jesus, just as he had rewarded Abraham with children; Noah with the ark; and Moses in his exodus from Egypt.

"And without faith it is impossible to please God, because anyone who comes to him must believe that he exists and that he rewards those who earnestly seek him." (Hebrews 11:6 NIV)

Chapter Fifty-Nine - Book of James

"God made so many different kinds of people. Why would he allow only one way to serve him?"
Martin Buber

It is now widely accepted that the author of this letter, addressed to the twelve tribes of Israel, is James the brother of Jesus. The address of the twelve tribes is generally interpreted as being that of the Jewish converts to Christianity. It seems plausible to me that this is in fact a relative or at least close friend of Jesus, as the author is quick to bless the poor and weak and curse the rich, just as Jesus had been quoted.

"The brother in humble circumstances ought to take pride in his high position. But the one who is rich should take pride in his low position, because he will pass away like a wild flower." (James 1:9-10 NIV)

"Has not God chosen those who are poor in the eyes of the world to be rich in faith and to inherit the kingdom he promised?" (James 2:5 NIV)

Not only is this just shameless popularist politics in an attempt to appeal to the masses, but it does seem somewhat harsh to lump all wealthy individuals into the corrupt basket and it does remind me of a scene from Monty Python's *Life of Brian*, in which John Cleese's character remarks after hearing Jesus' sermon, "Blessed are the meek? Well, Jesus has certainly got that wrong. It is the meek that cause all our problems!"

In this letter James unequivocally claims that prayers are not only listened to by the Almighty but they are also actioned upon. This is of little comfort now to the deeply religious majority of the American South, where hundreds of lifelong serving Christians prayed for saving during Hurricane Katrina, in their rooftop attics as the water levels rose higher and higher, until these poor souls eventually took the last breath before being consumed by a horrible death. Jesus didn't hear those prayers did he now? Proving the adage that nothing quite fails like prayer.

Yes I could list a shopping list of examples where Jesus stayed put on the sidelines to watch his sheep get slaughtered, which according to the Bible's claim makes him complicit in his ambivalence, but I will refrain, as the point is obvious. James writes:

"Is any one of you in trouble? He should pray. Is anyone of you sick? He should call the elders of the church to pray over him and anoint him with oil in the name of the Lord. And the prayer offered in faith will make the sick person well; the Lord will raise him up." (James 5:13-15 NIV)

If prayer cured illnesses and Christians believed this to be true, then why do believers bother with the cost of health insurance? And why visit a doctor? Why take medicine? Well the so called Christian Scientists amongst us do ignore the marvels of medical technology and healthcare in substitute for prayer and these dim-witted nuts end up watching their children suffer painful deaths from common ailments that could have been treated with a simple antibiotic tablet. The tragedy of ancient beliefs.

Chapter Sixty - Book of Peter 1

"How can the Church be received as a trustworthy guide in the invisible, which falls into so many errors in the visible?"
John W. Draper

The Book of Peter is a letter written by Saint Peter during his time as the Bishop of Rome, estimated to be approximately one hundred years after the death of Jesus. The intended audience church members scattered throughout the Black Sea coastal area.

The letter reads similar to many of Paul's preceding letters with the overarching theme being that of a Christian rally cry, to remain steadfast whilst non-believers persecute you. And a reminder to adopt the blood sacrifice of Jesus as the comparative bar for enduring suffering.

Peter urges followers to remain 'holy', obedient and steadfast and that salvation will come after death through their belief in Jesus. To this end Peter also includes the contentious claim that has divided many Christian observers throughout time:

"For unto this end was the gospel preached even to the dead, that they might be judged indeed according to men in the flesh, but live according to God in the spirit" (1 Peter 4:6 NIV).

A truly remarkable assertion given that it suggests that Jesus visited the dead in Hell before being resurrected three days after his death. That is some journey for even a Messiah to make. Can't imagine Satan being the gracious host and I am surprised the horned one didn't take the opportunity to take the son of God as his hostage. Surely God would have paid a handsome ransom?

Chapter Sixty-One - Book of Peter 2

"The reformer is always right about what is wrong.
He is generally wrong about what is right."
G.K. Chesterton

The second letter of Peter is addressed to all churches in common and reminds the followers of Jesus that the Messiah had promised believers salvation in heaven for obeying his word, maintaining faith and godliness.

> *"For if you these things, you will never fall and you will receive a rich welcome into the eternal kingdom of our Lord and Saviour Jesus Christ." (2 Peter 1:10-11 NIV)*

Peter warns against false prophets who will pretend to be the Messiah in the 'final days' and that slick wordsmiths will attempt to convince Christians to leave the church. However, Peter does not mince words when he warns against backsliding:

> *"It would have been better for them not to have known the way of righteousness, than to have known it and then to turn their backs on the sacred command that was passed onto them. Of them the proverbs are true: 'A dog returns to its vomit.'"* (2 Peter 2:21-22 NIV)

Prophecy Disclaimer

Peter makes a clever statement, more a sound-bite that current day Christians can hold onto in explaining why Jesus and Paul, falsely prophesized that the second coming of Jesus would occur in the living generation of the first century. Peter writes:

> *"With the Lord a day is like a thousand years and a thousand years are like a day."* (2 Peter 3:8 NIV)

Problem being that Jesus was a man, a human, and therefore he lived human days and human years. Further, this statement is made only from a Christian apologist and not from Jesus himself. As Jesus said quite clearly he would return before his disciples had passed. Peter tried to sneak a touchdown on a 4th down a long play, but more often than not the old Hail Mary gets swatted away by the defence.

Peter climbs aboard the 'fire and brimstone express', like his contemporaries, in painting a doomsday picture, in which the believers will be saved and the non-believers destroyed:

> *"But the day of the Lord will come like a thief. The heavens will disappear with a roar; the elements will be destroyed by fire and the earth and everything in it will be laid bare."* (2 Peter 3:10 NIV)

So watch-out you!

Chapter Sixty-Two - Book of John 1

"What is light must endure burning."
Victor Frankl

The author is believed to be the same author as that of the Gospel of John. Whilst a number of modern biblical scholars remain in disagreement as to the identity of this author, there is general consensus that it was written ninety years after Jesus death.

John states that he writes this book to warn his readers that evil men will try to lead the believers astray.

> *"Dear children, this is the last hour; and as you have heard that the antichrist is coming, even now many antichrists have come. This is how we know it is the last hour."* (1 John 2:18 NIV)

John also asserts that the reason that Jesus was sent to earth was destroy the devil's work. If this is true, he failed. And how is it that God permits the Devil to survive? God created everything and therefore can destroy everything. What is he waiting for? Why doesn't he just destroy the Devil now?

Must Beliefs

John makes four plain and simple statements as to what must be believed by Christians to join Jesus in Heaven at the time of the rapture:

- That Jesus is the son of God.
- That Jesus is the *only* son of God.
- That God is love.
- That Jesus is the Saviour.

Chapter Sixty-Three - Book of John 2

"The more I study religions the more I am convinced that man never worshipped anything but himself."
Richard Francis Burton

Comprising a mere thirteen verses, this book is the shortest of the Bible. The most remarkable statement in this book is the following:

> *"Many deceivers, who do not acknowledge Jesus Christ as coming in the flesh, have gone out into the world." (2 John 7 NIV)*

This suggests that not only were there those that refused to acknowledge Jesus as the son of God, but there were also many that refused to acknowledge that Jesus even walked the face of the planet. Arguably a fair claim, as the first recorded words of Jesus' life were written approximately one hundred years after he was alleged to have lived.

John does some damage to Paul's claim that Jesus' crucifixion effectively abolishes Old Testament law in writing that:

> *"The man who says, 'I know him', but does not do what he commands is a liar and the truth is not in him." (2 John 4 NIV)*

The 613 commandments are back in play Christians, so make sure your business suits do not contain wool and linen together, or it will be 'smackin' time at the Pearly Gates for you.

Chapter Sixty-Four - Book Of John 3

"I believe there is something out there watching over us. Unfortunately, it's the government."
Woody Allen

The second shortest book of the Bible, containing only a few more words than its predecessor. The Book of John is a letter written to a man named Gaius. It reads as a private letter, and complains about a man named Diotephes, who John claims has been spreading nasty rumours about him and thus causing division within his church.

> *"I will call attention to what he is doing, gossiping maliciously about us. Not satisfied with that, he refuses to welcome the brothers. He also stops those who want to do so and puts them out of the church." (2 John 10 NIV)*

Chapter Sixty-Five - Book of Jude

"Kill them all, for God knows His own."
Pope Innocent III, to his troops in the Albigensian Crusade of 1209

The Book of Jude is a letter written to no one church in particular and most interestingly he refers to himself as a servant of Jesus and a brother of James, which in fact makes Jude a brother of Jesus too. We assume both James and Jude were younger brothers of Jesus, because two of the four Gospels claimed that Mary was a virgin at the time of conceiving Jesus. If this nature defying immaculate conception were to be true, then at least we can say now that Mary didn't have any qualms about a good ole hanky-panky after giving birth to the proclaimed Messiah, as she and Joseph had a few years of getting down and dirty in their modest middle-class mud hut on the shores of Galilee.

The letter contains only a single chapter with a mere twenty five verses, but makes the promise of doom abundantly clear for the non-believers, as stated in the fifth paragraph:

> *"I want to remind you that the Lord delivered his people out of Egypt, but later destroyed those who did not believe. They serve as an example of those who suffer the punishment of eternal fire." (Jude 5-7 NIV)*

I really have trouble with the whole 'eternal fire' thing, as a punishment for those that may be ordinarily law abiding citizens but because of a lack of proof chose to disbelieve the merits of the Christian doctrine. I mean it is one thing for God to punish the non-believers with death, but torture for eternity? Isn't that extreme wickedness? Not to make light of a tragedy, but at least when Hitler sent the Jews to the gas chambers, their suffering was over once they died. But God on the other hand wants to inflict suffering forever and forever. Truly dastardly!

Jude promises that that time for perpetual torture will soon come for those that doubt the word of Jesus:

> *"See, the Lord is coming with thousands and thousands of his holy ones to judge everyone and to convict all the ungodly acts they have done and the harsh words ungodly sinners have spoken against him." (Jude 14-15 NIV)*

Harsh words spoken against God? Well I am royally screwed aren't I?

Chapter Sixty-Six - The Book of Revelation

"Kill them all. God will select those who should go to heaven and those who should go to hell."
Abbot Arnold de Citeaux, during the Fourth Crusade, 1205

I must confess that I have looked forward to writing this final chapter of the Bible more than any of the others, as Revelations could the basis for a book on its own. But like a child must complete his dinner before eating dessert, I too have kept the best for last, denying myself the temptation to summarize the most bizarre of books ever written before I had done so with the preceding sixty five books. Revelations is a trove of profound absurdity, that even the most imaginative fiction writer would have difficulty in equalling. If the title *One Flew Over The Cuckoo's Nest* had not been already taken, then I would have been quick to grab it as my own as the sub-heading for this chapter.

The book is a letter written by the gospel John and addressed to the seven churches in the province of Asia, that included: Ephesus, Smyrna, Pergamum, Thyatria, Sardis, Philadelphia and Laodicea. John penned this letter whilst exiled on the Greek island of Patmos. As this letter unfolds before you, you can assume John was either suffering from heat-stroke or one too many pool side piña-coladas whilst on his island retreat. John writes that this revelation from God was revealed to him in a dream. More likely a drunken stupor!

John's inspiration, or moreover plagiarism dressed as inspiration, stems from the Old Testament prophecy of Ezekiel. And if you return to the opening chapter of Ezekiel for a moment you will see the similarities.

Admittedly it is fairly safe to assume that John is writing in a metaphorical tone, as the unfolding story of this book emulates the story of Christ, that being rise, reign, ruin, resurrection, and restoration. Well let's hope it is a clever fiction, because this story will have you sleeping with the light on.

Heaven an Empty House... Still

John confirms Paul's and the Gospels proclamation that no one shall enter the kingdom of heaven until the end of times. NOW LET ME MAKE THIS CLEAR! (I apologize for shouting) You have been lied to by your Priest, Pastor, Clergy, there is no going to Heaven until everything in this prophecy comes to bear. In other words, THERE IS NO ONE IN HEAVEN ON THIS DAY EXCEPT FOR

JESUS AND GOD! But they never told you this in Sunday school, did they? The priest delivering the sermon at your grandmother's funeral never said this. This is, I believe, the biggest sin of propaganda perpetuated by the protectors of faith, the lie that Christian believers travel to heaven at the point of their death. *Wrong*! When one of God's good Christian soldiers dies today, he will be buried in the earth and the earth is where he shall stay until all events take place as promised in this book of Revelation. Which means that the earliest believers of Christ who died 2000 years ago are still buried in the top soil. They haven't gone anywhere. The big dirt nap, as Mafioso types like to say, is a big dirt nap. No doubt the disciples whom Jesus promised that the end of times would occur before their generation had passed are royally pissed off as their 2000 year sleep in the soil continues.

Revelations is going to reveal some crazy shit to you, but just remind yourself that if you want to travel to Heaven via Jesus Christ, then here comes your leap of faith...

The Prophecy Begins

The first three chapters of Revelations are letters individually addressed to the seven churches. Whilst the fourth begins the recount of his wondrous dream in which God spoke to him:

> *"After that I looked and there before me was a door standing open to heaven. And the voice I had first heard speaking to me like a trumpet said, 'Come up here and I will show you what must take place after this.' At once I was in the Spirit and there before me was a throne in heaven with someone sitting on it." (Revelations 4:1-2 NIV)*

Where would heaven be without harps and trumpets?

Description of Heaven

I have to hand it to John though, because unlike other prophets such as Moses and Abraham who claimed to have seen God and did not describe his features, John does provide a very descriptive narrative of what heaven looks like and according to him, it looks like this:

> *"A rainbow, resembling an emerald, encircled the throne. Surrounding the throne was twenty-four other thrones and seated on them were twenty-four elders. They were dressed in white and had crowns of gold on their heads. From the throne came flashes of lightening, rumblings and peals of thunder. Before the throne, seven lamps were blazing. These are the seven spirits of God. Also before the throne was what looked like a sea of glass, clear as crystal." Revelations 4:3-6 NIV)*

Ok maybe his description of heaven is confined to just the administrative office but I will credit him with at least making an imaginative, descriptive attempt. But thus far just the usual elementary school level imagery of heaven: gold, white, lightning, thunder, crowns and thrones. All images one would expect a 1st grade child to use to illustrate heaven. But John's illustration begins its bizarre twist hereafter:

> *"In the centre, around the throne, were four living creatures and they were covered with eyes, in front and behind. The first living creature was like a lion, the second was like an ox, the third had the face like a man, the fourth was like a flying eagle. Each of the four living creatures had six wings and was covered with eyes all around, even under his wings. Day and night the creatures never stopped saying, 'Holy, holy, holy is the Lord Almighty.'" (Revelations 4:6-8 NIV)*

Holy, holy, holy is more than likely what I too would have said if I was taken to this place in the clouds. 'Holy fucking shit,' would probably be more like it.

The Scroll and The Lamb

John watches on from his heavenly front row as a man seated in one of the thrones fumbles around in his hands with a scroll containing seven seals that he is unable to open. An angel walks in and tells the occupier of the throne that the seal cannot be opened because no one present is worthy for such a ceremonial duty. Next, in walks a lamb that appears to be slain, but as John makes closer inspection the lamb is not only still alive but has seven horns and seven eyes. This mutant lamb takes the scroll from the angel and all twenty-four elders of Heaven's throne fall down in worship before the lamb, whilst simultaneously all began playing harps and burning incense. Now, I can't be sure what drugs John was on, but I feel like I am having an acid flashback just retelling this.

The elders then all broke into song and sang to the seven eyed lamb:

> *"You are worthy to take the scroll and to open it seals, because you were slain and with your blood you purchased men for God from every tribe and language and people and nation. You have made them to be a kingdom and priests to serve our God and they will reign on the earth." (Revelations 5:9-10 NIV)*

The Opening of The Seven Seals

The obliging lamb then begins to open the first of the seven seals, which seems problematic given that lambs don't have the benefit of opposing thumbs. Regardless of my cynical observation, the lamb opened the first of the seals and my golly gosh *boom* a white horse flew out of the scroll, with a rider holding a bow and wearing a crown. The horse and its jockey rode off purposefully into the distance as if in a rush to go to battle.

The second seal was opened and *boom* another horse flew out of the scroll, but this time the horse was a fiery red in colour.

> *"It's rider given power to take peace from the earth and to make men slay each other. To him was given a large sword."* (Revelations 6:4 NIV)

The third seal produced a black horse, with its rider carrying a set of weighing scales in his hands.

The fourth seal produced a pale horse and its jockey was named 'Death'. This horse and rider were given power to slay a quarter of the earth's population by means of famine, plagues and wild beasts. Blood, slaughter, war, the end of times ain't pretty business!

The fifth seal produced no horse and thus the reason why scholars refer to the first four seals as the Four Horsemen of the Apocalypse. Seal number five enabled John a view to the graves of all godly men who had died till now, who in their state of death were asking for when the Lord shall return to rise them up to heaven. The dead were each given a white robe and reassured that they would only have to wait a little longer. Footnote: They are still waiting!

The sixth seal produced a tremendous earthquake, the sun turned black and the moon blood red in colour. The stars fell from the sky to earth and every mountain and island was removed from its place. John, with his ringside seat to the future, watched as non-believing men, from Kings to slaves, cowered in the refuge of caves as they watched the end of times draw near. Four angels then appeared to hold back the slaughter of the infidels until the angels had had their chance to place a seal on the forehead of all those living that were to be saved as servants of God. This is the total number of men to be saved into heaven at the time of the rapture.

But here comes the kicker: somewhat perplexing is that the number of men given keys to the city of heaven is not as high as I might expect considering there are more than 2 Billion people that consider themselves Christians today. The total number permitted into heaven when the end of times comes will be a staggeringly low number of only 144,000 souls. That's it! That is not a large number of tickets for the big dance! That leaves room for the Christian population of Albany, NY only. I pity the guy standing in the doorway of the pearly gates, as there is going to be a big line of disgruntled Jesus fans that were sold phoney entrance passes by enterprising ticket scalpers such as Billy Graham and the like.

With the 144,000 saved now standing around gleefully with the seal of God on their foreheads, it was time for the godly dead, dressed in their splendid white robes, to be given their entry stamps. As the dead approached, one of the elders asked John who these men were, to which he replied:

> *"These are they who have come out of the great tribulation; they have washed their robes and made them white in the blood of the Lamb. Therefore, they are before the throne of God and serve him day and night in his temple; and he who sits on the throne will spread his tent over them. For the Lamb at the centre of the throne will be their shepherd; he will lead them to springs of living water. And God will wipe away every tear from their eyes." (Revelations 7:14-17 NIV)*

My advice then is if you think you have missed the lottery like odds of being one of the 144,000 entrants to heaven, then *it's party time*! Let's order the cocaine and strippers now. Start dialling Pastor Ted.

Before moving on to the next step of God's doomsday scenario, I'd like you to think about this for a moment. Accepting that The Bible states only 144,000 lucky souls will enter the kingdom of Heaven at judgment day, then your chances by means of pure mathematical probability alone are slim. Let's, however, say that the sheer weight of odds runs with you rather than against and you do get the ultimate back stage pass, what then are the odds that everyone you know and love will enter with you? The odds just went from one in 5 billion to one in 100 trillion for that happening. Which means your wife, your husband, your children will all run with the odds, leaving them on the celestial outer. Isn't this some kind of Hell in its own right then? A psychological Hell! Knowing that the people you love most are not only not with you, but are now being tortured for eternity in Hell?

Think about it.

The Trumpets

Finally, the seventh seal was then opened and there was silence in heaven for about thirty minutes. Thank God! That incessant harp music would be driving me to hysterics too. But the elevator style music continued soon thereafter as seven angels appeared before God, this time playing trumpets, seven of them. Naturally you would assume the angels trumpeted to the tune of 'Oh when the Saints come marching in'. Makes perfect sense to me, but God commanded that each angel was to sound his trumpet individually upon his order. Henceforth, the first angel stepped forward, blasted out a pithy little tune and down rained hail and fire, mixed with blood onto the earth, resulting in one-third of the planet being consumed by fire.

The second angel stepped forth and as he hits his crescendo an enormous mountain, completely ablaze, was lifted out of the ground by an invisible hand and thrown into the sea, killing one-third of all living creatures in the sea. Willy, Flipper, Nemo all dead!

The fourth angel sounded his trumpet and a burning star came crashing down from the sky and landed on one-third of all of earth's rivers. Given that stars aren't as small as they seem without a telescope and are hundreds of times larger than our earth, I can't see how this is possible, but let's bear with it for a moment. The star made the water in a third of the rivers undrinkable thus killing many from thirst.

The fifth angel then belted out a Louis B. Armstrong classic and *bam* another star fell from space crashed into the earth causing a gigantic crater filled with fire and smoke. Out of the smoke emerged locusts with the power of scorpions, these nasty gnats were given instructions from the angel that they were not to harm the trees, or plants but only to attack those people that did not have the seal of God on their foreheads. What John foretells next is purely evil:

> *"They (scorpions dressed as locusts) were not given power to kill them, but only to torture them for five months. And the agony they suffered was like that of the sting of a scorpion when it strikes a man. During these days men will seek death, but will not find it; they will long to die, but death will elude them." (Revelations 9:5-6 NIV)*

So I don't know what you Christians against torture at Gitmo were on about, God loves torture! Which, no doubt, is where the Christian Inquisitors took inspiration from as they inserted hot irons into the anuses of those falsely accused of heresy and blasphemy during the dark and middle ages. When God sanctions torture, it makes it difficult for those in power with religious beliefs to challenge the morality of its use, don't you think?

Now if your kids aren't terrified yet, just read them John's description of the locusts before they go to sleep tonight:

> *"The locusts looked like horses prepared for battle. On their heads they wore something like crowns of gold and their faces resembled human faces. Their hair was like women's hair and their teeth were like lion's teeth. They had breastplates of iron and the sound of their wings was like the thundering of many horses and chariots rushing into battle." (Revelations 9:7-9 NIV)*

Never mind the kiddies, I just scared the crap out myself. If I read this to my children I'd need 5mgs of Xanax to put me out. Bang! Shit! What was that?

The sixth angel sounded his trumpet and four angels that had been assigned to the Euphrates River were released to kill one-third of mankind. *Bam* more slaughter. One-third of mankind wiped out in an instant, thus I assume this to be the attack on China. So goodbye all you Hindus, Buddhists, Taoists and Confuscists. And not a farewell Dear Friend, it's *au revoir* courtesy of plagues of fire, sulphur and wild horses with snakes as their tails. Surprisingly, more like unfuckingbelievably, it is written that the remainder of surviving mankind, having witnessed all this blood and gore, continued on their merry-way to worship other gods. What the fuck? If there was ever a time to convert to this brutish cult, then surely this is it.

The seventh trumpet sounded and against a backdrop of thunder and lightning, the twenty-four elders, who were seated on their thrones before God, fell face down and worshipped him, crying out:

> *"We give thanks to you, Lord God Almighty, the One who is and who was, because you have taken your great power and begun to reign. The nations were angry; and your wrath has come. The time has come for judging the dead and for rewarding your servants the prophets and your saints and those who reverence your name, both small and great – and for destroying those who destroy the earth." (Revelations 11:16-18 NIV)*

As the elders finished their praise of God, the temple in heaven was opened and within the temple was the Ark of the Covenant.

The Woman and The Dragon

As John continued on his Kontiki tour of Heaven he saw a woman clothed with the sun, with the moon under her feet and a crown of twelve stars on her head. We are talking about one gigantic behemoth of a woman! This woman was pregnant and she cried out in pain, as she was about to enter into labour. If this event wasn't fantastic enough, enter an enormous red dragon with seven heads and ten horns. The tail of the dragon swept through the sky knocking a third of all the stars out of orbit. Yes a big fucking dragon here folks. The dragon made its way over to the woman that was using the moon to rest her feet, so as he could devour the newborn child the moment it was born. The woman gave birth to a son, predictably so and God stepped in and snatched the child before the dragon could dine on his favourite baby-back ribs. (Sorry, bad joke!) The woman fled into the desert to a sanctuary prepared for by God himself and she stayed in this fantasy witness protection plan for the next 1,260 days.

A war then erupted in heaven between Michael and his angels versus the dragon, which smashes the illusion of heaven for me, because I would be ever so hopeful that if any place could be devoid of the horror of warfare then it would be heaven. We have too much of it here on earth, so where is the sanctuary? What kind of impotent God is this? Surely God had enough power to maintain a little peace and harmony in heaven for crying out loud? C'mon really? Anyway (huge sigh), the angels did battle and the dragon was hurled down to the earth and a loud voice shouted down to the surviving earthlings:

> *"But woe to the earth and the sea, because the devil has gone down to you! He is filled with fury, because he knows that his time is short." (Revelations 12:12 NIV)*

The dragon pursued the woman who fled into the desert, but she escaped once again.

The Beast Out of The Sea and The Beast Out of The Earth

John now witnesses a beast emerging from the depths of the sea, a monster with seven heads and ten horns. On each of its head were tattooed blasphemous words against God. John describes the beast as resembling a leopard, with feet like a bear and a mouth like a lion. The big nasty red dragon handed his power and authority to the beast and the non-believing men that remained on earth began to worship this beast as their new God. Remember this entire story is what Christians believe is going to occur in the end days, just in case you forgot the relevance of this story. But John's acid trip didn't stop with the creation of one beast, he now describes the emergence of a second ghoul, that climbs out of the earth. This monster had two horns like a lamb, notwithstanding the fact that lambs don't have horns and it spoke like a dragon. I've never heard a dragon speak, so I am hardly in a position to doubt John on this testimony. The sea beast passed on his authority to this earth beast and then this second beast began to perform terrifying miracles in full view of all men. The beast then ordered them to set up monuments honouring him and then demanded that all men and women receive a mark on his or her right hand. Without this mark no one was permitted to buy or sell any goods or produce, but I'm guessing this stamp could get you into some really cool nightclubs. The mark tattooed onto their right hand was the number 666.

The Lamb and The 144,000

John's celestial journey into the future then revealed the 144,000 men who had been saved and were now in heaven being led around by the Lamb. The saved followed the Lamb everywhere, whilst harpists played their harps. I am not making any of this up by the way! The Lamb taught these blessed men songs that only the 144,000 would have the ability to learn because they did not defile themselves with women whilst they lived on earth. Again a further implication of women as dirty temptresses, and evidence that there is no place in heaven for the fairer sex, according to the Bible. How did this passage go unread by those Nuns dressed like flying penguins that lead a life of miserable celibacy? Possibly the reason why Mother Theresa expressed her crisis of faith via a letter to the Pope in her dying days?

May I ask what is the point of converting to Christianity now when all the seats are sold? Believers, evidently, are as equally doomed as us atheists, but at least we are having earthly hedonistic fun!

The Three Angels

At this point three angels began buzzing around in mid-air whilst clutching the holy gospel. The angels, in turn, spoke to the remaining men on earth. The first angel said in a loud voice,

> *"'Fear God and give him glory, because the hour of his judgment has come.' Angel number two step forward and said in an equally booming voice, 'Fallen! Fallen is Babylon the Great, which made all the nations drink the maddening wine of her adulteries.' And the third angel proclaimed, 'If anyone worships the beast and his image and receives his mark on his forehead or on the hand, he, too, will drink the wine of God's fury, which has been poured full strength into the cup of his wrath. He will be tormented with burning sulphur in the presence of the holy angels and of the Lamb.'" (Revelations 14:1-10 NIV)*

The Seven Bowls of God's Wrath

John then heard a loud voice from heaven that yelled, "Go, pour out the seven bowls of God's wrath on the earth"

The first angel poured out his first bowl and all men that carried the mark of the devil broke out in painful sores. The second angel poured out his cup of wrath into the sea, killing every living creature in the ocean. Not sure what the dolphins did to deserve this, but this ain't my story. The third angel poured his bowl into all the rivers of the earth, turning the waters into blood. The fourth's was poured onto the sun which made the sun more powerful and a million times hotter so that it scorched people with fire. The fifth angel poured his over the throne of the beast, plunging his kingdom into darkness. Those that worshipped the beast gnawed their tongues in agony, but still refused to repent. The sixth angel poured his bowl into the Euphrates River causing it to dry up. Then finally the seventh angel emptied the contents of his bowl into the air, which caused an earthquake like no other earthquake that had ever occurred before. The quake was of such strength that it is powerful enough to make entire islands disappear. When the earthquake finished, hailstones that weighed more than 100 pounds each fell onto earth causing surviving men to curse the name of God. Well why wouldn't you utter a little "you suck dick God!" if you were being pelted by keg sized hail stones?

The Prostitute on The Beast

John was led away by one of the seven angels to see a woman in the desert who was on the back of a scarlet beast. The woman had tattooed to her forehead the wording:

> *MYSTERY*
> *BABYLON THE GREAT*
> *THE MOTHER OF PROSTITUTES*
> *AND OF ABOMINATIONS OF THE EARTH*

John writes that the woman is visibly drunk on the blood of those who bore testimony to Jesus. The angel said to John:

> *"The waters you saw, where the prostitute sits, are peoples, multitudes, nations and languages. The beast and the ten horns you saw will hate her to ruin and leave her naked; they will eat her flesh and burn her with fire. The woman you see is the great city that rules over the kings of the earth." (Revelations 17:15-18 NIV)*

The angel further explained that the ten horns on the beast's head represent ten kings who intend to make war against the Lamb, but the angel warns:

> *"But the Lamb will overcome them because he is Lord of lords and King of kings – and with him will be his called, chosen and faithful followers." (Revelations 17:14 NIV)*

Oh that's who the Lamb is, it is Jesus. Had me fooled for a moment, but I wondered why the 144,000 men were following the Lamb wherever it went. Which is the basis for the children's nursery rhyme, "Mary had a little lamb and everywhere that Mary went the sheep were sure to go. The Lamb's fleece was white as snow." Ok so a quick revision of Jesus: born to a virgin; walks on water; performs a few miracles; crucified; rises from the dead; and then morphs into a Lamb. That's fairly straight-forward then.

The fall of Babylon

This is just a matter of hopeful payback against the Babylonians that conquered Israel 500 years earlier. But since Babylon no longer exists, and the end of days has yet been cast upon us, the Bible falls short once again in its relevancy with reality.

An angel appeared by John's side and he showed him the destruction of Babylon, a city that had become home to evil doers and those that indulged in sexual immorality. The angel gave the Babylonians an ultimatum that they repent and accept Jesus or pretty soon another angel will hurl down a large boulder into the sea to wash Babylonia away. As promised Babylonia was no longer and a cry of "Hallelujah!" was heard throughout heaven.

The Rider on The White Horse

As the rejoicing of the fall of Babylon reached a crescendo, heaven opened up and out jumped a white horse whose rider was named 'Faithful and True'. The rider had a steely determination in his eyes with intent to perform justice by making war with the last of the remaining non-believers. The armies of heaven followed him, riding on white horses and dressed in fine linen. On the robe of the rider named Faithful and True, was the inscription:

KING OF KINGS AND LORD OF LORDS.

Shit I can't keep up, now Jesus has morphed back from Lamb to general of heaven's cavalry. Anyway, the army headed by Jesus, rode down to earth to slaughter all and in the process they captured the beast before throwing him into a lake of burning sulphur.

The One Thousand Years

The angel says to John that Satan has been captured and bound him into the Abyss for one thousand years. This course of action taken so that Satan could no longer deceive the world for the next millennia. But why not just kill Satan now that you have him as your POW? This is like a bad movie script where the bad guy is not given clemency or shown mercy but returns later to threaten the hero.

For those that stayed true to the cause, however and had not been stained with the tattoo of the Devil, they were risen into Heaven. John writes that at the conclusion of Satan's one thousand year incarceration, he will be released from his prison and will set forth to deceive all nations of all four corners of the earth, a reference to the fact that these first century wackos still believed the earth to be flat, to continue his recruitment of devil worshippers.

At the conclusion of one thousand years imprisonment Satan will be thrown into a lake of burning sulphur, which seems a difficult method for killing a guy that thrives in the boiling heat.

Heavenly Book Keeping

As John saw the death of Satan one thousand years into the future, Jesus appeared on a great white throne and according to John 'earth and sky fled from his presence', I am not sure what that means, but nevertheless Jesus opened what is called the 'Book of Life'. The equivalent of Santa Claus' 'Naughty & Nice' list. This book listed all those dead and alongside their names as a record of all the good and bad things they had done whilst alive. If your good deed outweighed your bad deeds you were given entry into heaven, if the opposite be recorded then you were tossed into a lake of fire. Ouch!

Then Jesus turned to John and instructed him to write the following words:

> *"It is done. I am the Alpha and the Omega, the beginning and the end. To him who is thirsty I will give to drink without cost from the spring of the water of life. He who overcomes will inherit all this and I will be his God and he will be my son. But the cowardly, the unbelieving, the vile, the murderers, the sexually immoral, those who practice magic arts, the idolators and all the liars – their place will be in the fiery lake of burning sulphur." (Revelations 21:6-8 NIV)*

Oh, the Christian myth of the caricature of a sweet loving forgiving Jesus. His command to throw all Hindus, Buddhists, Pagans, Muslims, Jews, Spiritualists, agnostics and atheists into a fiery lake of burning sulphur surely has to be at odds with the Mr. Nice persona that Christians are sold on?

The final words of Jesus and the final verse of the Bible reads:

> *"Behold, I am coming soon! Blessed is he who keeps the words of the prophecy in this book. I, Jesus, have sent my testimony for the churches. I am the Root and the Offspring of David and the brightest morning star. I warn everyone who hears the words of the prophecy of this book: If anyone adds anything to them, God will add to him the plagues described in this book. And if anyone takes words away from this book of prophecy, God will take away from him his share in the tree of life and in the holy city, which are described in this book." (Revelations 22:18-19 NIV)*

Jesus says the Bible is true, I will leave it up to you to decide for yourself.

THE END

Afterword

The intention of this book was never to attempt to disprove the existence of God, or gods because that is a fools' argument. It is no more possible for me to disprove the existence of Santa Claus, Apollo, Thor and Zeus than it is in nuking the claims for the God of Abraham. All gods maintain equal evidence to one another, that being none. But rather the objective was to use the Bible as an indictment against itself by demonstrating that if the God of the Bible were true then, like Richard Dawkins assertion, he is a racist, misogynistic, capricious, malevolent, infanticidal, homophobic, envious, genocidal ethnic cleanser.

The annihilation of thirty-one different Middle Eastern civilizations at God's demand in the Book of Joshua alone demonstrated his tribalist blood lust. The holocaust of the Passover, with the murder of Egypt's first born, proved his capacity and willingness to murder innocent children as a means to an end. His disdain for homosexuality, a natural occurring phenomenon in all walks of nature, articulated in Leviticus and via Paul's divisiveness in Romans. The fact that women, in God's eyes, are worth little more than an Ox or an Ass on a man's balance sheet is a theme perpetuated throughout almost all sixty-six Biblical books. His petty, insecure and jealous ways are not only presented in black and white via the first four of the Ten Commandments, but also throughout Israel's journey from slavery to statehood.

This is the God, according to Bible lore, that created mankind, then wiped out all of its inhabitants because they didn't abide by his rules, rules that he had not yet provided, which we estimated the death toll of his flood to be thirty-million men, women and children. A God that calls for the death and destruction of any society that practices religious freedom and tolerance, including your own children if required. A God that says that not only may you sell your daughter into slavery, but you may also bludgeon her brains out should she call you a 'dithering old twat', being a sign of parental disrespect. A God that thinks so lowly of women that he deems it better to give your daughters up to be gang-raped rather than male strangers that you met only five minutes earlier.

Certainly a dangerous book, a dangerous book because it decrees all manner of actions that we as a morally evolved society now deem to be barbaric. But unfortunately God hasn't released any new best sellers of late, and believers are left with this book from antiquity to perform actions that they believe would please this wicked monster. Thus believers of all faiths will continue to kill in his name because the Bible and the Koran make the ugliest aspects of the human condition righteous and virtuous.

Civilization is left with a stark contrasting choice on how we move forward together in solidarity or in conflict. To borrow Bill Maher's words from his movie *Religulous*:

"Either we grow up or we die."

Bibliography

The God Delusion, Richard Dawkins (Mariner Books 2008) 978-0-552-77429-1

God Is Not Great, Christopher Hitchens (Atlantic Books, 2007) 978-1-84354-574-3

A History of God, Karen Armstrong (Ballantine Books, 1994) 978-0-34538-4560

End of Faith, Sam Harris (WW Norton & Company, 2004) 978-0-7432-6809-7

The Year of Living Biblically, AJ Jacobs (Simon & Schuster, 2007) 978-0743291477

Religulous, Bill Maher, DVD (Lionsgate Films, 2008), ASIN B0027Z83V4

Me of Little Faith, Lewis Black (Riverhead, 2008) ISBN 978-1-59448-994-5

The Quotable Atheist: Ammunition for Non-Believers, Political Junkies, Gadflies, and Those Generally Hell-Bound, Jack Huberman (Nation Books, 2006) 978-1560259695

God: The Failed Hypothesis. How Science Shows That God Does Not Exist, Victor J. Stenger (Prometheus Books, 2008) 978-1591026525

Everything You Know About God Is Wrong: The Disinformation Guide to Religion (The Disinformation Company, 2007) 978-1932857597

CJ Werleman

Author, Columnist, Speaker, Comic

If you add the total sum of life experiences of CJ's life, you reach a total of 128 years for a guy that is still only in his late-30s. He has owned and operated businesses, managed an international software company, lived in the world's largest Muslim country for nearly a decade, represented Indonesia in cricket, witnessed a suicide bomb, travelled to all continents, and contributed to foreign newspapers. Interestingly, CJ believes that all his trials, and tribulations have taught him only one thing: THAT EVERYTHING IS FUNNY! And those that do it more often tend to live longer and happier.

CJ is a contributor for the Bangkok Post, and has cultivated a popular following on Twitter. For stories and articles contact CJ directly:

Email: CJ@CJWerleman.com
Website: www.CJWerleman.com

Lightning Source UK Ltd.
Milton Keynes UK
03 June 2010

155064UK00001BB/31/P